ORTHODOX PERSPECTIVES
ON PASTORAL PRAXIS

HOLY CROSS 50TH ANNIVERSARY STUDIES

VOLUME ONE

ORTHODOX PERSPECTIVES ON PASTORAL PRAXIS

Papers of the Intra-Orthodox Conference on Pastoral Praxis (24-25 September 1986) Celebrating the 50th Anniversary of Holy Cross Greek Orthodox School of Theology (1937-1987)

Edited by

Theodore Stylianopoulos

HOLY CROSS ORTHODOX PRESS
Brookline, Massachusetts 02146

© Copyright 1988 by Holy Cross Orthodox Press

Published by Holy Cross Orthodox Press
50 Goddard Avenue
Brookline, Massachusetts 02146

Cover design by Mary C. Vaporis

Library of Congress Cataloging-in-Publication Data
Intro-Orthodox Conference on Pastoral Praxis
(1986 Brookline, Mass.)
Orthodox perspectives on pastoral praxis.

(Holy Cross 50th anniversary studies; v. 1)
Bibliography: p.
Includes index.
1. Pastoral theology—Orthodox Eastern Church—Congresses. 2. Orthodox
Eastern Church—Clergy—Congresses. 3. Orthodox Eastern Church—Doctrines—
Congresses. 4. Holy Cross Greek Orthodox School of Theology—Congresses.
I. Stylianopoulos, Theodore G. II. Title. III. Series.
BX341.6.I58 1986   253'.088219   88-8087
ISBN 0-917651-19-7 (pbk.)

To my mother, Vassiliki —
for her Christian example and
prayers through all the years.

Contents

Contents

Editor's Note

AS PART OF THE HOLY CROSS FIFTIETH ANNIVERSARY celebrations a number of conferences were held on the campus of Hellenic College and Holy Cross during the 1986-1987 academic year. Among them were the Intra-Orthodox Conference on Pastoral Praxis (September 1986), the Symposium on Christian Faith Facing Science, Education, and Politics (March 1987), and the Third International Conference of Orthodox Theological Schools (August-September 1987). The papers of these academic gatherings will appear in three volumes in the Holy Cross Fiftieth Anniversary Studies edited by faculty members of Hellenic College and Holy Cross and published by Holy Cross Orthodox Press.

This first volume, *Orthodox Perspectives on Pastoral Praxis,* features a variety of contributions. Next to the historical reflections on the founding and mission of Holy Cross, the papers included in this volume deal with Orthodoxy in America, pastoral care and education, the place of women in the Church, the question of divergent practices of receiving converts, and monasticism. All of these topics were the foci of the Intra-Orthodox Conference on Pastoral Praxis which generated animated discussion among the participants. It is hoped that these contributions will be of wider interest to readers not only for providing honest perspectives on basic issues discussed by Orthodox Christians, but also for offering insights into the ways Orthodox thinkers are dealing with new challenges in the North American milieu.

Theodore Stylianopoulos

Introduction: Reflections on the Fiftieth Anniversary of Holy Cross

"And you shall hallow the fiftieth year . . .
It shall be a jubilee for you . . .
It shall be holy to you" (Lev 25.10,12)

DURING THE COURSE OF THE 1986-1987 ACADEMIC YEAR, Holy Cross Greek Orthodox School of Theology marked its fiftieth anniversary with a series of festive events, symposia, and conferences. It was a jubilee year shared by faculty and students, hierarchs, and faithful, as well as sister Orthodox seminaries and affiliated theological schools of the Boston Theological Institute. Thanks be to God for his bountiful blessings and for the mission that he has entrusted to us to proclaim the good news of his love and redeeming work to the world. Celebrating the fiftieth anniversary, we are mindful of how Holy Cross has tried to fulfill its own mission from its establishment to the present. The following reflections touch not only on the past, but also the present and the future of the witness and mission of Holy Cross.

The expectations of Holy Cross were very modest when it was founded in Pomfret, Connecticut in 1937. At that time the primary goal of the School was to provide preparatory education for young men who would subsequently go to Athens or Constantinople to study for the priesthood. With the advent of the Second World War, however, it became obvious that such a plan was not realistic. Ever since that time, Holy Cross has been developing and has matured to a point where it is now a fully accredited and internationally recognized School of Theology.

From its humble beginnings in a small rural town, Holy Cross has developed into a recognized center of Orthodox theological learning. Today, Holy Cross and its undergraduate Hellenic College are located in Brookline, MA, on fifty-two rustic acres of prime land overlooking Boston, our nation's greatest educational metropolis.

The School is known by many names. Some remember it as Pomfret, while others call it Brookline, names derived from its host towns. Others call it the Hill from its geographical setting. Many prefer to refer to it by its name, Holy Cross. Those, however, who have been intimately involved with its life and mission affectionately call it the *Schole* — the School.

The move from Pomfret to Brookline was accomplished during 1946-48. In its new surroundings Holy Cross was obliged to think of itself and its mission in a broader ecumenical perspective. It had to measure itself against the established institutions of higher learning that had now become its neighbors. The seminary models of the old world, which had helped shape its early years, had to be adjusted. The challenge to strive for excellence became more urgent. The transfer to Brookline catapulted Holy Cross into a new era of development with far-reaching ramifications for the School, the Church and the Orthodox theological enterprise.

Holy Cross was no longer an experiment. It had become embedded in the consciousness of the Church, thanks to the productive pastoral ministries of its early graduates; the sacrifices and unfailing dedication and work of its first administrators and faculty; the commitment of its trustees; and the great promise it held for the future, as epitomized by its presence in the "Athens of America." The School became the pride of the faithful. It was pledged to the mission of upholding and reinforcing the riches of our religious and cultural heritage and to advance with vigor and strength Orthodox theological thought and life in the Americas.

In the early 50s the decision was made to link the School's educational program with those of the accredited mainstream theological schools and seminaries of our nation, while retaining in clear focus its own unique character and goals. Progress and growth have come in stages since then. The original five-year, post-high school plan of study, which integrated liberal arts and theological studies, was expanded first to six and finally to seven years. Little by little, the ground was laid for the distinction between a general and theological education, which would eventually lead to the establishment of a liberal arts college, Hellenic College, and the graduate School of Theology, Holy Cross. The final stages of this development, begun in the late 60s, were to culminate in the accreditation of both institutions in 1976. In 1981 the entire institution was re-evaluated according to normal procedures, and was granted the maximum ten-year period of accreditation. During these times of innovation and daring decisions, Holy Cross has remained the faithful daughter of the Church, helping men and women fulfill their calling in various ministries.

Holy Cross has been the seminary of the Greek Orthodox Archdiocese of Americas. Since the priestly ministry is essential to the life of the Orthodox Church, the education of men who are called to be priests has always been and shall always be central the life of Holy Cross. The faithful of the Archdiocese look to Holy Cross for the preparation of the future priestly leadership of the Church. They also rejoice that Holy Cross serves as the seminary for the students of other Orthodox jurisdictions in the Americas, as well as in Europe and the missions in Africa and Asia. This is certainly one of the important ways in which Holy Cross has demonstrated its commitment to Orthodox unity and cooperation.

Holy Cross exists to serve the Church in her sacred mission and witness. In addition to preparing and educating qualified and approved candidates for the holy priesthood, which is its primary objective, the School provides professional education for men and women for specialized ministries in the Church and otherwise satisfies a variety of academic interests and professional objectives.

Holy Cross is concerned with the advancement of Orthodox thought and life. Through research, publications and ecumenical encounters, it seeks to provide sound theological reflection on vital issues facing the Church. It is a source of renewal and continuing education. It provides theological training for lay people in cooperation with local dioceses, parishes and institutions. Holy Cross maintains ongoing relationships with other Orthodox schools of theology in the Americas, Europe, Africa, Asia, and Australia. It is also a member of the Boston Theological Institute, a consortium of nine theological schools in the Greater Boston area.

For fifty years Holy Cross has faithfully served the Church and nourished the souls of countless people. Like a great river which flows through the towns and cities of the heartland of a country, the ministry of Holy Cross reaches and touches the life of every parish and every parishioner of our Church. It is the emblem of the promise and the strength of Orthodoxy in the Americas.

The clergy and faithful of the Church have invested Holy Cross with great expectations. They have come to see the School as the heart of the Church in America. Certainly, they continue to expect Holy Cross to be the seminary where young men are prepared for the holy priesthood both in the undergraduate and their graduate years of study. Yet, in addition to this, the clergy and faithful also expect Holy Cross to be a dynamic center of Orthodox theological education and spirituality. The School is looked upon as the place where the values, traditions, and faith of our forefathers are preserved and transmitted in a special way.

As we look toward the future, we must accept the challenge that faithfulness to our Greek Orthodox heritage must include a bold recapturing of the fearless creativity of the great Fathers of the Church. To be the genuine guardians of the Faith once delivered to the saints requires that we also be pioneers in theological scholarship and activity.

We must choose to uplift the theological consciousness of the Church. For, without serious theological witness and theological criticism, the Church cannot be worthy nor capable of fulfilling her saving mission in the world. The practical everyday life of the Church must have theological substance. Holy Cross is the spiritual, intellectual, and reflective center of our Church in the Americas. If it is to be the devoted, faithful daughter of the Church and the resolute servant of the truth, it must have a sense of urgency about the Gospel, about doing the work of theology for the Church, about informing the mind of the faithful, about providing meaningful theological education for a variety of church ministries, and about bringing unique perspectives to priestly formation. It is time once again for a new and thunderous martyria for effective theological work.

In the year of jubilation we have stood firmly upon the shoulders of those who had gone before us, so that we may better know from whence we have come and so that we may more clearly see the vast horizons of the School's ministry that lie ahead. As we have recalled the past with reverence and deep gratitude, we have looked confidently to the future, being ever-mindful of our commitment to preserve and advance the faith.

Invoking the blessings of our triune God upon our School, we will dare to be a ray of the Kingdom in this wounded and broken world.

Alkiviadis C. Calivas

Patriarch Athenagoras and the 50th Anniversary of the Founding of Holy Cross Greek Orthodox School of Theology in America

DENO J. GEANAKOPLOS

IT IS A GREAT HONOR TO BE A PARTICIPANT IN THIS VERY special celebration of the 50th anniversary of this theological school and one which also honors the 100th anniversary of the birth of its founder, Archbishop Athenagoras, who later, as we all know, became the Ecumenical Patriarch of Constantinople.

This is a celebration not only for the Greek Orthodox community of America, which is, of course, under the jurisdiction of the Ecumenical Patriarchate, but in a larger sense for all the world of Orthodoxy. For it was Patriarch Athenagoras who made the first heroic efforts in modern times to bring about the close relationship among all the various Orthodox churches of the world. Not only did his patriarchate envision a closer bond among the various churches of the Orthodox ecumene but, during his patriarchal term, it was he who made the first attempts since the 15th century to bring about a reconciliation between the Roman Catholic and Orthodox segments of Christendom. Thus not long after his election by the Holy Synod as Patriarch he suggested a meeting with Pope Paul VI in Jerusalem. And some months later, the two hierarchs, in simultaneous announcements, in the Vatican and the Phanar, proclaimed the annulment of the historic anathemas of 1054, thus paving the way for an eventual complete reconciliation of these two great sections of the Christian Church, which had been, originally, as we

1

all know, united in one faith in the early period of the great Fathers of the Church.

Now the founding of this Holy Cross Greek Orthodox School of Theology by Archbishop Athenagoras exactly 50 years ago was the act of a man of genuine vision — one who realized that if the Greek Orthodox Church of America was to survive and prosper among a still immigrant people, as the Greeks then were in America, the church needed, above all, an institution for the training of new young priests. Of course, he did not know then that his own beloved patriarchal seminary on the island of Halke in Constantinople, at which he himself had studied, would one day be closed by the Turkish government and that this seminary here in distant America would, in a certain sense, take its place as the training ground of new Greek Orthodox priests in America.

The relationship between these two theological schools has physical parallels: Halke, situated on a verdant little island in the Bosporus, redolent with the fragrance of trees and vegetation and with its imposing building which, let us not forget, housed (and still does) a rich library of rare Orthodox books and manuscripts. On the other side of the world, this theological seminary is situated on an eminence filled with woods and vegetation, on the old estate of the patrician Cabot family overlooking the great city of Boston, also with its own excellent, constantly growing library. As one who taught at this school during its still formative stage, from 1953 to 1954, I feel a special pride in having been at one point in its history a part of this unique institution.

Because this year marks the centenary of the birth of Patriarch Athenagoras as well as the 50th year since the foundation of this theological school of Holy Cross, I think it would be entirely appropriate to focus now on a discussion of the development of this school's prototype, the patriarchal Academy in Constantinople during the late Byzantine and post-Byzantine times, that is in the Turkish period and later. For as we all should realize, the patriarchal Academy at Halke and this theological school in Brookline both constitute part of a continuous 1500-year-old tradition of Orthodox theological teaching and education. So, I think it would render more meaningful for you the significance of today's dual celebration to know something about the past history of the patriarchal school or Academy in late Byzantine and more modern times. Indeed, there can be no doubt that the education provided by the patriarchal Academy of Constantinople and also by this Holy Cross School of Theology constituted one of the most meaningful concerns in the entire life and career of Patriarch Athenagoras.

From the very emergence of Constantinople as a patriarchate at the ancient Second Ecumenical Council of 381, the patriarchate possessed a school or, as it soon came to be called, an Academy for the training of priests and theologians. At the same time the Byzantine Empire always maintained an imperial University, or higher school, where law, medicine, and advanced secular philosophy were taught, especially for the education of the governmental bureaucracy. In Byzantium two kinds of learning existed, outer or profane learning (meaning the classical pagan tradition), and Christian theology, or inner learning. The secular university's existence, as might be expected, was ended in 1453 with the Turkish capture of Constantinople, but the patriarchal Academy continued to exist up into the modern era. It was, then, the patriarchal Academy under the aegis of the patriarch which played a very significant role in preserving the Orthodox religion, as well as, in considerable part, even secular Greek learning.

Many Orthodox are today amazed to hear that in the early centuries of the Christian Church there was grave danger that the great literary and philosophic legacy of classical Greece would literally perish, since not a few rather important early Christian theologians believed all literature that was anti-Christian, that is pagan, should be destroyed. The salvagers of the classical Greek tradition were primarily the fourth-century Cappadocian Church Fathers, Basil the Great, his brother Gregory of Nyssa, and "the" theologian, Patriarch Gregory of Nazianzos. All three churchmen believed that through the use of ancient Greek literature and philosophy, its methods and especially its lofty, moral tone, so similar to that of Christianity, the New and Old Testaments, that is the Bible itself, could be better understood and interpreted. Of course, they advocated a selective reading of the Greek classics, omitting those passages concerned with a plurality of gods and the foibles and immoralities of these gods. Indeed, Basil asked in his famous essay, *Discourse to the Christian Youth on Study of the Greek Classical Literature*:

Why should we destroy ancient Greek literature and philosophy when its beautifully expressed morality and ethos can do so much to interpret and even strengthen the similar moral message of Christ?

Throughout the 1,000 year life of Byzantium, the patriarchal Academy often shared distinguished professors with the institution of the imperial university. There was a frequent exchange between them. Photios, perhaps the best known of all Orthodox patriarchs, was originally a professor of higher philosophy in the university, and, after becoming patriarch, devoted much time to renewal of interest in its opposite number, the patriarchal Academy. Indeed, Photios is usually credited with beginning, in the ninth century after the dark period of the Arab incursions, a renaissance of classical Greek learning as well as of Christian theology and Christian literature. Among the persons connected with the patriarchal school in his time were probably the Byzantine scholar — monks Cyril and his brother Methodios, both later to become the famous Slavic Apostles, that is, missionaries bearing Christianity to the Orthodox Slavic peoples.

Despite the difference in the eyes of the Byzantines between inner and outer learning, it cannot be said that the secular Greek learning of the ancients was under-appreciated throughout Byzantium's long life. Indeed oftentimes it was the high ecclesiastics themselves who showed a particular liking for the secular pagan classics. The attitude of qualified tolerance to pagan literature and philosophy, as advocated by Saint Basil, was most sensitively expressed, I believe, later in the 11th century by the Metropolitan of the Church John Mauropous. He was so impressed by the similarity of Plato and Plutarch's moral sentiment to gospel teaching, that he even pleaded to Christ himself to save the philosopher and in a lovely, very touching epigram (my translation):

If perchance, my Christ, you wish to except certain pagans from eternal punishment, may you spare for my sake Plato and Plutarch. For both were very close to your law in both teaching and way of life. Even if they were unaware that you as God reign over all, in this matter only your charity is needed, through which you are willing to save all people, while asking nothing in return.

Noble, deeply moving words reminding us somewhat of the beginning lines of the *Inferno* in Dante's *Divine Comedy* in which Dante, with the same sentiment in mind put the souls of the pagan Greek and Roman philosophers not in hell, but in limbo, just outside of hell.

In the Byzantine period the patriarchal Academy took boys early and kept them on to do their specialist studies in theology. At times of economic or cultural depression when the imperial university was in decline or even fading out, higher education was carried on mainly by the patriarchal Academy. Indeed, in the last three centuries of the Byzantine era, the church's (as well as private individual) schools had become very enlightened.

In the 13th century, during the period of the repressive military and political occupation of Constantinople by Western Latin armies (that is, from 1204-61), of course, neither the Byzantine patriarchal school nor the university existed any longer. Indeed in those years the Roman Church sought forcibly to convert the Greeks to the Roman faith. But when in 1261, the Byzantine Emperor Michael VIII Palaiologos of Nicea in Asia Minor recovered Constantinople from the Latins, one of his earliest acts was to reestablish higher learning, including the patriarchal Academy. Indeed he reorganized the Academy. At this time, the patriarchal Academy seems to have covered much the same ground of instruction as the state university, though always with greater emphasis on theology. Under Michael's son Emperor Andronikos II the two institutions were again reorganized, and in about 1400, under Emperors Manuel II and John VIII Palaiologos, the patriarchal Academy received its final form. Emperor Manuel moved the site of the patriarchal Academy to buildings — there were then no permanent ones — around the monastery of Saint John the Baptist in Studios where there was a good library. And he put it under the Studite monk and scholar Joseph Bryennios, who became its director and professor of scriptural exegesis. In this condition the patriarchal Academy remained in operation until the tragic fall of the imperial city of Constantinople to the invading Ottoman Turks in 1453.

It was in education that the Greek Church felt the effects of the subsequently long servitude to the Turks most disastrously. At Constantinople after 1453 the university in fact disappeared, and all that was left of the wreckage was remnants of the patriarchal Academy. Now during the Turkokratia, that is the Turkish occupation, more than ever in the face of continual and barbaric Turkish oppression, the Church had to devote itself to training clergy. As his choice to be the first patriarch under the Turks, conqueror Sultan Mehmed II appointed the anti-unionist Greek monk Gennadios Scholarios, a man of broad education and a deep religious sense. It became Patriarch Gennadios' policy to establish the patriarchal throne as the best means of continuity not only of the Orthodox Church but of the very life of the Greek people. Under Gennadios, the Ecumenical Patriarchate, denied the use of Hagia Sophia by the Turks (they had converted it to a mosque), was first situated at the Church of the Holy Apostles. Later the Patriarchate was moved to the convent of Pammakaristos, then in the 16th century to the church of Theoleptos Paramphea, afterwards to the church of Saint Demetrios, and, finally, in 1601 to the little church of Saint George in the Phanar district of Constantinople, where it still remains.

In 1454, the year that Gennadios became patriarch, he reestablished the patriarchal Academy but now higher philosophy was no longer studied there. A kind of hostility to philosophy gradually in fact seemed to pervade the high clergy and gradually was handed down by them to the lower clergy and masses throughout almost the entire 400 year period of Turkish rule. Indeed during this period the educational level of the Greek people in Greece proper, though much less than in Constantinople, sank very low. But this decline is understandable, given the lack of a Greek government, an organized Greek society, and the terrible conditions of servitude to the Turks. In my view the lowest point in the existence of the Greek people during the interminable 400 years of Turkish occupation was probably reached in the late 16th and early 17th centuries.

But the tragic fate of the Greek people was already foreseen not only by Patriarch Gennadios himself but by one of the greatest of the Greek scholars and ecclesiastics who went as refugees from Constantinople to Italy, Bessarion, Archbishop of Nicea. After the signing of the false ecclesiastical union with Rome in 1439 (the Byzantine emperor had hoped through religious union to secure papal aid against the Turks), Bessarion returned to Italy and became a Cardinal of the Roman Church. And in this capacity as a Roman prelate, he acted as protector of many Byzantine intellectuals who fled to the West, many of whom played an important role in furthering the spread of Greek learning in the Italian Renaissance, a subject which has very much interested me. In 1472, Bessarion, in his will, bequeathed the celebrated collection of 800 Greek manuscripts he had laboriously amassed to the city of Venice, where, in time, there had been developing the largest Greek colony of emigres. As Bessarion wrote so prophetically (and his words were completely overlooked until I was able to find and publish them some years ago in my book *Greek Scholars in Renaissance Venice*:

> I leave my manuscript collection to Venice in order, partly to benefit Italian humanists, but much more important, so that our own precious Hellenic heritage may be kept alive among our Greek people, who, under Turkish domination, are in grave danger of perishing, or worse, becoming barbarous and slaves.

It is notable that Bessarion's manuscript collection, which still exists as the nucleus of the great Marciana library of Venice, served as the textual models for publication of the first printing of most classical Greek authors in the Italian Renaissance as well as of the first publication of many Greek liturgical works. Indeed, remarkably, until as late as the 19th century the chief place for publication of the Greek Orthodox liturgical and ecclesiastical books was still the Greek-owned printing presses of the Greek colony in Venice. This was true for the liturgical works utilized by monks on Mount Athos and even for books used by the prelates of the Holy Synod in the patriarchate itself.

During the long Turkish period from 1453 to 1821, there is little doubt that the most important learning center in the Greek East was the patriarchal Academy. And its establishment, as we have seen, in 1454, was undoubtedly Patriarch Gennadios' most significant cultural achievement. For it did nothing less than propagate and keep alive the intellectual and especially ecclesiastical tradition of the Greek people. Now, the subjects taught at the Academy were not only grammar and the basics of Aristotle's philosophy (Platonism with its dualist mysticism was usually considered too dangerous for theology students), but the rhetoric of the early Byzantine Hermogenes, and, most important, of course, Orthodox theology from the standard textbook of the famous 9th century Byzantine theologian John of Damascus. Scores of youths from Greece and the Balkans attended the patriarchal Academy, especially after it was again revitalized in the 17th century on order of the patriarch by the Greek philosopher Theophilos Corydalleus, its principal. Earlier in Patriarch Gennadios' time the very first scholarch (or head of the Academy) had been Matthew Kamariotes, a student of Gennadios. And the first professor to receive the high patriarchal title of Grand Rhetor, an old one carried over from Byzantine times, was Manuel Corinthios, in the 16th century. Meanwhile, scores of Greek students seeking to study not theology but secular Aristotelian philosophy (that is higher philosophy) or medicine emigrated to Italy, in particular to the liberal University of Padua. Padua, the possession of Venice, now became the leading university in Western Europe, and one which, as one modern Greek scholar has accurately put it, "become a kind of cradle for the emerging modern Greek nation — so many Cretan and other Greek young men studied there. It should be noted that up to the capture of the island of Crete by the Turks as late as 1669, Crete remained the only important Greek territory in the Greek East, not under Turkish rule but under the Venetians. Hence the emigration of so many Greeks from Crete and also from Venetian Cyprus to the great city of Venice.

Aside from the patriarchal Academy in Constantinople and a few isolated schools in the Venetian-held Greek islands, elementary and intermediate schools in the Greek East under the Turks in time virtually disappeared. Under such deplorable conditions village priests in many areas, seeking to preserve at least elementary knowledge of the Greek tradition, had to hold classes in the narthexes of churches or even in monastic cells. It was then that on the walls of many Orthodox churches on mainland Greece, images of the great pagan philosophers Plato, Aristotle, and the moralist Plutarch were sometimes painted. This was in accordance with old Byzantine tradition — reverting back to Saint Basil himself — to honor those whose oral teaching had seemed to foreshadow the beliefs and doctrines of Christianity. It was of course also a way of teaching Greek children something of the meaning of ancient Greek philosophy and, not least, to inculcate in them in this modern period a sense of inchoate national Greek feeling.

In the dark centuries of Turkish enslavement, it was thus largely the work of the ecumenical patriarchs, aided, we should certainly not forget, by the often semiliterate village priests, who preserved at least a semblance of learning among the desperately ignorant and oppressed mainland Greek population whom the Turks frequently harassed or even threatened with death unless they converted to Islam. During these long, dark centuries a number of important patriarchs were trained in the patriarchal Academy. These included Jeremiah II, ho Tranos (the formidable), a learned theologian as well as philosopher-historian who, despite the time of unsettled conditions, as patriarch went to Russia in 1598 and presided over the creation of a new patriarchate, that of Moscow. He also became involved in epistolary discussions with the emerging Lutheran Church of Germany whose theology to their surprise he condemned as unorthodox. Jeremiah took a deep interest in the patriarchal Academy. In order to strengthen it, he tried to persuade several noted Greek scholars living in the thriving Greek colony of Venice, such as Maximos Margounios, to come to teach at the patriarchal Academy but with little success.

It is interesting that, though the Turkish government actually suppressed or looked with extreme disfavor on schools in Asia Minor and Greece, it never really interfered with the operation of the patriarchal Academy in Constantinople itself. But of course there the patriarch was constantly and directly under the thumb of the powerful Sultan. Meanwhile in mainland Greek society and the church, conditions grew worse and worse outside of Constantinople. Among other things the patriarch therefore sought to establish centers of religious culture on Mount Athos in Greece, where Patriarch Cyril V in 1753 founded the Athonite Academy. This, after initial progress, however, was not very successful.

During this long period of extreme vulnerability for Orthodoxy, the papacy, in order to attract young Greeks to the Roman faith, established in 1577 in Rome, the still existent Greek college of Saint Athanasios. Not a few young Greek students did attend school there (sponsored by the Roman Church), but despite their thorough training in Roman theology, when they returned to their homes in the Greek East they almost invariably reverted to the Orthodox faith. In the 17th century the memorable Patriarch Cyril Lukaris, who believed the salvation of the Greek people could come only with the spread of higher education among the Greek youth, sent promising graduates of the patriarchal Academy westward to finish their studies in Protestant Holland, England, or Germany. He even founded the first printing press at the patriarchate in Constantinople and of course he is well-known for his relations with the Western Calvinist Church of Geneva with which some scholars believe he became much too close. Still another patriarch early trained at the patriarchal school in Constantinople was the noted Cretan scholar-patriarch of Alexandria, Meletios Pegas.

Because of the stultifying and corrupt atmosphere of the Turkish court, corruption, quite understandably, also gradually entered the court of the Sultan's subordinate, the patriarch. But the origins of venality in the patriarchal court may above all be traced to the demands of the Turkish government which forced the patriarch to pay gradually larger and larger sums (bribes, that is) for assuming his ecclesiastical office. Patriarchs were consequently installed and removed at the mere whim of the Sultan. This is only one indication of the worsening cultural and moral conditions that slowly began to spread within the patriarchal court in the Phanar during the first three centuries of Turkish oppression. It was probably not until as late as the mid-17th or early 18th century that the Greek people at last began to awaken from their long turpor, and to begin to think seriously of possible liberation from the Turks. As we all know, in 1821, the Greek Revolution finally burst forth. The immediate Turkish reaction in Constantinople was to hang the Ecumenical Patriarch Gregory V, who was technically, of course, a governmental official of the Sultan, before the gate of the patriarchate. Thus the patriarchate, though a logical support, at least clandestinely, for the success of the Greek Revolution, was constrained by its extremely vulnerable position to say nothing publicly to the struggling Greeks. Its true sentiments, however, must have been clear to all thinking Greeks.

After suffering through the critical events of the Greek War of liberation without being able to give overt aid to the Greek people, the Ecumenical Patriarch in Constantinople, a few decades after the Revolution, was finally given permission by the Turkish government to erect a building as the site of a revivified patriarchal Academy, which had virtually ceased to function after the Revolution. The structure, which was erected in 1844 on the small nearby isle of Halke, was an imposing building constructed through the generosity of the Orthodox Skylitzes family.

It was at this newly built Academy that there was trained and educated the young Athenagoras, in whose hands was to lie the fate of the Orthodox Church in very recent times. But as I mentioned earlier, the new theological Academy now established at Halke did not enjoy much more than a century of life. In 1972 it was in fact closed by order of the Turkish government, thus ending, at least for the present, the patriarchal Academy's fifteen hundred years of continual existence from the fifth century onwards.

This tragic event of 1972, the result of retaliatory Turkish political motives in connection with the difficult problem of Cyprus, must have been a truly painful one for the then Patriarch Athenagoras. But it is this very closing of the patriarchal Academy which makes the 50th anniversary of the foundation of this theological school of the Holy Cross all the more poignant. It goes without saying that in our Orthodox Church, which prides itself, above all, on preservation of the doctrinal beliefs of the seven ecumenical synods and of the work and ideals of the Cappadocian Fathers, theological teaching on a high level must always continue. And so, aside of course from such theological schools as Athens and Thessalonike Universities, the torch of Greek Orthodox theological learning was, so to speak, transplanted by Patriarch Athenagoras from Halke across the ocean to the new world, and, more specifically, to this theological school of the Holy Cross which he founded exactly fifty years ago in 1937.

The aims and ideals of Patriarch Athenagoras, who died in 1972, the same year that the Academy of Halke was closed by the Turkish government, must not be lost or diluted, for his extraordinary contribution to Orthodoxy — in education, in ecumenical affairs, and always on behalf of the greater unity of Orthodoxy — have made him the very symbol of Orthodoxy, an immense source of pride and inspiration to all members of the Orthodox Church throughout the world. You members of the faculty and students of this school must understand that you have a unique opportunity, indeed a sacred duty, to carry on the vision and ideals activated fifty years ago when this theological school of the Holy Cross was created by Patriarch Athenagoras, whose bust very properly stands on this campus before the jewel-like Byzantine chapel you erected with such devotion.

We Orthodox of America are extremely fortunate in that we have at present as president of this school and Archbishop of North and South America a prelate who was the chief disciple and protege of his great lamented mentor, Patriarch Athenagoras.

Here in this school of theology, and also in its component of outer learning Hellenic College, you faculty and students are carrying out the injunctions of Saint Basil the Great. As I noted earlier, when the very existence of our precious classical Greek heritage was woefully threatened by misunderstanding zealots of early Christianity, Saint Basil insisted not only on the preservation of Hellenic learning but that it even be grafted, so to speak, onto Christian belief itself, to the advantage of both. The foundation and development of this school, then, with its combined emphasis on Hellenic learning in Hellenic College, and on the Orthodox faith and religion in its theological school, Holy Cross, seem perfectly to embody not only the ideals of Saint Basil, but also of his most distinguished modern Orthodox successor, the Ecumenical Patriarch Athenagoras I. May both their memories remain eternal.

Orthodoxy in America:
Continuity, Discontinuity, Newness

STANLEY S. HARAKAS

Introduction
MY TASK IN THIS PAPER IS TO ADDRESS THE TOPIC "Orthodoxy in American Culture: Continuity, Discontinuity, Newness." I will seek to summarize my conclusions at the end of this presentation precisely on those themes. But in order to do so, it will be necessary to take a different tack on developing the topic. First, there is need, in my judgment, to address briefly in outline fashion, the issue of "The Orthodox Tradition and the 'World,' in History," in order to focus on the "Orthodox" side of the theme. Secondly, in order to give concrete content to the other side of this endeavor, an assessment has to be made of "America as the 'world' into which we have entered." We wil ask the questions, "What was characteristic of America when it was founded?" and "What has it become today?" The final part of this effort to deal with Orthodoxy in America will take a more normative stance and will seek to provide some direction in terms of Orthodoxy, American culture and their continuity, discontinuity, and newness.

The Orthodox Tradition and "The World" in History
It has become a commonplace to note that within Christianity there are two opposite tendencies as the Church addresses the world in which it finds itself.[1] One is a radical rejection of the world.

---

[1] I have addressed the theme of this section in several articles to which I refer the reader for a more detailed development. This and the final

13

In this vision only the "people of God" are holy, while the world by definition finds itself in full submission to the demonic. Such a perspective has a long history, traceable from the earliest pages of the New Testament, many of the Apologists, and most fully embodied in the monastic system and the ideal of desert asceticism.

The other tendency is contrasted to this essential denigration and rejection of the world in what might be called the incarnational vision of the world. Here, the Church sees itself as obligated to reach out to the world, to be somehow a vehicle for injecting at least some measure of the divine in an environment which has rejected it, but which cannot find its own purpose and fulfillment without it. Christian evangelization seeks to convert it; philanthropy to correct its worst effects upon the lives of people; and social concern to modify its structures for the sake of fairness and justice.

Unlike sectarianism on the one hand which adopts a radical discontinuity with the world's culture, and unlike some forms of liberal Christianity on the other hand which have effectively championed a radical identity with the world's culture, Orthodoxy, with other churches rooted in the long history of the Christian tradition, has held these tendencies together in an unresolved, yet mutually influential paradox.

Theologically expressed, this standard Orthodox position can be described with three terms: confrontation, incarnation, and transformation. Ideally, this theological stance demands that wherever evil and the demonic is encountered it must be met in a spirit of confrontation, in a spirit of discontinuity. That discontinuity may mean escape, but it also may mean condemnation and

---

section of this paper selectively draw upon the conclusions of these papers: "The Church and the Secular World," *The Greek Orthodox Theological Review,* 17.1 (1972) 721-43; "Greek Orthodox Ethics and Western Ethics," *Journal of Ecumenical Studies,* 10.4 (1973) 728-51. See also, a treatment which largely parallels these writings in the volume which will be the basis of the second part of this paper, Robert N. Bellah, and others, *Habits of the Heart: Individualism and Commitment in American Life* (New York, 1985). The perspectives of my earlier writings on this topic are remarkably summarized by Bellah's statement: "If there is to be an effective public church in the United States today, bringing the concerns of biblical religion into the common discussion about the nature and future of our society, it will probably have to be one in which the dimensions of church, sect, and mysticism all play a significant part, the strengths of each offsetting the deficiencies of the others," p. 246.

spiritual warfare. In any case, it is a negative stance which high-
lights the difference between God's ways and the ways that are
not his.[2]

Nevertheless, this is not the central thrust of the Church's encounter with the world and its culture. Its central way is the Lord's
way: it seeks to address the world in an incarnational mode, i.e.,
somehow to infuse the Spirit of God into it, to sanctify it, and unite
the divine with the created order as much as the world will bear
it in any given place or time.

Thus, in the realm of priorities and goals (idealistic and
unrealizable as it may appear) the theological ethos of the Orthodox
Church seeks in as many ways as possible to transform the world's
culture, and to turn it from its apostasy from God to communion
and union with him. The Church's goal is not to consign the world
to hell, but to transfigure the world by absorbing it into the life
of the kingdom of God, of which it itself is its chief manifestation
on earth. The Church's prayer is its Lord's prayer: "Your kingdom come; your will be done, on earth as it is heaven" (Mt 6.10).

There are other ways of articulating this same truth within the
theological world view of Orthodox Christianity. Thus it is to say
a similar thing when Orthodox proclaim that the Orthodox Church's
approach to the world is sacramental, eucharistic, and icono-
graphic.[3] Examples are many: regarding the sphere of aesthetic
culture. Orthodoxy offers the holy icons;[4] in reference to the

---

[2]For more about the Orthodox approach to evil and the struggle to reject, combat and exorcise it from created life, see chapters 4 and 5 of
my book, *Toward Transfigured Life: The Theoria of Orthodox Christian
Ethics* (Minneapolis, 1983).

[3]I have in mind writings, to mention only two, such as Alexander
Schmemann, *For the Life of the World* (Crestwood, NY., 1982) and Ion
Bria, ed. *Martyria/Mission: The Witness of the Orthodox Churches Today*
(Geneva, 1980), in which note the concept of the "liturgy after the Liturgy." For a thorough treatment of social and philanthropic institutions
in Orthodox Byzantium, see Demetrios J. Constantelos, *Byzantine Philanthropy and Social Welfare* (New Brunswick, NJ., 1968). An excellent
sourcebook of Byzantine cultural life is Deno John Geanakoplos, *Byzantium: Church, Society, and Civilization Seen through Contemporary Eyes*
(Chicago, 1984).

[4]Constantine D. Kalokyris, *The Essence of Orthodox Iconography*
(Brookline, 1971) and Leonid Ouspensky, *Theology of the Icon* (Crestwood,
NY., 1978).

State, the Orthodox have developed the ideal of mutual cooperation, yet distinction of Church and State as expressed in the political
theory of "symphonia";[5] in the area of science, for example,
scholars have just recently uncovered the remarkable history of
the development of the medical hospital within the confines of
church institutions.[6]

What emerges from this tradition is a vision of the corporate
reality of life. Thus, the vision of the Church for the world is that
it reflect as much as it is able the image of the Church as the body
of Christ, in which all the members are related to each other by
their unity with their divine head, and their mutuality of service
and love for each other. This comprehensive corporateness is inclusive of genuine human values: spiritual and material values,
all human knowledge and its proper application, as well as a genuine balance and harmony between the personal and social dimensions of human existence. The Church thus affirms "personhood"
as a reflection of the truth that every person is created with the
purpose of becoming in fullness the "image and likeness of God."
But what it rejects is "atomism," that is, the kind of self-perception
which sees others only as means for the fulfillment of one's own

subjective needs and desires. Its ultimate truth in this issue, as
with all others, is that ultimate reality is a community of persons —
the One God who is a Holy Trinity of persons. Thus in its vision
of the relationship of the Church with the world, sin is excluded,
but all else is capable of inclusion.

Moving and articulate expression of this vision can be found
in various places of the liturgical life of the Orthodox Church, from

---

[5]See, as the most recent contribution to this Church-State understanding, J. M. Hussey, *The Orthodox Church in the Byzantine Empire* (Oxford, 1986) and in particular, Part II, ch. 2, "The Patriarch of Constantinople and the Emperor."

[6]Timothy Miller, *The Birth of the Hospital in the Byzantine Empire*
(Baltimore, 1985). More generally about the Church and medicine, see
John Scarborough (ed.), *Byzantine Medicine, Dumbarton Oaks Papers
Number Thirty-Eight, 1984: Symposium on Byzantine Medicine* (Wash-
ington, D.C., 1986).

the use of the Psalm 103 in every Vespers Service, to the latter part of the Great Eucharistic of the Liturgy of Saint Basil with its fully inclusive and wholistic vision of the life and mission of the Church, to this prayer of Saint Gregory the Theologian:[7]

Hymn to God

You are above all things
    and what other way can we rightly sing of you?

How can words sing your praise
    when no word can speak of you?

You alone are unutterable
    from the time you created all things
    that can be spoken of.

You alone are unknowable
    from the time you created all things
    that can be known.

All things cry out about you,
    those which speak,
    and those which cannot speak,

all things honor you,
    those which think,
    and those which cannot think.

For there is one longing, one groaning,
    that all things have for you.

All things pray to you that comprehend your plan
    and offer you a silent hymn.

In you, the One, all things abide
    and all things endlessly run to you
    who are the end of all.[8]

---

[7]Recited by Holy Cross Greek Orthodox School of Theology Dean and Administrative Director, Rev. Alkiviadis Calivas, as the opening prayer to the Conference on Pastoral Praxis, at which this paper was delivered.

[8]*Saint Gregory Nazianzen: Selected Poems,* translated with an introduction by John McGuckin (Fairacres, Oxford, 1986), p. 7.

Nevertheless, this vision rarely has an opportunity to find full expression, much less accomplish it. In the first place, even with the best of conditions and intentions, the reality of sin is ever present, foiling repeatedly the implementation of the vision. But the fact is that the "conditions," that is, the openness and receptivity of any given culture in any given historical period to the presence and transforming grace of the kingdom, vary greatly. As we tell our Orthodox story — a story which is repeated with its own variations, successes, failures and betrayals in every local history of the encounter of Christianity with culture — we observe an uneven trajectory.

Where Orthodoxy was formally allied with power and authority, such as in Byzantium, the vision of the incarnational transformation of culture was accepted somehow as normative. There were impressive successes, as well as tragic failures; but the vision, to the very end, remained alive and empowering. But in periods of slavery where there was sharp discontinuity between the dominant culture and core Orthodox Christianity, such as in the 500 year experience of the "Tourkokratia" under the Ottoman Turks, withdrawal was the norm, survival and preservation the goals. As Orthodox Christianity entered the modern world, the situation became more complex. For a while it seemed that the incarnational impulse of Orthodoxy succeeded with the formation of a constellation of "Orthodox nations" but the result has been an inability to sustain them. In some cases, we have what we might call a "mixed condition," exemplified by pre-revolutionary Russia, the modern Greek state, and even some of the contemporary Balkan nations with socialist regimes. In other cases, there is a vigorous antagonism between Church and culture because such antagonism is defined by the culture. I have in mind the reincarnation of pagan Rome in the Marxist regimes, and in particular, in the Soviet Union.

By historical progression, we have come to the consideration of the Orthodox Church and America. What is the cultural situation of America, *vis-à-vis* Christianity, and what is the relationship of Orthodox Christianity to America? In order to address this question we need to make some kind of assessment of the essential nature of American culture and character.

The American Scene as a "World" into Which We Have Entered
We cannot make sense of an Orthodox approach to America,

unless we somehow have a handle on what it is we are dealing with. We need some definition of what it is that we Orthodox have come into, before we can assess our continuities and discontinuities and before we can articulate what this may demand of us.

There is a long and complex history of American self-analysis which seeks to understand the unique character of the American experiment. All nations and peoples are involved in this kind of enterprise, seeking to discover their unique genius which sets them apart, as a people unto themselves. However, the American genius seems to be generally recognized as a nation of another kind, by others as well as by ourselves. The methods applied to this American search are many and varied: religious visions, constitutional patterns, economic systems, geographic modes, and psychological patterns have all been used as heuristic devices to plumb the American character. Not the least, and perhaps the most successful, have been sociological analyses of the American scene.

In 1985 the most recent of a long series of sociological studies dealing with the American character appeared. Written by five sociologists, with Robert N. Bellah of the University of California at Berkeley at their head, the book was the result of hundreds of interviews with Americans, primarily of the white middle class. The book made an important contribution to plumbing the essence of American culture as it was originally. But the book's new contribution is that it traces out the course American culture has taken over two hundred years to the present day. The title, *Habits of the Heart: Individualism and Commitment in American Life,* is a good summary of its themes.[9] One of the book's major sources

---

[9] I wish to thank the members of the Boston Ministers' Club, of which I am privileged to be a member, for introducing me to this book, through one of its regular program meetings at which a full oral review and discussion of *Habits of the Heart* was offered in May of 1986. It was an exciting evening of discovery! Also, many deep thanks to Jack Sparks of the Evangelical Orthodox Mission of the Antiochian Orthodox Church whose unpublished 68 page duplicated summary and review, "A Brief and Preliminary Examination of *Habits of the Heart*," was made available to me at the Annual Meeting of the Orthodox Theological Society in May, 1986. Both of these sparked my own interest in the topic, and directed me to the careful study of the volume, and to the decision to use its insights, especially in this second part of this paper. I am grateful that

is the assessment of American character in the classic study *Democracy in America* by Alexis de Tocqueville, the French social philosopher who, in 1830, published what the authors call "the most comprehensive and penetrating analysis of the relationship between character and society that has been written."[10]

De Tocqueville focused on the central phenomenon of American character and culture which he identified as individualism. One reviewer properly described *Habits of the Heart* as "an extended gloss on this sentence from Tocqueville's *Democracy in America:* "Individualism is a calm and considered feeling which disposes each citizen to isolate himself from the mass of his fellows and withdraw into the circle of his family and friends; with this little society formed to his tastes, he gladly leaves the greater society to look after itself."[11] Both de Tocqueville and Bellah recognize this individualism as the core dimension of American character and see in it many good things, in particular, its fostering of the spirit of equality, justice, equal opportunity and a democratic mind set. Yet de Tocqueville's perception was that this individualism had the potential to harm public life. Bellah and his colleagues are also convinced that in the last analysis, unchecked individualism in America also harms private life. They are convinced that unchecked individualism cannot long sustain itself and that if left unchecked, threatens the fabric of American life.

Thus, individualism is seen as the primary element in American character. In this analysis, originally the positive consequences of individualism were protected, and its harmful consequences were muted and limited in the early period of the nation by two other dynamic influences on American character, the "biblical tradition" and the "republican tradition." These two terms are used to define social phenomena central to the makeup of American character.

The biblical tradition came to these shores with the first dissenters from England and Holland. They came here to find freedom

---

Father Sparks, in his analysis, was kind enough to include reference to some of my previous work in aiding him to raise significant questions and issues from an Orthodox perspective, in regard to the fundamental evaluation of the volume.

[10]Ibid. p. vii.

of worship and saw America as a "city set on the hill," a kind of this-worldly "Promised Land." It was not hard to think of this new place under the sun as a gift from God, with whom Americans entered into a covenant relationship, and consequently, like a new Israel, Americans were in fact God's chosen people. Sociologically, this biblical tradition served to provide America with a set of transcendent values which placed the dominant individualist tradition under God, and thus provided a control and restraint upon it from outside of itself.

A second historic element limiting the negative consequences of individualism in American tradition was what *Habits of the Heart* calls the "republican tradition." Here the focus is on the life of early America which focused on the small town, its life of community, and the commitment (to which the sub-title of the book refers) to the public good. The founding fathers (especially Madison in the *Federalist* No. 45) assumed that virtuous character would result in a concern for the public good, in which individuals pursuing their individual interests would also be "reasonable men" who recognized that the "democracy of opportunity" which they promoted needed a public virtue among the citizens to restrain individualism from self-destruction. Such a self-destruction was understood as the reimposition of tyranny as a result of the chaos unrestricted individualism would most certainly produce.

In spite of these observations, neither the description of the American culture, nor the evaluation of it, is an attack on individualism. The themes of freedom, equality, the suspicion of those who exercise power and the validity of pursuing one's own self-interest are still central to the American ethos. The economic expression of individualism in marketplace capitalism and its political expression in movements for justice are positive aspects of American individualism. For a long time, the authors hold, the restraining influence of the transcendent referents of religion and the republican tradition of civic responsibility made for a dynamic, growing and healthy tension in American culture.

However, Bellah and company now perceive that the restraining influences have weakened and fallen away in the post-World War II period. The balance has disintegrated. The transcendent dimension has been lost from public life as religion has been subjectivized, relativized and privatized. In Richard John Newhouse's term, the "public square is naked" of transcendent spiritual and moral values.[12] In the same manner, the national and international corporations have been breaking the local commitments and loyalties of community. There is less and less claim of the historic "republican tradition" on mobile Americans. Patriotism is countered by a disenchantment with the authority of the Constitution, which now is clearly seen as subject to manipulation by politics and interest groups. It seems to me that the recent congressional debates regarding the appointments of Chief Justice Renquist and Justice Scalia are a witness to this.

In the view of the authors of *Habits of the Heart* and many others, the result is that the moral glue of American society has lost its power. It is precisely this moral glue which de Tocqueville called "the habits of the heart." Without the balancing and countervailing power of religion and civic virtue, individualism is rampant. In their place a subservient "therapeutic culture" has arisen to help individuals cope, but it provides only a normless "adjustment" to personally chosen, yet essentially philosophically groundless, socially rootless and personally meaningless, choices. At best it allows the basic "utilitarian individualism" to be transformed into a less grasping, exploitative mode, which Bellah calls, "expressive individualism," according to which many Americans are simply content to "do their own thing."[13] This lack of internal coherence is expressed in a culture which in its main lines today is judged to be materialistic, fragmented, atomistic and in danger of dissolution.

Orthodoxy and America

Of course, all is not so pessimistic as my description of this important assessment of American character might suggest. Not all of America has bought into this middle-class malaise. Neither religion with its transcendent verities and community life is dead, nor has the "republican tradition" of civic virtue disappeared completely. Yet, the danger bell is ringing, and the need to do something about it is generally recognized. I read fourteen book reviews of *Habits of the Heart* published between mid-1985 shortly after

---

[12]Richard John Newhouse, *The Naked Public Square: Religion and Democracy in America* (Grand Rapids, 1984).

[13]See *Habits of the Heart,* especially chapter 6.

its publication and early 1986.[14] It was a good experience: the political leftists thought it was a rightist book; the political rightists thought it was a leftist book; the socialists criticized it for middle-class focus; the religious reviewers found disparate messages for themselves, some positive, some negative, some critical, especially in terms of practical prescriptions to change the situation for the better. None, however, denied the validity of the book's central evaluation of the American culture of today. All recognized that something is going wrong with the American vision.

For us "johnny come lately" Orthodox, however, there are several messages. The first, of course, is that in the pages of this book we find a tool for analyzing some of the weaknesses and failings which we are experiencing as a church in this nation. It is not that we are not aware of the powerful forces which are at work in our society, and consequently, at work influencing our own membership. The American environment has produced strong currents which are expressive of the kind of individualism described in *Habits of the Heart,* producing a "multi-option society" in which Orthodox Christians find themselves. The Orthodox are beginning to sense the danger to them, reversing an almost uncritical immigrant's appreciation for their adopted land. Thus, in a workbook prepared for the 8th All American Council of the Orthodox Council in America on *Church Growth and Evangelization,* the alternatives to an Orthodox way of life are discussed as "options (which) stand in direct opposition to the life and faith of Orthodox Christianity." The membership was warned, thus, against "secularism . . . humanism . . . dualism . . . relativism . . . and civil religion."[15] Similarly, over the years, the Greek Orthodox

---

[14]Martin E. Marty, *The Christian Century,* (May 15, 1985) 499-501; ibid. (May 22, 1985) 523-24; Jack Beaty, *Commonweal,* (May 17, 1985) 308-09; Michael Novak, *National Review,* (June 28, 1985) 36; Benjamin R. Barber, *New Republic,* (May 20, 1985) 33; Peter Stienfels, *New York Times Book Review,* (Apr. 14, 1985) 1; Sal Alfano, *Psychology Today,* (June, 1985) 72-73; Barbara Ehrenreich, *The Nation,* (Dec. 28/Jan. 4), 717-18; Deborah Meier, ibid., 719-20; Lynne Sharon Schwartz, ibid., 720-21; Michael Zuckerman, ibid., 721-22; Norman Birnbaum, ibid., 723; Alvin P. Sanoff, *U.S. News and World Report,* (May 27, 1985) 69-70.

[15]*Church Growth and Evangelization,* (Syosset, NY.) 23.

Archdiocese of North and South America, at its Biennial Clergy-Laity Congresses has on numerous occasions focused on issues of "Moral Disintegration and Secularism" and many other social problems of our American society, in particular the 18th (1966), 19th (1968), and the 21st (1972) Clergy-Laity Congresses.[16] At its 28th Clergy-Laity Congress in 1986, the Congress Church and Society Report focused strongly on the issue of the contemporary family. As an indication of the importance of the topic for the Church, this report was not summarized as were the others, but it was published in full in the Archdiocese newspaper, the *Orthodox Observer*."[17] Clearly the membership of the Orthodox Church is not uninfluenced by these forces in American society.[18]

Nevertheless, as we turn to the theological and ecclesial message which Orthodox Christianity has for America, there is something

---

[16]See Stanley S. Harakas, *Let Mercy Abound: Social Concern in the Greek Orthodox Church*, (Brookline, MA., 1983).

[17]Wednesday, September 24, 1986, p. 2.

[18]A few of the theological efforts in the realm of the Orthodox world dealing with the nature of culture and society are the following: Michael Azkoul, "The Greek Fathers: Polis and Paideia," *St. Vladimir's Theological Quarterly*, 23.1 (1979) 3-22 and 23.2 (1979) 67-86; Archbishop Iakovos (Koukouzis), "Looking Toward the Twenty-first Century," *The Greek Orthodox Theological Review*, 29.3 (1984) 219-32; Vigen Guroian, "The Americanization of Orthodoxy: Crisis and Challenge," *The Greek Orthodox Theological Review*, 29.3 (1984) 255-68; Stanley S. Harakas, "Alexander N. Tsirindanes on the Present Age," *The Greek Orthodox Theological Review*, 2.1 (1956) 75-82, and "The Church and the Secular World," *The Greek Orthodox Theological Review*, 18.1 (1973) 167-99; Peter Carl Haskell, "American Civil Religion and the Greek Immigration: Religious Confrontation Before the First World War," *St. Vladimir's Theological Quarterly*, 18.4 (1974) 166-92; George Khodr, "The Church and the World," *St. Vladimir's Theological Quarterly*, 13.1-2 (1969) 33-51; Daniel F. Martensen, "A Synopsis of Eastern Orthodoxy and the Secular: A Historical Instance," *The Greek Orthodox Theological Review*, 13.1 1968) 41-64; *The Orthodox Approach to Diakonia: Consultation on Church and Service* (Geneva, 1980); "Consultation on Christianity and Traditional Cultures," *St. Vladimir's Theological Quarterly*, 26.4 (1982) 245-50; Alexander Schmemann, "The Problem of the Church's Presence in the World in Orthodox Consciousness," *St. Vladimir's Theological Quarterly*, 21.1 (1977) 3-17. For a more general bibliography of Orthodox involvement in issues of social concern, see the footnoted bibliographies in Stanley S. Harakas, *Let Mercy Abound*, (Brookline, MA., 1983).

poignant about the book when it looks to possible resources for a solution. Those of us attuned to the Eastern Orthodox theological vision of a cosmic Christ, of a sacramental, incarnational, transfigurational, comprehensive and wholistic Christian tradition most surely must hear the pain in the sociologist's cry for coherence for our disjointed and fragmented society. Hear the words:

> If our culture could begin to talk about nature and history, space and time, in ways that did not disaggregate them into fragments, it might be possible for us to find connections and analogies with older ways in which human life was made meaningful. This would not result in a neotraditionalism that would return us to the past. Rather, it might lead to a recovery of genuine tradition, one that is always self-revising and in a state of development. It might help us find a coherence we have almost lost.[19]

Bellah calls the loss of the biblical and republican tradition, the loss of our "second language," with individualism as the "first language" actually losing power as a result of that loss. It would be easy to spend a lot of time talking out of the salvific vision of Orthodoxy as fully capable of providing for America the content of that so badly needed second language. We could develop the balance in Orthodoxy of the personal, ecclesial and outreach dimensions which have characterized its theological and ecclesial vision. We could expound on the greatest contribution we Orthodox may have for America, that is, our understanding that communal life and genuine personal life are essential to each other's existence, a truth taught to us by our most serious and most central theological affirmation: the doctrine of the triune nature of the one God. It would be easy to do all this, but I won't.

And this, because our historic discontinuities with the American scene are so great; our continuities so abysmally uncommunicated, that to make such pronouncements and to gratuitously offer solutions off the cuff is the worst kind of self-delusion. Within the last fifteen years or so, we have made gestures in this direction. The Greek Archdiocese, for example, declared itself officially as being in the mainstream of American society a while back, and the

---

[19]Robert N. Bellah and others, *Habits of the Heart*, p. 283.

Russian Metropolia adopted a name identifying itself with America and the Antiochians were the first to adopt the language of the land wholesale in worship.

But all of us have done this without having seriously struggled with the issues and problems of America. I believe that Orthodox Christianity *is* the answer to America's problems, because I believe that Orthodox Christianity is the answer to every person's and every society's and every nation's problems. Orthodoxy is God's answer to the human problem. But until we get our own house in order, we are useless to them and to ourselves.

In the short run our ethnic identities help us cope, for they provide us with strong "second languages." But as far as America is concerned, unless we are able to develop means to address the common life of this nation, to institute vehicles for plumbing the meaning of our tradition for America, to assume an activist role in the dialogues of public life, not sporadically and occasionally, but on a daily basis, we will have denied to America our contribution toward the solution of her problems, and perhaps even her survival as a free people.

Till now our immigrant mentality has allowed to assume the stance of a pilgrim minority, fundamentally estranged from the heart and soul of the nation in which we live. We need now to assume a serious sense of responsibility for this nation, just as we have in generations past for dozens of other nations.

We need to study, reflect, write, and communicate the wisdom of our tradition as it may be incarnated in the American society in which we live. But we need to do more than talk. We need to form Pan-Orthodox action-groups, coalitions of Orthodox people in major fields of endeavor, develop projects of service and commitment, perhaps an Orthodox Service Corps to move beyond our Glendia, Haflis and Balalaikas. We must first see, study, debate, communicate, and practice the implications of our Faith among ourselves, before we can be so bold as to proffer solutions to our neighbors. But as Orthodox we cannot stop there.

Our ethnic heritages are precious and we have as much right to them in America as do every other group. Precious also are our ethnic mother tongues. We do a disservice to ourselves and our people, even to America, if we allow them to die and disappear. But the thrust of Orthodox theology demands of us much more. Orthodoxy has always had a tradition of culture-building and

America has tremendous need of our special "second language" which is the truth of Orthodox Christianity. There are many things which we must do, but concurrently with the kinds of activities I have suggested above, we need to cultivate something more than a ghetto mind, something more than thinking and talking about Orthodoxy and America, something more than activism. God has put us here in this place for a purpose. We need to become aware of it; we must reject negativism and pessimism about our future in this country. We have to turn toward America with a message.

Among the things we must tell America is that it has too high expectations of itself. America is not the kingdom of God. The assumption of the authors that somehow the American reality must have and is capable of achieving a totally full solution to its problems is an idolatry. It is no less achievable here than in any other nation of the world. Perhaps it is precisely our long history with cultures of many kinds, with periods of power and prestige contrasted with periods of suffering and humiliation, that can provide America with a message she has to hear.

We have spoken of continuities; and we have spoken of discontinuities. What is the new that is demanded of us? It would appear to be that Orthodox Christians in America need to put off the old self-image of being strangers and foreigners in this land. The other side of this coin is not passivity, assimilation, nor accommodation. Rather, Orthodox Christianity in America needs to develop a realistic and conscious sense of mission to America. This, I believe, in the mid-eighties of our century, is precisely what is new in the equation, "Orthodoxy in the American Culture."

In the Place of a Conclusion

The moving picture, *Moscow on the Hudson,* is a comedy of sorts about the first experiences of a Soviet defector in New York City. There are three scenes in the film which strikingly illustrate some of the major points which were made in the first part of this paper. Please let me begin by describing them to you.

The protagonist's story is essentially a description of his good faith efforts at entering into the American spirit and making his way in American society. He quickly learns that he must be enterprising, that money is very important in America, and that he has the opportunity in America to get ahead. He becomes romantically attached to a lovely Italian immigrant woman who is studying in preparation for her citizenship examination. During a relatively modest sex scene, the heroine is assisted by the protagonist as she studies the questions for the citizenship examination. He asks her to enumerate the freedoms guaranteed by the Bill of Rights. After mentioning several, she becomes playful and adds two of her own, the right to meet (by which she clearly is referring to her tryst with her lover) and the right to sex. Individualism very subjectively understood and lived is the hallmark of American life, the scene seems to say.

The second scene I wish to bring to your attention follows the protagonist's attendance at a party and dance with fellow Russian emigres. He has drunk a little too much and he is, as they say, "feeling good," as he returns to his tenement home. As he enters the corridor he is mugged, robbed and beaten. It is the 4th of July. He calls a friend and they go to an all night restaurant where he loudly asks, "What good is freedom, if you can't walk the streets in safety?" He is confronted by another Russian immigrant who challenges him to go back to Russia if security is what he is really looking for. The point of the scene is that somehow not everything is going well in the American commonwealth, raising questions about the adequacy of the American dream.

The third scene follows directly. Orientals, Blacks, and Caucasians of other nationalities join the discussion. They note that it is Independence Day, and they mutually rediscover the promise of American democracy: "life, liberty, and the pursuit of happiness." The camera focuses on an Oriental walking past the window of the restaurant. In his hand he holds a burning sparkler. The camera zeroes in on the intense white light of the sparkler till it fills the screen with transfiguration-like brightness. In the background is patriotic music. The scene evokes strong patriotic emotions. The film seems to be saying that America has a special and unique promise for the transfiguration of life, and that the American vision demands it be much more than what other nations are expected to be.

Regardless of the critique, and in spite of the dangers, I believe that in many ways, America's potential remains a light for the world in its vision of freedom, personal dignity, respect for multiple traditions, and equality of opportunity.

If we Orthodox have a mission to America — and I believe it exists and is unavoidable — it is because in part it is an imperative of the Orthodox Faith, and because in a special way this nation is still a beacon and light. One of our tasks as Orthodox Christians in this land is to contribute our share so that this light burn brightly and permanently, as a beacon set high upon a hill. We have a mission in America.

Response to Stanley S. Harakas' "Orthodoxy in America: Continuity, Discontinuity, Newness"

VESELIN KESICH

FATHER HARAKAS IN HIS PAPER APTLY SUMMARIZES THE Orthodox Church's attitude toward the world. What is particularly attractive in this presentation is his valuable effort to give us an evaluation of the American religious scene, the new world for the Church.

He rightly brings out two tendencies in the Orthodox Church. One is the "world-negating" tendency, and the other the "world-affirming." On the basis of our own everyday experience, we see the validity of pointing to and stressing these two predispositions. We meet people in our churches who express a negative feeling toward the world. To them it is beyond the pale of salvation. The world is full of evil; there is no need to teach or preach to the world but only to pray and wait for the apocalyptic end. We also know those whose vision of the world is imbued by a spirit of transfiguration and resurrection, or what Father Harakas characterized as an incarnational vision of the world. Yet these two tendencies or attitudes toward the world are not so clearly separated either in the life of the Church as a corporate body in history or in the life of individual believers. The "ascetic" and the "incarnational" views of the world are often mixed or overlapping. Father Harakas perceptively observed that the Church "has held these tendencies together in an unresolved, yet mutually influential, paradox." Undoubtedly, it was the predominance of the incarnational vision of the world which inspired the Church to conquer the world. The Church accomplished this by transforming the aspiration of the human mind and thus fulfilling God's plan and work in history.

31

In one sense, it neither negated nor affirmed the world but accomplished an inner transformation.

During my visit recently to Asia Minor, to the great Hellenistic sites in western Turkey, I saw vivid evidence of how the Church confronted the world. The ruined cities of the early centuries of the Christian era attest to it. In Sardis, for instance, there are the ruins of an imposing temple to Artemis, built in 300 B.C., replacing an altar which had been there for two or three hundred years. In the fifth century A.D. a Byzantine church was erected just at the head of this enormous structure to Artemis. The ruins of both temples, pagan and Christian, we see even in our own time, and they teach us that Christ was the fulfillment of the yearning of pagan religious aspirations as well.

In Pergamon, however, we have a different picture, which complements what we see in Sardis. Here there was a temple to Serapis. Sanctuaries to this deity, of the most syncretistic cults of the Hellenistic period, blending Egyptian myth with Greek elements, have been discovered in several cities. Unlike temples devoted to the numerous Hellenistic deities, these sanctuaries to Serapis had large assembly halls instead of a small inner sanctuary. The "Red Temple" of Serapis in Pergamon, built of reddish brick during the reign of Hadrian (second century A.D.) could accommodate at least a thousand people. During the Byzantine period, this temple was converted into a church. Here the church was not built at the head or beside the ancient temple; the pagan sanctuary was transformed and the inner hall was converted to serve the Christians in Pergamon.

The temples in Sardis and Pergamon and the churches that succeeded them illustrate the Church's attitude toward its contemporary world. The church at the head of the temple in Sardis represents a fulfillment, whereas the church in Pergamon points inner transformation. The power of early Christianity was not the power to destroy but to incorporate and thus transform its world.

Of course, this "incarnational" vision has never been fully realized. It would be utopian to believe that it ever will be. But whenever the vision has been alive and the power of transformation that accompanied it has been manifested in human conditions, the Church has known what its role and responsibility should be in the world and for the world.

Relying on good authority, Father Harakas isolates "individualism" as "the primary element in the American character," but limited above all by "biblical" and "republican" traditions. He offers us a clear analysis of how transcendental values (i.e., biblical) and commitment to the public good (i.e., republican) protect the positive and keep in check the negative consequences of individualism. What Father Harakas does not discuss in this connection is the fact, new to the Orthodox experience, that in this environment the people feel free to move from one religious group to another. We may assume that this is due to American individualism. Not only may they switch from one religious community to another, but they may also be tempted to start their own new religion. Individual conversions are common in this country. In the last few decades many joined or were converted to the Orthodox Church. This, however, is not due to evangelical efforts of the Church but primarily to the religious search of these men and women. They "discovered" the Orthodox Church for themselves, and upon being received they found their home.

Orthodoxy is not "strange" or "exotic" for those engaged in religious study or in a search for religious commitment. Anyone who has had contact with college students and experience in teaching the history or theology or spirituality of the Orthodox Church in American schools will concur with the above statement. On the basis of my own experience teaching courses in comparative religion at a secular college, I am aware of the impact Vladimir Lossky's *Mystical Theology of the Eastern Church* has upon those who read and study it. Through this book they become acquainted with the tradition common to universal Christianity, the tradition of the universal undivided Church. Lossky's book expanded their vision and answered some of their spiritual needs. The ecumenical character of the book, the author's positive attitude, free from empty polemic, evoked admiration from students, whatever their background. Without promulgating one point of view, Lossky clearly presented "the indivisible treasure for both parts of a divided Christendom." And this "treasure" they recognized as belonging to them too; here they found their roots defined.

With his rather short but rich paper, filled with important information, analysis and insightful comments, Father Harakas introduces us to "the American scene" and helps us to understand

what is "the unique character of the American experiment." We
welcome the clarity of his presentation and his appreciation and
understanding of the new culture into which the Orthodox Church
has entered. Possibly for lack of space, certain important aspects
of the American religious situation and its makeup are only implied or vaguely suggested. In the opinion of this respondent, the
following phenomena deserve more explicit comment: civil religion, pluralism, the nature and meaning of the turmoil of the sixties and seventies, and the rise of cults. Of course many other
topics need to be discussed for a full picture of the American religious scene, but we shall select these for their importance both
for religion in America in general and for the Orthodox Churches
in particular.

The existence and practice of civil religion adds to the com-
plexity of the American religious scene. Every president of the
United States, beginning with Washington at the time of his inauguration, as a rule mentions God but not Christ. "The God of
the civil religion is not only rather 'unitarian,' he is also on the
austere side, much more related to order, law, and right than to
salvation and love," writes Robert N. Bellah in his analysis of civil
religion. He goes on to say that God is actively engaged in history
and his particular care is now for the American people. Civil religion selects and applies well-known and recognizable elements from
the biblical and Christian tradition, and yet it was not meant to
be a "substitute for Christianity." Like any other religion, it is
not immune to various distortions. Not to see the difference between a transcendent God and the country is one of them. Probably this fusion of God with the country is the worst among the
distortions, leading to many others. But the civil religion at its
best, argues Bellah, "is a genuine apprehension of universal and
transcendent religious reality as seen in or, one could almost say,
as revealed through the experience of the American people."
America is a free nation under God. Christian and non-Christian
religions are free in the free society. They are not under the control of the state, nor do they control the state. This leads us to
the question of pluralism.

In this pluralistic society all major religious groups are actively
engaged in influencing the course of events, inspired by the spirit
of their own traditions. A chaotic situation is avoided by acceptance of and respect for the body of law by all these groups. The

preeminence of the law as the vital, dominant core of this pluralistic society is taken for granted. This society is based upon the law and ruled by the law.

American religious pluralism, due particularly to the Great Awakening of the eighteenth and nineteenth centuries, tends to minimize differences in doctrinal teachings among the Christian churches. They are important, for they exist, but not so important that they should occupy the first place. One of the most perceptive evaluations and analyses of American religious pluralism was offered by the late John Courney Murray, an outstanding Roman Catholic theologian. For him pluralistic society "is a pattern of interacting." Various groups work for their own good and hopefully for the common good of the society to which they belong. There is the highest political goal, which is a just, free, peaceful, united society. This is the goal, but it is not yet realized. There is "the search for religious unity, the highest spiritual good," but it always encounters dissensions and warfare. "Religious pluralism," observes Murray, "is against the will of God. But it is the human condition; it is written into the script of history." Then what may we expect, what is the solution of the problem of religious pluralism? To hope to make American society the perfect society "based on a unanimous consensus" is nothing but utopian. But he adds that "we could at least do two things. We could limit the warfare, and we could enlarge the dialogue." He is pleading for a unity, "the unity of an orderly conversation." He uses the word "conversation" in its Latin sense, that is, "living together and talking together." If we do not attain "unity of conversation," then we shall fall into barbarism, which Murray defines as "the lack of reasonable conversation according to reasonable laws."

To participate in dialogue, an Orthodox must first of all study and learn from his own rich tradition. This is well-emphasized in Father Harakas' paper. The Orthodox Christian has been accustomed to see pluralism exclusively in a negative light. But he should see it as a challenge and opportunity, which a free pluralistic society offers him. It really forces him to go deeper into his own tradition, to bring out its treasures and share them with others. The Orthodox Church in a free pluralistic society can bear witness to its faith, proclaim it, defend it and contribute to the common good of the society. In other words, those who belong to the Church can be at the same time good Orthodox and good Americans. To advance unity among Christian bodies, there is no other way in the pluralistic society, the free society, but dialogue. There is nothing so important for the Orthodox Church in this "human situation" as having strong theological schools and well-educated pastors.

During the 1960s and 1970s there occurred a proliferation of American religious pluralism. At this time particularly Oriental religious cults and movements entered the American scene and the American campuses. The practice of Eastern meditation spread throughout all strata of American society. The emergence of new cults affected the lives of many and shaped their attitude toward institutionalized religion. Some saw in these new developments signs of religious vitality, and awareness of the importance of religion in the lives of young people. Others were more critical and perhaps more perceptive. They regarded the new flowering of religious groups rooted in the Eastern vision of ultimate reality as a clear sign pointing to the weakening influence of the "biblical" and "republican" traditions on the American character. The sense of the transcendent was under radical question, while the commitment to the public good had been turned into a commitment to "my group." All this was accompanied by a rise in the popularity of occult practices, astrology, and divination. A new sense of sacredness replaced the traditional, biblical sense of holiness. And, as had happened before, the sense of the sacredness of nature and eros produced new gods and new lords. Religion, it was claimed, has nothing to do with "institutions," the Church, but with a "new consciousness," which is not rooted in or controlled by anything beyond itself. All these signs, if not signs of a "new age," were certainly signs of a "new syncretism."

It is worth noting that in the 1960s we had a decline in church attendance, as the Gallup poll reported. Then, around the middle of the seventies this decline was arrested. These data prompted some observers to conclude that the new cults of the sixties had been here for a short period, that they were already exhausted, their spiritual energies in decline, that they were temporary, and that their impact upon the life and ministry of the Church would be negligible. What really happened in the 1960s was much more serious for the traditional Christian churches than simply a temporary decline in church attendance and a loss of revenues.

In *A Religious History of the American People* (1979), Sydney E. Ahlstrom wrote that the 1960s opened a new stage in American religious experience. It is true, he observed, that "some sensational cults came and went (as fads and fashions will)," but what stayed with us was "the existence of a basic shift in mood, rooted in deep social and institutional dislocations," which proved anything but "ephemeral."

Basic Christian beliefs have been questioned ever since. The institutions have been under attack. The generations of the sixties and after have been more interested in experiencing the divine, in whatever sense, than simply in talking about God. They turned to "other religions," and from them received mantras and methods of mediation. The Christian churches, they felt, could not offer them what they were looking for in the field of meditation and spirituality. The so-called "Western spirituality," with its own mantras, needed to be "discovered" and used.

In an essay on "The Jesus Prayer," Huston Smith, a respected authority in the field of comparative religion, describes his visit to Mount Athos, where he came "face to face with the kenotic, or self-emptying, tradition within Christendom; with hesychasm . . . with the *Philokalia* and its science of the prayer of the heart; and above all with that nineteenth-century classic of Russian spirituality, *The Way of a Pilgrim*." The Jesus Prayer ("Lord Jesus Christ, Son of God, have mercy on me a sinner") is "a Western mantra if I ever heard one." But this mantra, a properly repeated hymn or formula used in worship and meditation, was unknown to our students. They received a large variety of other mantras. "In these our curious times," Smith concludes, "when magic and divination are being seriously practiced on every major university campus in our land, is it possible that the Jesus Prayer might come into its own?"

We should not forget that this prayer is also a theological and christological prayer. Spirituality without theology, as we are well aware, may lead anywhere, and theology without spirituality may be reduced to an intellectual exercise composed on concepts and deprived of the Spirit.

Father Harakas rightly insists that we must first study and practice our faith before we turn toward our neighbors for dialogue. Until we do it, we are "useless to them," and the "treasures" we are called to communicate will remain unknown unless they are discovered by those who thirst for authentic "lost Christianity." We share a common language with those around us, but this is not enough without serious study.

What is the role and potential contribution of the Orthodox Church to an America characterized by religious pluralism?

First of all there is the Church's theological contribution: to strengthen and clarify among Christian groups the basic Christian beliefs and practices. At the same time we bear witness to the universal, common tradition of both Eastern and Western Christianity. The vision of God and Christ, the Holy Spirit in the life of the corporate worship of the Church as well as in the life of individual Christians belong here.

Christianity everywhere in the world has been under attack in our time by secularists, for whom the only world is the temporal one and religion is a "purely private matter." The secularist is critical of organized worship, of the community coming together and praying together. He is critical of the idea of transcendence. Only the Christian vision of a transcendent God enables us to grasp that the heart of humanity and its future is linked with transcendence and otherworldliness. In the words of the Elder Zosima, from *The Brothers Karamazov,* "what grows lives and is alive only through the feeling of its contact with other mysterious worlds . . . If that feeling grows weak and is destroyed" in us, then we will be "indifferent to life and even grow to hate it." Rejection of the divine or eternal served as the basis for a new aggressive paganism, deifying either a particular economic class or race.

By its contribution to the strengthening or "discovery" of common tradition and a vision of the future, the Orthodox Church can bring closer the churches of the Catholic and Protestant traditions and quicken the process of healing among them. She may thus help them to remove the rifts accumulated from the past and overcome conflicts and wars of previous centuries by a new relationship and a new history. Many even among Orthodox will not share in this hope or in the role ascribed here to the Orthodox Church in this country. Yet there is some basis for hope. We have hope for the future because there are grounds for it in the past. The process of healing is slow and not easily observable. There have already been some movements which may serve as signs of the future importance of the very presence of the Orthodox Church in the West to promote healing. Theologians and scholars at

St. Sergius Institute in Paris between the two world wars brought about better relations between French Catholics and French Protestants. Donald A. Lowrie in his book, *Saint Sergius in Paris,* wrote: "Thanks to friendly relations of both Catholics and Protestants in France with St. Sergius, the two French confessions have come into closer touch."

In conclusion, it is clear that we can no longer discuss the role of the Orthodox Church in this country without acquiring a more complete knowledge of the American religious scene. We cannot make a significant contribution here without studying and participating in our own tradition. This is the message that comes clearly from Father Harakas' valuable and challenging paper.

Orthodox Parish Life and Changing Interpersonal Relationships

JOSEPH J. ALLEN

IF THE PASTORAL PROBLEM AT HAND IS TO DEAL WITH THE two crucial aspects of the Christian community, "Orthodox parish life" and "changing interpersonal relations," then that problem must be filtered through the screen of pastoral *praxis* ("practice"). In short, both aspects must be seen through the ministry (*diakonia*) of the "leader" (*proestos*) of the community since communal life (*koinonia,* "communion," "community") and its development are his central concern. It should also be said, from the start, that within the interpersonal relationships of the Christian community, how a pastor "practices" his ministry has a crucial bearing upon not only the relationship among the persons within that community, but also his *own* relationship with those same persons; his relationship with them is just as central to the communal life of the Church as is their relationship with each other. This is the broadest base of what we mean by the use of the term "interpersonal," and our intention in this presentation is to include both sets of relationships throughout our various points.

It is Saint Basil the Great who can give us a lead into our exploration when we notice his great emphasis upon the term *proestos* ("leader," "pastor," "shepherd"). His frequent use of the term, found in both his *Great Ascetic Work* and *Small Ascetic Work,*[1] has as its fundamental purpose the praxis of

---

[1]Cf. Paul Fedwick, *The Church and the Charisma of Leadership in Basil of Caesarea* (Pontifical Institute of Medieval Studies, Toronto, 1979).

leadership and the development of all that is involved in the communal life of the parish.[2] Studying what he has written in those sources, we see that our own stress must be precisely upon the praxis, the "practice" of the pastor, now as it is brought to bear upon the Christian relationships for which he is responsible.

Inclinations in Praxis

The praxis of the pastor can be inclined in various directions. But there are two inclinations within that praxis which, if pushed to the extreme, cannot be circumvented if we are honestly to look at the effect that that praxis may have upon communal life. With the patience of the reader, I should like to begin by describing these two inclinations, so important to our task, by recalling a circumstance which occurred early on in my own ministry. As the reader will see, it is an event which most adequately describes these inclinations, and it is probably not unique to any one pastor; it is most likely shared by every pastoral leader at some time or another.

It was soon after ordination that an old Orthodox priest, who served in a different parish every three to four years, took me aside and advised me: "Do not be a 'bully.'" A very short time later, another old priest similarly took me aside and advised: "Do not be a 'chicken.'" Growing up in a rather rough and tough

---

Also see Saint Basil, *The Rules*, ed. Ray DeFarrare, in the series entitled *The Fathers of the Church* (Washington, D.C., 1950). Saint Basil, of course, is writing for the monastic community (which was the *cenobitic*, or communal type, rather than the hermetic type) but there is a natural connection in meaning with the Church-in-the-world. In his *Small Asketikon* he uses this term seven times, in his *Great Asketikon*, about fifty times.

[2]It should be made clear that when we use this term, "communal life," we do not mean the reception of the Holy Eucharist in the narrow sense, i.e. the sacramental act itself. Of course, the sacrament is the true and final "symbol" and destination of communal relations, but one can (wrongly and unfortunately) "take" the Holy Eucharist and not truly be "in communion" with the persons of the Father, Son, and Holy Spirit, as well as the persons of our brothers and sisters in one mind and faith. In using this term, "communal life," as a Christian way to express "interpersonal relations," we can see that both terms are most fully expressed in the sacramental act of the Eucharist.

neighborhood (the ethnic "sixth ward" of Allentown, Pennsylvania), I knew very well what each one meant, although there were other "neighborhood names" which were used to describe these two types of personalities and behavioral patterns.

As I later continued to practice my priestly ministry, as well as to teach in our Orthodox theological schoolss in the area of Pastoral Theology, my studies brought me into contact with other "specialists" in this area who gave different and more sophisticated — even more "scriptural" — sounding titles to these two types (which we shall shortly explain). However, for our immediate purposes, regarding the ministry of the *proestos* and the interpersonal relations in the communal life, Saint Basil knew of what he spoke: it is no secret that clergy are themselves either a source of unity or division in the Church, and very often this depends upon how the pastor understands his own task of pastoral praxis. Furthermore, many times he understands this task precisely in the behavioral terms as those just mentioned. We must briefly look at these inclinations with a little more depth.

To begin, the condition is not exclusive to the clergy; many people perceive themselves as either "the beaten" or "the beater," the chicken or the bully. However, regarding our particular concern — and using that "more scriptural" language previously mentioned — we often hear it said, especially among the Orthodox, that this *proestos* is either the "pastoral-type" or the "prophetic-type," as if each type precludes the inclination of the other within his praxis. What is often true is that beneath the surface of each of these exclusively "prophetic-types" there is a "bully," and beneath the surface of each of these exclusively "pastoral-types" there is a "chicken" (note the word "exclusively").[3] In whatever way such inclinations have developed, and whether or not they are brought into one's current leadership pattern from before ordination, i.e., from an earlier age in the person's life, the Orthodox pastorate has very often become a haven for persons who are either "bullies" or "chickens." In the interpersonal relations of the community, they either push or they get pushed around. In the end, of course, each extreme on the part of the pastor creates an

---

[3]Brown Barr, "Prophets and Pastors: Personality Tendencies which Interfere with Balanced Ministry," *The Christian Ministry*, (March, 1985) 5-8.

atmosphere which is detrimental to the proper development of the Christian community.

If we look still further, it becomes obvious that we may never be able to eliminate these extreme inclinations in the church leadership (human personalities, as any father confessor and/or spiritual director can attest, are very complex), but we can at least begin with this approach: many of these prophetic-type pastors have not taken charge of the "bully" within them, and many of these pastoral-type pastors have not conquered the "coward" within. Rather, these inclinations seek to take control of him. As a result, the community suffers in a multitude of ways since his relationship, as shepherd, is axial to its entire life. This damage is simply incalculable to those to whom he is sent to minister and lead, because they remain either uncomforted or unchallenged. This intolerable scenario is only exacerbated when this acting-out bully and this acting-out coward are justified and canonized under the scriptural cloak of "prophet" or "humble parish pastor."

But before we explore some few chosen ways to explain how these inclinations actually affect the communal life, it would be helpful to pause and to take brief note of the nature of such inclinations in themselves. Many inclinations, of course, are born of very deep and stubborn "passions," often buried in one's ego. Although it would be beyond the range of our present concern to delve in depth into this particular area of the inner life of the one who ministers (that would take another type of study — and for different reasons than our present ones), nevertheless it is still important to at least briefly mention this connection. The chosen source for this point is Saint Gregory of Nazianzos.

Among other points in his *On the Flight to Pontos,* Gregory the Theologian is telling us that the leadership of the community requires that one, through an "internal warfare," take charge of one's passions, that, like one experienced and aged enough to have "hoary (gray) hair," he must act "with maturity and propriety," and that, finally, all this so that he be "balanced." In fact he likens the task, from which at first he fled, to "walking a tightrope":

This I take to be generally admitted: that just as it is not safe for those who walk on a lofty tightrope to lean to one side or another (for even though the inclination seems slight, it has no slight consequences since their safety depends on perfect balance): so is the case of one of us if he leans to one side or the other . . . such is the case with our passions, and such is the matter in the task of the good shepherd if he is to know properly the souls of his flock, and guide them according to the methods of pastoral care which is right and just, and worthy of our True Shepherd.[4]

Even more succinctly, the Theologian shows this connection between the inner life of the *proestos* and his praxis as leader of the community:

A man must himself be cleansed before cleansing others; himself become wise before making others wise; become light and then give light; draw near to God, and so to bring others near; be hallowed, then hallow them; be possessed of hands to lead others by the hand; be possessed in wisdom to give others advice.[5]

Such examples — and there are many more — only serve to remind us that the pastor must indeed be in a constant "internal warfare," i.e. in which his own desires and passions, so often present in the form of such inclinations, must be encountered. It is only in light of this struggle that one can be led to a continuously increasing "priestly consciousness" (*ieratiki syneidesis*), a matter deeply related to the development of true Christian relations.

Taking seriously what Gregory says, then, it is important for the leader to ask himself who he thinks he is, what he could mean to those entrusted to his care, and what are the observable fruits and consequences of his relations. It is only in light of his own inner struggles, e.g. against such inclinations, that he may then ask: "Before God, unto whom all hearts are open, who am I? Are my relationships redemptive, evasive, destructive? Do I move toward persons affiliatively, away from them evasively, or against

---

[4]Gregory the Theologian, *On the Flight to Pontos* in *The Nicene and Post-Nicene Fathers Vol. 7 (Grand Rapids)*, p. 211; also see pp. 212, 224, and 227.

[5]*Ibid.* p. 219.

them destructively?'' An honest facing of such personal questions is a necessary first step in the validation of one's response to be a servant of God, one who is to lead the community to a true *koinonia.*

Praxis Extremes and Communal Life

Our concern for a proper pastoral praxis, now including our brief but important note regarding the pastor's inner life, serves as a perfect *passage d'entre* into our broader exploration of the interpersonal relations in the Christian communal life. But we still must ask: "How is this so? How *is* the praxis of the pastor consequential to the life of the parish, to the interpersonal relations within that parish?" Among the many examples which can be noted, we can use our two extreme examples to show this dynamic.

It is precisely when these two inclinations are taken to the extreme that we see a distortion so severe that the very exercise of the pastoral ministry borders on a type of ecclesiological (although not necessarily "doctrinal") heresy. For example, although as Saint Basil instructs, the *proestos* is to be responsible for *all* types of people in the community (and even for all types of problems which they have), we could easily begin to suggest that the people should "search out" a parish where their "spiritual needs" would be met more satisfactorily by this or that type of pastor. Thus, if they are too comfortable and need to be challenged (or even "smitten" a bit), they could be sent to some neighboring Orthodox parish (or even, for some, to some non-Orthodox parish!), where some confrontational, prophetic-type was the leader. In this case, such a person is broken from relationship with his present comunity; chaos, insecurity, transience, etc., are the result. If they say they were afflicted and wanted to be comforted, they could be sent to the more sensitive, pastoral-type. Again, such a person is broken from his present community.

What is the price paid for this? What happens when, because of this pastoral typology (which, as we have said, we *know* is extreme), we are content to free the prophetic-type from pastoral responsibility, and the pastoral-type from prophetic responsibility? As we shall presently see, in an age of unthinkable outer peril and immense inner turmoil, these leadership types — when practiced to the exclusion of the other — are a luxury and an indulgence of personal preference on the part of the clergy that we can no longer risk in the Church; such extremes merely distort the totality of the good news.

As Orthodox, we may have wanted to believe that this prophetic-type was the *only* one influencing and confronting the life-and-death issues of the day, and persons who are to be so "awakened" and "challenged" are to be sent to them. Unfortunately, although there is indeed some truth in this, such extreme types all too often influence only those who already agree with them. On the other hand, the more non-confrontational pastoral-type has not shown convincingly that he is doing much to shake the citadels of the Devil which exist both within and without the Church. This deficiency is also unacceptable since we cannot justify any leadership praxis that will not challenge the persons of the community to judge themselves and their relationship with their fellows in light of the gospel of Jesus Christ. The truth, however, is that every pastor must be prophetic, and every prophet must be pastoral, adjusting with "discernment" to the ever-changing conditions which exists within the community to which he ministers.

And so we have it: either the scriptural-sounding "prophet and pastor," or the neighborhood-sounding "bully and chicken." Many have come to believe that it is to be one or the other, and that certain persons of the Church best belong to the pastoral care of the one or the other.

One Response to the Problem

What are we to do? How is this to be dealt with by those who are training the future leaders of our Orthodox communities? The time has certainly come for the Orthodox — both seminary and Church — to begin shaping the true scriptural model of leadership which draws profoundly — and gratefully — upon both the prophet and the pastor, *but which protects the Church from the bully and the chicken!* The scripture certainly calls us to be prophets and pastors, but also certainly not to become bullies or cowards.

One definite response to this sad condition is for the Church to begin paying attention, precisely as we are currently doing, to the problems and challenges related *specifically* to the *praxis* of the pastor. *Mirable dictu,* this has already begun! In our present circumstance, we Orthodox have only lately begun to realize that, along with history, liturgics, doctrine, etc., the ministry *as a subject* in itself within the theological curriculum, is crucial to the ongoing life of the Church. Furthermore, this condition can only improve as we begin to plan learning experiences through the various symposia which have as their exclusive focus pastoral praxis. All too often, for the Orthodox, such a focus belongs to the Catholics and Protestants alone. This means that we can continue to live "as if," that is "as if" the matter of the unity and Christian relationships within the Body of Christ; "as if" the matter of the people *living* as Christians; "as if" the matter of making crucial decisions and ethical choices dependent upon faith-stances (rather than "popular" current trends); "as if" the matter of *implementing* the gospel in the flesh of each new generation — in other words, "as if" such issues do not have to be the concern of the Orthodox, as they are of the others. The ministry of the Church is not practiced when such issues are circumvented in such "as if" attitude.

It is when we are sincerely willing to deal specifically with the *praxis* of the pastor that certain lessons can be learned — or "relearned" as the case may be — by those serving in the priestly ministry. For example, more than ever, does the pastor not have to remember that this is not his *own* ministry, but that of Christ's; he is not a free-wheeling ecclesiastical entrepreneur, but a "disciple" of the Master (the *only* High Priest, the *only* mediator) *in* whose priesthood and *under* whose discipline he is "allowed" to practice (as indicated in the Ordination Service)? Furthermore, does he not need constantly to dialogue with fellow-clergy who could only serve to remind him (and each other) of such truths by which they both "build up the Body" (Gal 4.15-16)? And even more specifically to our point, does he not need a true and trusted father confessor who can continuously remind him of the need to "control and tame" whatever extreme (e.g. "bully and chicken") which will rise up to ensnare and impede his praxis within the community? Such sources and experiences can only help in the clarification of his task, as well as in his capacity to truly discern with a "priestly consciousness" as he directs the "flock." In such a way, we can at least struggle against the dangerous limitations of either the narrowly "prophetic" or the narrowly "pastoral," both of which too easily become the "bully" and the "chicken."

Although much more could be said along the line of such extreme inclinations and their relationship to the communal body, we must at this point move on to explore where such a pastoral praxis, if it is *not* endangered in this way, should be leading us in the development of interpersonal relations within the Church. But certainly, the development of the Christian community does begin with the proper "praxis of the *proestos*," the practice of the leader of the community.

Where, then, should a proper pastoral practice be leading the community? Or better, using Saint Gregory the Theologian's language, where should "the method of pastoral care which is right and just, and worthy of our True Shepherd" be leading the relationships within the communal life? We move from concern with the central impact of the pastoral praxis on communal life, to exploring the *nature* of that communal life itself, although, at each point, such an exploration will always be inclusive of the function of the leader. Our exploration must include three components: 1) the meaning of relationships in a distinct Christian context, i.e. the "theology of relations," 2) the actual *experience* of communion and 3) the activity of the Spirit which must be "stirred up" (2 Tim 1.6) rather than be "quenched" (1 Thes 5.9) for the sake of the community's mission to God's created world. In our third and last point, we will emphasize the relationship of the Christian community to our contemporary world which is so radically and rapidly "changing." Once the Spirit in the community is "stirred up," then that community must seek to "stir up" the world. We now turn to these three points.

The Theology of Relations

What is there about "relations" which is distinctly Christian? Why must the leader be concerned with this relational element? And where do we learn the basis for such Christian relations? These, and questions like them, take us into the consideration of the ministry which has, as its basis, the "theology of relations."

The community of believers is, therefore, by its very nature, 'for others.' Individually and collectively, believers are united in the communion of the Holy Spirit to the Father and the Son. At the same time, the believing members of the Body of Christ are united together by that same Spirit. And by their relationship to each other and God, believers are directed toward all of humanity.[6]

With these words Edward Malatesta capsulates and summarizes the entire range of Christian relations. The basis for interpersonal relationships in its distinct Christian context is that it is a relationship of fidelity in which one lives precisely "for others." From Genesis to Revelation, the scripture unfolds what God intends to be a relationship of reciprocal fidelity with those he has created in his image. Of course, what God intends is not always what the people receive; they are always wavering — one time rejecting, another time receiving — in this relationship of fidelity to God and each other. Thus we see in scripture a history of darkness and light, sorrow and joy, division and union, which will only be finally resolved when God and his people dwell together forever in peace (Rev 21.1-4). The gracious deeds of Father, Son, and Holy Spirit are God's attempt to show us what is to be our own way. He shows us that "he loved us with an everlasting love" (Jer 31.3), and that "he who is love (1 Jn 4.8 and 16) remains faithful (Is 40.8). Finally we see that the greatest reality of this fidelity toward us is given "in the fullness of time" with the person and deeds of Jesus (Heb 1.2), who is the faithful and true witness (Rev 3.14), the merciful and High Priest (Heb 2.17), the one who loved us perfectly to the end (Jn 13.1); this is the same one who now both intercedes for us in the presence of his Father (Heb 7.24-35) and dwells in our midst by the Holy Spirit (Mt 18.20 and 28.20). His fidelity toward us is to be our fidelity toward each other. This is the basis for all Christian relations between persons; it begins with God's initiative toward in creation and redemption, but it is our part to respond by assuming it to be our own way.

We see in this truth that if the supreme revelation of God himself is given to the world in the Incarnation — the "enfleshment" of his Word (Logos) in the "person" of Christ — then personality

---

[6]Edward Malatesta, "The Mystery of Faith," *The Way* (1971) 220.

is raised to a level of unique significance.[7] Furthermore, if
God's salvific work is done through various "personal" relationships, i.e. through his appointed personal agents, then again, personal relationships are also raised to a level of unique significance.

A study of human relationships reveals that the communication
and communion of one person with another embodies a unique
spiritual reality that cannot be denied and should never be
distorted.[8]

There is no relationship between human persons which is in-
significant. That this must be constantly transmitted by the pastor, there must be no doubt, and he begins to show this by *himself* living in this way. Again, his praxis could be the crucial beginning point, although it cannot end there; his relationship with
the persons of his community can be diffuse in such a way that
it creates an atmosphere of mutuality within it. This means that
when the leader is a "teacher," he is teaching *persons* with sensitivity and concern; when he is "priest," he is offering up the
gifts on behalf of *persons* (for a priest is nothing else than one
"who offers"); when he is "prophet," he is challenging *persons*
who, although gone astray, he believes are "worth it"; when he
is confessor and spiritual director he is guiding, encouraging and
disciplining *persons* to help them make certain choices (which
truly must be their own, and not his). In short, in these ways, and
many more, when he is the leader, he is leading *persons*. These
persons are not objects, nor are they merely "sheep" (animals),
as Saint John Chrysostom warns; indeed they are a "rational
flock."[9]

In very specific terms of relationships, it is Martin Buber who
made this the central point in his famous work, *I and Thou*. Buber's important contribution to our understanding is that the
world of objects does presuppose an "I," and that that "I" does

---

[7]Earl Furgeson, "A Relational Theory of Ministry," *Pastoral Psychology* (1976) 268-81.

[8]Ibid. p. 268.

[9]Cf. Book Two of Chrysostom's *On the Priesthood* in *Nicene and Post-
Nicene Fathers*, Vol. 11 (Grand Rapids, 1968), pp. 39-44.

arrange and appropriate these objects. But then, he says, the world of *persons* is constituted of "others," who *cannot* be appropriated. For an "I" to relate to a "Thou" as if were an "It," would be to deny the sacred element in personal relationships.[10] This is a basic lesson in the "ethics" of personal relationships. Are we not taught the very same lesson about Christian relationships in the Epistle of Saint James? Only now we are given specific direct and ethical instructions, for example: "If a brother or sister is naked, or destitute of daily food," we cannot merely dismiss them saying, "Depart in peace, be warm and filled, as if we do not have to give them the things that are needful" (Jam 2.15-16). (Actually the entire epistle gives this lesson, but especially chapter two).

In truth, any two persons are in relationship when each makes a difference to the life of the other. Although such a definition may be a very wide one, we learn, by extension, that *if* every relationship "makes a difference," then no single one can ever be neutral. In fact, "if we tend to think that some of our relationships are neutral, we should ask ourselves whether we are talking about 'relationships,' or simply about co-existence. A relationship is either growth-producing or life-destroying."[11]

What is it, though, which makes a relationship "growth-producing?" In the end, for the Christian it is always a true love, and it is one which is most adequately defined in the word, *agape.* Of course, the meaning of this *agape* is fully embodied in the Christ of God. When we note the Christ-event we see, at once, a "suffering-love" and an "affirming-love"; we see the cross and we see affirmation of human worth in the hope and forgiveness of the resurrection. However, these forms are already given to us, i.e. they are proleptically demonstrated before the death and resurrection, in the daily ministry of Jesus of Nazareth.

Among many examples of this, for instance, we see his willingness to "turn his face up to Jerusalem" (Lk 9.51) which indicates this "suffering-love," and we see his "affirming-love" — despite the suspicions of the Pharisee Simon — of the prostitute who washed his feet (Lk 7.37-49). Taken together, these two qualities

---

[10]Martin Buber, *I and Thou,* trans. R. G. Smith (1937).

[11]Jacques Pasquier, "Healing Relationships," *The Way* 16 (3, 1976) 208-15.

suffering- and affirming-love, are the hallmarks of true love, and it is through persons who live by such Christian qualities that that work of Christian interpersonal relations is realized. This is true because such qualities, after all, require the capacity fully both to receive and express love, not only in the simpler, more natural forms of affection (*storge*), e.g. toward one's family, or in brotherly love (*philia*), or again in sexual attraction (*eros*), but also in those seemingly unnatural forms of loving those whom one does not necessarily like (Mt 5.44). Here is the quality of being willing to accept those who are unacceptable, of always struggling to differentiate between the *nature* of the person and the *act* of the person (or as the Orthodox like to teach, especially in ascetic literature, between the sin which is hated and the sinner who is loved). This, of course, is no easy task and we try whenever possible to circumvent this "narrow way," especially in face-to-face relations. The sad truth of things is bluntly put into the mouth of Ivan Karamazov by Dostoevsky: "I have never been able to understand how one can love one's neighbor. To my mind, it is just one's neighbor one cannot love, although one might love those *at a distance*" (Book 5, chapter 4).

But the Christian cannot avoid this truth of the gospel of Christ: unlike popular views of feelings, of "falling in love," etc., his is a demand to love, and at that, to love precisely face-to-face and not "at a distance." This demand means his acceptance of persons as they are (even if not approving of what they are doing), i.e. to affirm and accept them as having a right *to be* rather than *not to be*. Here is the true meaning of *sympathein* ("co-suffer") of which the Epistle to the Hebrews speaks when pointing to Christ, our High Priest who sympathizes (*sympathesai*) with us; the exact meaning of this term in our present context is our willingness to "be touched with the feeling of the infirmity" of the other person (Hebrews 4.15). In fact, this means that it is to feel or suffer "as if within the other person's frame." This must be done without such sympathy (or better, "empathy") degenerating into emotional sentimentality. It is a delicate balance, to be sure, but one required in a true Christian context.

In perfect line with this, if one looks to the true meaning of the Apostle Paul's definition of *agape* in his most beautiful "hymn to love" (1 Cor 13) — and now in terms of our present point — he sees what this could mean: this love is never blind to evil, but rejoices only in the good; it rejoices in the excellence of the beloved, while not condemning what is less than excellent. Such love, then, is reverence for the other in that it does not seek to absorb the other into one's self, nor want to be absorbed by the other, or as C. S. Lewis says it in his usual paradoxical way, it keeps its distance as it draws near.[12] This love desires the beloved to be what he truly is, created in God's image, and thus valued, without attempting to refashion him into *my* image. Furthermore, this love seeks knowledge of the other, not by way of curiosity (which so often merely satisfies one's "lust of itchy ears"), nor to seek power over him, but only to understand, and in this understanding, to enter into communion with that other (for such knowledge, born out of this agape, *is* communion with that other).

Finally, this love in the interpersonal relations of the Christian, does not evade suffering, but is willing — precisely because suffering so often is the touchstone of true love — to participate in it. In this way, as the Apostle says, "love never fails," for if one lives by this "demand," love will *not* fail. In the practicalities of communal life, however, this again begins with the leader, who in such sympathy (empathy) must "sit where the people sit." As the Prophet Ezekiel put it: "I sat where they sat, and remained astonished among them for seven days. And . . . the word of the Lord came upon me . . . " (Ezek 3.15-16).

Relations, then, are "growth-producing" (rather than "life-destroying") for the Christian, when he is following the way of the Lord Jesus because *agape* is at the center of a true "theology of relations."

The Experience of Communion: Sharing the Spirit

If Christians live by the true love within the communal life, what then are they to *experience*? This is our second crucial component. Although there are no doubt many ways of describing this experience, one of the most comprehensive is that to which Saint Paul points: "For freedom (*eleutheria*) Christ has set us free" (Gal 5.1). Apart from the redeeming work of Christ, man finds himself captive to his own limitation, weakness and impulse; he is imprisoned by his sinfulness and selfishness; he is dominated

---

[12]C. S. Lewis, *The Four Loves* (London, 1960), p. 100.

by pressures and influences of wickedness, both within and without. He cannot truly love others, because he is too self-concerned and inward-turned; he cannot be one-for-others because he is bound to himself. By the power of Christ, however, Paul is teaching that he is liberated into love, that is, he is given freedom to love and be loved. Here is the true meaning of the word *eleutheria* (liberty, freedom), and its implication for our present point.

However, when we look carefully at this word *eleutheria*, we find that the Lord himself, especially in the Johannine literature, is telling us that the agency by which such liberty is experienced, is the Holy Spirit whom the Lord promises to his Church (cf. Jn 14.16). In fact it is only within the communal experience of this freedom that Christians are made *aware* of the presence of the Spirit in their midst. This is the reason why Paul could also write, "Where the Spirit of the Lord is, there is freedom" (*eleutheria*) (1 Cor 3.17). And in still another place, the great Apostle describes the *effect* of the presence of the Spirit when it is experienced among us: "But the fruit of the Spirit is love, joy, peace, patience, kindness, goodness, faithfulness, gentleness and self-control" (Gal 5.22-23). To the degree that we experience *these* things which are the "fruit of the Spirit," not merely as desirable, but actually made possible through a "power" (*exousia, dynamis*) given to us in faith, we experience the presence of God's Spirit among us. And, of course, in the Christian communal life, this happens *together*; we share this experience, we "share the Spirit."

However, this communal experience begins, paradoxically, when we forsake total reliance upon ourselves, and in this case, even upon our own ability to create community. After all, Christian community is *God's* gift, created through his Spirit. Our part, i.e. our human task, is to open ourselves up to the Spirit so that, in whatever we are able to accomplish, it will clearly remain in our minds that this is a "response" to the activity of the Spirit. As it applies to communal life, this gives to us the true meaning of "cooperation" (*synergia*) in which everything we have and can do comes from God, our human "will" responding to his initiative. This is a crucial understanding because, when we forget it, we come to believe that Christian community can rest solely upon our human technique and mechanism. It is not that what we do as human persons is unimportant, but if that is all we live by, there will be no "fruit of the Spirit" experienced in the communal life, only "groupings of people," perhaps sharing a common task or goal. It is the efficacy of the Spirit which makes the community a Christian one.

Thus "cooperation" does imply our human response. Saint Paul best captures this dynamic of the *synergia* of God's grace and human response within the communal life, when he addresses the community of Christians at Corinth:

> I, therefore, a prisoner of the Lord, beg you to lead a life worthy of the calling to which you have been called, with all lowliness and meekness, with patience, forbearing one another in love, eager to maintain the unity of the Spirit in the bond of peace (Eph 4.1-3).

Appealing to their human will, Saint Paul is urging them "to lead a life worthy of the calling," i.e. he is asking them for their own human will and virtue, that they may live "with all lowliness, meekness, patience and forbearance." Furthermore, showing again that they do have a part in this communal process, his hope is that they will seek the unity which they "should be eager to maintain." For us who now read this epistle, Paul is also inviting us to share this experience which is, precisely, to respond to the promptings of the Spirit. But no mistake should be made regarding where it begins: community is, at once, created by the Spirit and conferred upon us by the Spirit.

Of course, this divine communication into which we ourselves enter through our cooperation, has as its deepest source and symbol, the life of the Trinity itself. God establishes a "community" as Father, Son, and Holy Spirit, three persons in the truest of interpersonal relationships. The eternal life which these three persons have together overflows in the act of creation and redemption in such a way that we, in the human community of persons, may share with them in the life of love and joy which describes their own eternal life. This is so fundamental to the Orthodox ethos and teaching of communal life, including the very meaning of the Eucharist, that little more need be said. The sole reason that this essential and theological truth is raised at this point in our presentation is the reminder that, in the experience of our interpersonal relations as Christians, we are united not only with each other, but also with the Father and the Son through the Spirit. In fact, this truth is expressed by Paul's closing words of blessing to the community of Corinthian Christians: "The grace of our Lord Jesus Christ, the love of God, and the communion of the Holy Spirit be with you" (2 Cor 13.14). (We find this blessing also in the Anaphora of the eucharistic Liturgy.)

However, we also cannot forget that, by definition, "experience" is something which is "seen, looked upon, touched," etc.; it is something which, although inexplicable to our human minds and limitations, is nevertheless felt and sensed. Regarding *this* particular experience of Christian communion, it is received by us from those who, before us, have themselves experienced it, and who now "bear witness" and "testify" to us that that very experience is now to be our own. This is what Saint John, in his First Letter, means:

> That which was from the beginning, which we have seen with our eyes, which we have looked upon, and touched with our hands, concerning the word of life . . . we saw it, and testify to it, and proclaim it to you, the eternal life which was with the Father, and was made manifest to us — this we proclaim to you so that *you* may have communion with us; and our communion (with each other) is with the Father and his Son, Jesus Christ. And we are writing this that our joy might be complete" (1 Jn 1.1-13).

One cannot fail to notice the development of this passage. After recounting the tangible and visible experience which is received by John in the communication of God (in the Incarnation), John proceeds to proclaim that those who willingly receive this communication in faith, will themselves be drawn into that very same experience by God's Spirit. Thus it is the Spirit who is one and the same in Christ and in us. In this way, i.e. by the experience of the Spirit, we become ourselves "sons of God": "For all who are led by the Spirit of God, are sons of God" (Rom 8.14), in fact, "it is the Spirit himself bearing witness with our spirit, that we are children of God, and if children, then heirs: heirs of God and fellow-heirs with Christ, provided we suffer with him in order that we may also be glorified with him (Rom 8.15-17).

Having now pointed to the communal experience of "sharing

the Spirit'' in the inner life of the Christian community, we move now to the ''stirring of the Spirit,'' but now for the sake of God's created world.

The Community for the World: Stirring up the Spirit

After addressing the inner communal experience of ''sharing the Spirit,'' we must finally move on to ''stirring up the Spirit.'' With this aspect we have to point, even more strongly and clearly, to the distinct human endeavor and activity which is to respond to the Spirit, but now in terms of the community's relationship of mission to God's created world. In this way, we move from within to without, from the community out to the world.

Looked at from our present perspective, *we* become a source for the giving of life, a means whereby God transmits his Spirit into the minds and hearts of others. Here there is an openness to receive from God our gift of community, and then a willingness to be ''used'' by God in order to share it with his very own creation. Is this not what our Lord is telling us to do, as he prays to the Father: ''That they may be one as we are one, I in them and thou in me, that they may become perfectly one, so that the world may know that thou has sent me and has loved me'' (Jn 17.21-23).

It should also be said that, at this final point, we can address, at least in part, the problem of such radical ''changes'' which we find in our world, and in turn, which often take an antagonistic position *vis-à-vis* the Church. These conditions do not only affect the ''outsiders'' to Orthodoxy. The persons of the Orthodox parishes who are living in that same world, are subject to these very same pressures. Thus, we can speak of the problem of such changes which we find in our task of exploring ''*changing* interpersonal relations.''

When we begin to speak of ''stirring up the Spirit,'' as we have previously mentioned, no human person can presume that God will act without our cooperation, although God will certainly do what he will do. If this *were* presumed, there would be no basis for our concern about God's judgment (as in Mt 25), no human self-determination to live by virtue, nor to do good (e.g. as in the patristic insistence of the *autoexousion,* the ''will of the reasoning soul,'' as Saint John of Damascus calls it). In fact, all would be magic, something in which we as humans would have no part.

This is not the case, however, and the "fruit of the Spirit" is experienced by us only inasmuch as we are willing actively to share the Spirit through our human endeavors. In short, we are asked to share what we receive. How misguided, then, would be our effort to seek perfection in isolation, simply for oneself, i.e. in a supposed union with God which is cut off from a concern for others (cf. our former point regarding *agape*, sharing the Spirit, and the like). In other words, attempting to receive the gifts of God's grace (*charismata*) without our actively *seeking* to share them, and to do so generously, is analogous to a heart attempting to live and beat for itself, and not for the rest of the body. Again, just as we are asked to share what we have received *within* the community, so we, *as* community, are asked to share what we have received with our larger world. This is the evangelical impulse which was so alive in the apostolic Church; it is a critical part of our present concern.

Each of the many ways, more than possibly can be included here, in which the Spirit is to be "stirred up" and not "quenched," has to do with our seeking to activate the Spirit who is always trying to engage human persons. But as we face God's created world, we must ask, "Why do *we as humans* have to be concerned at all?" The answer is not complex, although it is so very simple to "bury one's head in the sand." Jesus commands it as the way that the Spirit will work. "Go," he says to his Apostles, and in every generation, Christians stand shoulder to shoulder with those same Apostles. The particular problems with which we are faced today make us no less "apostles" than those mentioned in the Gospels.

We can see our current task in light of this reasoning when we note two recent books, *Christianity Confronts Modernity,* and *Summons to Faith and Renewal.*[13] One of the central points in these two books is that the Christian faith *vis-à-vis* the world (or better, society), is now more than ever in history in a life-death struggle; the war being fought is more potentially devastating to the life of the Church. Here enters the concern with "changes," for both books locate this powerfully negative stream of influence

---

[13]*Christianity Confronts Modernity,* ed. P. Williamson and K. Perrota (Ann Arbor, 1981) and *Summons to Faith and Renewal* (Ann Arbor, 1983) by the same editors.

as occurring between persons, e.g. in familial relations, sexual relations, occupational relations, and the like. Such changes as are
occurring in these arenas are almost beyond the human grasp;
our world seems to be falling apart, in terms of what was considered socially "normative." (*Is* there anything "normative"
today?)

> Modern cities, national bureaucracies, corportations, labor
> unions, school systems, and the rest have appeared. The
> churches find themselves pushed to the periphery of society by
> this expansion. In this new technological order, Christianity
> seems of questionable importance to some, who look to science,
> technology, and government to answer questions or solve
> problems.[14]

To this is added:

> At the same time, the impressive growth of technology has
> strengthened the temptation to place man, his accomplishments
> and his potential, at the center of all consideration.[15]

These statements, and the many social and ancillary problems
that accompany them, tell us that we must direct the multitude
of gifts of the Spirit, given to the Christian community, *out* to the
world. As obvious as this is, it still must be reiterated because there
are always those who hold the thesis that in such contemporary
changes, there is "nothing new." However true that may be (and
there is much doubt about that when one considers, for example,
the many bio-ethical scenarios today!), we are still challenged as
a Christian community living in the world, to be a particular *type*
of people, one which has a mission to that world. But perhaps in
this we should simply allow the great Apostle to speak, as he did
when writing to the Christians at Philippi. There he tells them that
they were "children of God without blemish in the midst of a
crooked and perverse generation, among whom you shine like lights
in the world" (Phil 2.15). The *fact* of our Christian task is the same,
regardless of whether or not the forms have changed: the world

---

[14]Ibid., *Summons*, p. 13.
[15]Ibid. p. 13.

is essentially without that which it needs most, a living relationship with its Creator and Redeemer.

This being the case, we must re-learn how to "stir up the Spirit" in today's world (cf. Mt 5.16). By this, of course, the call is not to a careless and reckless relationship with the world, e.g. merely in supporting this or that political position, nor in some sacramental sense of inter-communion. Rather, what must be done is to show the *light* which the darkness of the world prefers to hide, to display *forgiveness* in a world of revenge, to *comfort* in a world which prefers to ravage. "Stirring up the Spirit," in our present and final point, regardless of the programmatics involved, means precisely this: the Christian community, with all that we have claimed in this presentation comprises it, must be constantly approaching the the world. The ministry of the Church, commanded by the Head of this body, must be at the very cutting edge, and it must be so with these three messages: *light, forgiveness, and comfort.*

It is with mention of these three distinct Christian virtues, so badly needed in our world, that we should like to conclude our presentation. This seems to us logical since any "changes" which the Christian community can effect in order to counteract those pressing and negative forces imposed upon persons living in the world, can only be realized in light of these three virtues.

Our first obligation is to give *light.* We are required to communicate to the world the light which we have received in our own lives: "Let your light so shine before men that they may see your good works and give glory to your Father who is in heaven" (Mt 5.16). This is required because light, it if is merely received and not acted upon, can be mere information. But, "the fruit of light is found in all that is good and right and true" (Eph 5.19). Orthodox Christianity has an obligation to proclaim to the world all that "is good and right and true." Thus from practicing such elements of the light as might be experienced within the community, the movement must then go outward.

Our second obligation to offer is *forgiveness.* The commission given to the disciples on Pascha is one of forgiveness. "Receive the Holy Spirit, and if you forgive the sins of any they are forgiven; if you retain the sins of any they are retained;" this is preceeded by, "As the Father has sent me, so do I send you"

(Jn 20.21-23). Paul repeats this meaning for the Christians at Colossae: "Put on then, as God's chosen ones, holy and beloved, compassion, kindness, lowliness, meekness, and patience" — and then as if summarizing it all Paul continues, "forbearing one another, and if one has a complaint against another, forgive each other; as the Lord has forgiven you, so you must forgive others" (Col 3.12-13). These words directly connect with the community's message to the world. In even clearer terms, Saint Paul would at another time describe this message of forgiveness in terms of a "ministry of reconciliation": "God was in Christ reconciling the world to himself, not counting their trespasses against them, and entrusting to us the ministry of reconciliation. And so we are 'ambassadors' for Christ, God making his appeal through us" (2 Cor 5.19-20).

The third and final obligation is *comforting*. We must be concerned with comfort because light and forgiveness do not automatically remove what is hurtful and painful in our lives. Christians, therefore, both look to God to receive comfort and strength from him, and turn to the world to share with others the comfort they have received: "The God of all comfort . . . comforts us in all our affliction, so that we may be able to comfort those who are in any affliction, with the comfort with which we ourselves are comforted by God" (2 Cor 1.4). This comfort, again, does not mean the elimination of all suffering from life, but rather the ability and the strength to endure, a strength that comes from both the power of God at work in us, and from the support of the brethren with whom we share an interpersonal relationship in the Christian community.

These three gifts, then, each which is received in the community as a gift of God's Spirit, are not only the basis of the interpersonal relations which are experienced within that communal life; they are also to be "stirred up" as a basis for the Church's relationship with the world, *for the sake of the world*.

Looking at the whole picture of Orthodox parish life and interpersonal relations, therefore, we see that this process, which must begin with the praxis of the pastor, must then flow through the communal relations and into the world.

Response to Joseph J. Allen's "Parish Life and Changing Interpersonal Relationships"

DANIEL J. SAHAS

IN RESPONDING TO A WELL THOUGHT-THROUGH PRESENTATION made by someone who specializes in pastoral theology, I become even more conscious of the fact that I, with no formal qualifications in psychology or in pastoral theology, and with no vocational experience as a priest, am out of place. If there are any redeeming reasons which might make my participation less objectionable, these are, simply stated, the meaning and implications of *laicos* in the Orthodox Church as an integral part of the people of God which consists of priests and laypeople alike, the understanding of an Orthodox parish and of its experience in North America, the meaning and the function of the Orthodox *diakonia*, and finally, the imperative of a balance that the Orthodox Church strikes and cultivates between theology and *praxis*.

These redeeming factors, however, have not, nor will they now absolve me from misunderstandings or statements of naivete. Such defects are, certainly, personal risks, which I often take for the sake of my own elucidation, not necessarily for the sake of that of Father Allen and of the participants.

Father Allen's paper is clear and its theses are lucid. The structure and the main points of his paper, if I am allowed to reiterate them, are the following:

1. The topic itself identifies the problem; this is "the pastoral praxis," that is, the relations of the pastor to the parish and of the parishioners among themselves.
2. The example of the *praxis* of the *proestos* (leader) is to be

63

found in the ascetic works of Saint Basil.

3. The praxis of the priest can range between the "bully" and the "chicken," or the "prophet" and the "pastor."

4. The praxis of the priest has consequences upon the life of the parish. Any inclination taken to its extreme is an "ecclesiological heresy."

5. The training of priests in pastoral theology should be an integral part of theological education provided by the Church and the seminary.

6. An analysis of the character of communal life involves consideration of three things: the meaning of relationships (i.e. the theology of relations), the actual experience of communion, and the activity of the Spirit.

   a) What makes a relationship grow and be growth-producing is love, in its comprehensive Christian sense.

   b) The fruit of communal love is freedom; the agent which makes freedom to be experienced is the Spirit, and experience of communion means sharing in the Spirit.

   c) The community lives not for itself but for the sake of the world; the ministry of the Church in the world is summarized in light, forgiveness and comfort.

The first part of my response will be to these particular points. With regard to the first point, it seems to me that "Orthodox Parish Life and Interpersonal Relationships" as a topic can mean different things to different people, and all of them be valid. Father Allen's introductory assertion that

> If the pastoral problem at hand is to deal with the two crucial aspects of th Christian community, "Orthodox Parish Life" and "Changing Interpersonal Relations," then the problem must be filtered through the screen of pastoral praxis,"

contains, from the beginning, a limitation and it implies an abstraction. It represents, I think, a limited methodology in dealing with the "problem" (why is it a problem?) by filtering it through the screen of pastoral praxis. Any discussion of changing interpersonal relationships and their implications for parish life (or the opposite) must deal with the praxis and life of all those persons and factors involved, but before even that it must engage itself in some reflection of the basic theological presuppositions of person-hood.[1] It is necessary also to state and keep in mind that when we are talking about Orthodox parish life, we must be fully conscious of, and sensitive to a concrete reality in space and time (in this instance, I suppose, the local immigrant or semi-immigrant Greek, Russian, etc. parish in North America), without either confusing it with, nor separating it from, the mystical body of Christ in its unity and catholicity.[2]

Although one can hardly call an Orthodox community "a parish" without a eucharistic *proestos,* that is an ordained leader, parish is, nevertheless, a much more complex reality. At this point I would like to emphasize that theological immaturity and lack of eucharistic sacramental relationships make interpersonal relations, on the functional level, even more complex and problematic. There is a direct reciprocity between personhood and sacramental relationship which we need to understand and cultivate further. Interpersonal relationships, therefore, are part of a more complex network that involves not only the relations between the priest and the parishioners, but also the relations of the parishioners with the priest, the relations of the parishioners among themselves, the priest and his own social environment, as well as the parishioners and their own social environment. Again, in the section of the meaning of relationships, or the theology of relations, Father Allen is *practical* in stressing love as the center of a true "theology of relations." There are no qualms about this. But again, we must broaden the meaning of relationships, or the theology of relations, as something beyond and in spite of love. Personhood is a gift and a state of being which does not depend on loving or being loved. Loving and being loved do not define personhood, as sin also does not

---

[1] I have been forced to use for this paper this new word "personhood" in order to relate the state, condition, quality, and character of being a person, as neither "personality" nor "personage" yield this meaning. For interesting material and remarks on the philosophical and theological meaning of "person," see Christos Yiannaras, *To ontologikon periechomenon tes theologikes ennoias tou prosopou,* (Athens, 1970).

[2] John D. Zizioulas' *Being as Communion. Studies in Personhood and the Church* (Crestwood, N.Y., 1985) is now a "must" for Orthodox ecclesiology and for any discussion on personhood. Cf. especially what Zizioulas writes in chapters 3 and 4 with regard to the unity of the Church and its catholicity, pp. 123-69.

define human nature. I would tend to think that holocausts (Armenian or Jewish), Shabras and Shatilas, political, religious, or ethnic persecutions and atrocities against people, do not annihilate the person; they expose what is "non-person." We must cultivate the meaning and the significance of personhood in spite of any emotional considerations. Personhood is a given. It is something that is affirmed (or actually celebrated) by acknowledging it, but it loses nothing of its own, even if it is not affirmed, or loved.

On the second point, I would like to question whether we can equate the role of the *proestos* in an ascetic community, and the *proestos* in a parish community. Not that the principle stated by Father Allen, that "the praxis and life of the *proestos* is fundamental to the development of those involved in the communal life" does not hold true in both instances. But the presuppositions of a monastic, let alone of an ascetic, community are markedly different from those existing in an Orthodox community-parish anywhere, especially in North America. Firstly, the members of a community-parish are not celibate members. Secondly, they have not taken the vows of poverty. Indeed, if they have taken any such vows, these are towards the opposite end! And thirdly, and most importantly, they have not taken any vow to be obedient and submit themselves to the will of the *proestos* as if this were the will of God. Along with these essential differences there are also the contextual monastic presuppositions of contemplation, prayer, communal life, work, fasting, and others, which are not the characteristics of a community-parish. All these characteristics change radically the nature and the implications of interpersonal relations. One thing, however, is absolutely certain: that one gains a great deal of insight, and enriches and refreshes himself immensely when one looks into, and draws from, the tradition of Orthodox spirituality and praxis, and especially from the monastic and ascetic ethos of the Fathers. This is a precious and valuable resource that we Orthodox have. The challenge for us must be not how to exhibit it or transplant it in the world. The challenge for us must be how to knead this ethos with, and make it part of, our modern intellectualized, rationalized, compartmentalized, consumerist and technological mentality and praxis. Along with that we need both to know and to acknowledge the changes which are taking place in human life in our society, these being either "crises" or "passages."[3] We *must* acknowledge and take into account the socio-political context within which our parishes in North America live. These are not normative circumstances under which Orthodox life, as we have received it, can be cultivated and Orthodox community-parishes can develop today, and in this part of the world. We *must* acknowledge and take into account the historical reality of our Orthodox community-parishes, as well as the jurisdictional maze of the Orthodox diaspora in North America. These are not matters which we can easily overlook when we talk about "Orthodox parish life" and "interpersonal relations."[4] After all, neither Orthodox parish life nor interpersonal relations take place in the stratosphere or in the abstract.

On the third point, I was somehow taken aback by the equation of the "bully" with the "prophetic type," and the "chicken" with the "pastoral type" of priest; particularly the latter pair of names. I have experienced and have always pictured in my mind the shepherd (that is the pastor) being raggedly dressed, wearing rough, heavy boots, constantly moving, running, throwing stones to alert his flock, using his staff made of unpolished wood with knots on his impertinent and disobedient sheep, fighting wolves, and searching to find the not so single lost sheep. This is at least the biblical image of the pastor and that which I have experienced in the rural and ragged countryside of Greece and of the Middle East, especially in the Sinai desert. I can hardly equate, therefore, such an image of a pastor to a "chicken." Pastors of opulent offices, surrounded by framed degrees and well-bound books hardly ever opened, do not resemble shepherds, not even chickens!

On the fourth point, I must say that I am particularly gratified by Father Allen's somewhat derogatory use of the word "inclination" (and especially inclination in praxis) because, indeed, it is "inclination" that defines accurately that which is not orthodox. It is about time that the word "orthodox" be understood properly and used not as a name for triumphalism, or as a convenient fortification to defend idiosyncrasies, but as a name which

[3] See, for example, the findings in such popular empirical surveys as in Gail Sheehy, *Passages, Predictable Crises of Adult Life* (New York, 1974).

[4] See the papers presented at the Third International Theological Conference of Orthodox Theologians in America, *The Greek Orthodox Theological Review*, 34 (1979) 2, 3.

has tangible implications and measurable manifestations, *vis-à-vis* "inclinations." The question is not whether an inclination is of doctrine or praxis, and then whether it is towards the right or towards the left. Inclination itself is, precisely, an abnormality, because it is an individual preference or mood. This is what unorthodox is in essence: ignoring or negating the "royal way" which inclines neither to the right nor to the left; resorting to an individualism instead of integrating inclinations and extremes, being idiosyncratic instead of balanced (*orthos*) and comprehensive (*doxa*, that is, faith and expression), losing the sense of the body.[5]

On the other hand, the identification of a behavior inclination with an "ecclesiological *heresy*" might not be accurate in this context. Any personal behavioral inclination speaks more of the reality of the Church as a *living body* of human beings, and it does not necessarily need to be viewed as heresy. The parish, although the microcosm of the Church, is not necessarily the absolute and exclusive definition of the Church. The parish is the Church, but the Church transcends the borders of the parish. The catholicity of the parish is affirmed and safeguarded by its sacramental life, but its physical, visible dimension is not coincidental to the Church at large. In other words, the pastor of a parish is not the Church, or the equivalent to all the pastors, let alone to priesthood itself.

It seems to me that, beyond behavioral personal characteristics, the sacerdotal ministry of a priest in its full sense, and his role as one who paves the right path (*orthotomei*) of the word of God's truth, are much more essential and central ecclesiological issues. Whether a priest is a "bully" or a "chicken" might be in the end immaterial; both are needed and a big variety in between, and all of them preferably in one and the same person. What is a more significant thing to consider is, I think, whether the priest views his parishioners as reasonable sheep destined to salvation,[6] and each one of them as a unique and unrepeatable person. This is the inherent meaning and implication of *person*: to face each other *tête-à-tête*, to recognize in someone else a person, and to respond to this person directly. Only then a relationship is meaningful when

---

[5] See "The Christological Dimension of Orthodox Catechesis" in Daniel J. Sahas, *Catechesis: The Maturation of the Body* (Brookline, 1984), pp. 59-73.

[6] Cf. 1. Pet 2.2.

it is personal — meaning, when it is responding in a personal (not institutional) way, and in the way required by the particular person and the circumstances. Paul's "I have become all things to all men"[7] points, I think, to a comprehensive and balanced, rather than to an unstable or inconsistent person.

On the fifth point, there is little to be argued against apple-pie and education. And yet I am tempted to ask the question and broaden the issue: Are not education and students influenced by teachers? What about, for example, a "bully" or a "chicken" curriculum, teacher, or institution? Should not pastoral education be treated as something broader than a formal institutional exercise, and be inspired to become a constant personal struggle for intellectual and spiritual enrichment of the individual, and a responsibility of the Church as a whole?

I have no qualms with what Father Allen says on the sixth point about the distinct Christian elements of "relations." Perhaps I would have stressed more the distinct Christian meaning or person on account of the personal character of God known in Trinity, the meaning and the significance of sharing in the recreation and the redemption of the new Adam,[8] or the meaning in sharing a common spiritual womb, the baptistry of the Church. The uniqueness of Christian theology is to be found in the experience of God the Father, God the Son, God the Holy Spirit, that is, in a personal God. Father Allen tends to overemphasize the role of the priest in interpersonal relationships: "if God's salvific work is done through various 'personal' relationships, i.e. *through his appointed personal agents* (the emphasis is mine), then again, personal relationships are also raised to a level of unique significance." If the question at stake is interpersonal relationships in the proper meaning of the word, then persons, priests and laypeople, who see each other as being subject to the same conditions, with similar quests and yearnings, have a better chance of relating meaningfully with each other.

---

[7] Cf. 1 Cor 9.19-23.

[8] John of Damascus is particularly helpful in this context by reminding us of the inherent value of human nature and its glorification after the incarnation, to the extent that human beings are even superior to the angels! *Imag.* 3. 26, 64-67 in P. Bonifatius Kotter, *Die Schriften des Johannes von Damaskos*, vol. 3, (Berlin, 1975), p. 134.

I must admit also that I cannot see easily freedom as the fruit of communal love, as Father Allen suggests. I can see more clearly the reverse connection: personal freedom yielding love and expressing itself in love. Personhood presupposes freedom. A free person is at ease with himself and can see and relate to man and to God easier. Interpersonal relationships are primarily the outcome of freedom; and the characteristic of such relationships is, indeed, love. But, somehow, when I am faced with a rationalization or prioratization of such spiritual, mystical and God-like categories as person, freedom, love and their explanation in terms of cause and effect, I am not sure of myself. Do these notions not gain in value by being left at the apophatic and mystical realm as a personal experience, each one being of its own right and value? I would leave the entire section on "The Experience of Communion" in the hands of a more competent theologian than myself, to review and evaluate.

Towards the end, I felt that the focus of the paper had shifted from the topic of interpersonal relationships to the missionary nature of the parish, or of the Church. There is very much of substance in this paper to be digested. On a topic like this, it is difficult for one to decide whether to be theoretical and talk about notions, or be practical and talk about concrete empirical instances. One thing is certain; our theological tradition and our empirical church life provide us with plenty of opportunities and food for thought, contemplation, study, and integration of both, especially integration!

The key issues in our topic are (Orthodox) parish life, persons, relationships, and change. In this second part of my response, allow me a few remarks on each of these four issues as a way of amplifying Father Allen's contribution and integrating these issues together.

Change

My reading of the topic leads me to believe that the thrust of the subject under discussion is the *changing* interpersonal relationships — something which, I think, one must take as a given. After defining and evaluating these changes one then is asked to discuss their impact upon the Orthodox parish. Interpersonal relationships, by definition, are not something static, but changing. The responsibility of thinking people and leaders is to discern changes correctly, respond to them and affect their course to the better.

It seems to me that change in interpersonal relationships in the context of parish life have to do mainly with the following agents and roles:

a) the priest and his role in relationships to his parishioners;
b) the parishioner and his or her relationship with the rest of the parish;
c) the relationship of sexes and their role in the parish life in general; and
d) the church administration in relationship to the parish.

Changes in these areas and in the persons involved should not be seen with surprise as isolated or independent phenomena. Priests, parishioners (men, women, and children), and administrators all live in a wider community of people where significant changes in social and interpersonal relationships are taking place constantly. Such broader changes are easily discernible in relationships between spouses, parents and children, authorities and subjects, friends and neighbors, countries and governments, offenders and law-abiding citizens, homegeneous or pluralistic societies.

Some expressions of by-products of such changing interpersonal relations are (not necessarily in any particular order): the proliferation of special interest groups, associations or clubs (singles' clubs, victims' associations, divorced mothers' or fathers' associations, delinquincy clubs, etc.), divorce and alternative ways of cohabitation or marital relations, proliferation and complication of statutes, legal or paralegal bodies and organizations, proliferation and sophistication of defensive and offensive personal or military weapons, commercialization of sex, aggravation of crime, narcotics, suicide, and others. There are, also, proliferation of charitable and welfare organizations, resurgence of religious fundamentalism, socialization and politicization of ethics, acceptance of universalism, adoption of religious, social, political, and cultural pluralism, rise of idealism and popular spirituality, and others.

There is a widely expressed complaint that we are moving steadily farther away from the person towards de-personalization. Indeed, critics cite as causes of this trend the computer and television, the transportation and the high-technological communication achievements of our times; the growth, compartmentalization and specialization of knowledge and skill; the intense emphasis on speed and movement; the isolation and glorification of the qualities and expertise of the individual rather than of the group or of a given society; the present-day socio-economic demands on the individual, the family, the country; the emphasis on techno-logical productivity, consumerism, and others. Personally, I am not sure that we are moving from person to de-personalization as fast as the pessimists maintain, or that the real causes of de-personalization are the ones they cite. Optimists tend to point to a growing sense of human solidarity, albeit the different solu-tions which are proposed, on broad issues of peace, the environ-ment and its survival, social justice, responsible research, toler-ance, religious and cultural pluralism, and others as signs of a grow-ing awareness of the inherent value of human nature and of personhood. Regardless of what explanation or meaning one may give to person and what reasons one may cite for it, the truth of the matter is that the notion of person is at the center of aware-ness and concern of people today, possibly more so than in past generations. However, individualization, isolation, and frag-mentation of the person *is* a characteristic of our changing times, although individualization should not be confused with indivi-duality. Individuality is a gift which matures and fulfills itself in a community with others. Cultivation of individuality and of uniqueness should not be equated with de-personalization. Or-thodox theology has stood by this principle for centuries: "Man is condemned alone, but saved with others"; a principle which upholds individuality and condemns individualism and de-personalization. Salvation means salvation of persons being in communion with others. Monasticism, for example, even in its most extreme form of individual asceticism, is not an affirmation of de-personalization, but a search for discovering the real person in one's own self, and in others. Monasticism is the search of true relationships, beginning with the discovery of the relationship of the individual with God that will lead, simultaneously, to a true relationship with others as persons, as icons of God. That is why monasticism, by definition, and in an antinomical sense, is an affirmation of communal life *par excellence* and of social con-cern. Monasticism which is anti-personal is a contradiction in terms.

The Parish

A parish is not defined by the physical confines of its establishment, but by its broader living and ontological perimeter. Parish is the community of people of God in space and time. If the parish does not extend to the work place, to the family and social life, and to the realm of influence of its parishioners into the world, then that parish does not exist, but only as a kind of religious organization or club. Parish life should not be measured by what is happening exclusively within the confines of the parish premises, but by the fruit its members bear and its impact on the life of real people in the world. An apple tree is not evaluated by its own shape and form, but by the quality of its fruit available at the market stall and on the family table.

A parish is not a museum; it is a movement and a statement. A parish is a living organism, ontologically the whole of the catholic Church. Parish is the clergy and the laity together, with no more or less responsibility resting upon any one of them separately in manifesting the historical reality of the mystical body of Christ. A parish is not a ghetto. It is the microcosm of the cosmos, of the world: "and the earth, and its fulness, is of the Lord." This is not a triumphalistic statement. It is the ontological reality of parish which, in its true simplicity, humility, and unassuming character points to the truth of the divine and integrating presence in the midst of an otherwise fragmented world.

Nothing justifies fossilization of a parish for the sake of tradition, doctrine, history, or ecclesiastical structure. Doctrine, tradition, and ecclesiastical structures are, and must remain, dynamic forces which animate and keep a parish growing and maturing.

What an Orthodox parish has to offer in a world of changing interpersonal relationships are:

    a) the balanced (*to orthodoxon*) or upright sense and content of faith, practice, and view of the world;

    b) the quest for excellence and the pursuit of that which is really good and perfect;[9]

    c) the consistency, interrelationship and integration of faith and practice, proclamation (*martyria*) and witness (*martyrion*),

---

[9] Mt 5.48.

       ideology and policy;[10]

d) the liturgy in its broadest sense: the symphony, comprehensiveness, integration and interaction between the sacred and the mundane, the spiritual and the material, the otherwordly and the worldly, the eternal and the temporal, the wholly other and each other;

e) the phenomenon of the icon: the witnessing, that is, of the deification of the human and the glorification of the material creation, as a means of communicating with and sharing in the divine life;[11]and

f) the art of Orthodox living, "walking on a tightrope," being alert, vigilant, informed, *ex-hypnos* (out of sleep), living in the world and being of another world — the commonness and at the same time "otherness" of Orthodoxy.

If an Orthodox parish makes Orthodoxy something recognizable and familiar only to itself, Orthodox parish will become something base and common. If an Orthodox parish makes Orthodoxy merely something "other," then Orthodox parish will become irrelevant. None of these is God-like. God is the "wholly other," but at the same time able and willful enough to empty himself and become one of us. God is the unfathomable "silence," but a "silence" so transcendent and tangible as to reveal himself through his own *Logos,* and in flesh — theological presuppositions with immense implications for interpersonal relationships within the parish, and of the parish with the world.

Persons and Personhood

    Personhood is a divine quality, as God is the personal Being *par excellence,* the true and only Being that relates to himself and to the world fully, eternally, and in love.[12]

---

[10]Cf. Mt 7.21.

[11]In the thought of John of Damascus the icon is precisely this constant reminder and manifestation of the redemption of human nature by its union with the divine, and of the glorification of the material creation. Cf. Daniel J. Sahas, *hyle* and *physis* in John of Damascus, "Apologetic Orations to Those who Distort what the Holy Icons are" (1987, unpublished).

[12]See Vladimir Lossky, *The Mystical Theology of the Eastern Church* (Cambridge, 1957), chapter 3, pp. 44-66.

Man is a person, and a sharer in personhood on account of being created "according to the image and likeness" of God.[13] For man to be able to see through all the mirrors[14] and the conditions imposed by the density of our body in somebody else, the person, that is, the image of God in all its potential to become like God, is the outcome of the incarnation and a gift of grace. How easy or difficult, but how imperative as well, is it for a priest to see his parishioners as persons in the midst of so many ideological, political, or administrative conflicts and deeply rooted polarizations? How easy or difficult is it for a parishioner to see other fellow-parishioners as persons in the midst of competition, envy, personal conflicts and disagreements, or in the context of a formal administrative membership in the parish?

The discovery of personhood in somebody else is a matter of *metanoia,* turning one's mind away from the external and non-essentials and delving into the mystery of the person itself. It is also a matter of constantly rediscovering and celebrating one's own personhood in himself; a delving into the mystery and glory of God inside one's own self. Self-esteem is the prerequisite for discovering, honoring, and celebrating personhood in somebody else as the extension of the divine presence in the life of human beings.

One cannot talk about the *theosis* of human nature, unless one experiences the presence of God in one's life and in the life of others. The Transfiguration is not a story about *something* extraordinary, but the event about *someone*[15] — the rediscovery of the ontology of human nature in the New Testament, and the gift of personhood in its ultimate fullness. The disciples would not have been able to recognize Jesus transfigured if they were not disposed properly to see and witness to him; if they were not called apart from the others; if they had not gone to the top of the mountain; if they were not willing to see Jesus of Nazareth as "the Son of the living God." The Transfiguration followed, it did not precede, the confession of Peter. To them Christ, indeed, was not some Elijah, Jeremiah, John the Baptist "or one of the prophets."[16] That is why they were able to see Jesus as transfigured Christ, to recognize and contrast him to Moses and Elijah, even though they had never met these other two in person.

---

[15]Cf. Mt 17.1-8.
[16]Cf. Mt 15.14.

What we learn also from the monastic spiritual literature of our tradition is actually the story of rediscovering the qualities and manifestations of personhood behind concrete and ordinary human beings: the saintliness of the *gheron* (the elder), the light of his sharing in the light of the Transfiguration; the depth of his humility; the breadth and intensity of his love for humankind; the power of his prayer. The ever-contemporary value of our spiritual tradition is to be found in its power to break the idols and the external shells of anthropomorphism, and allow a glimpse into the ontology of human personhood. Monasticism is not a denial of the world and of human beings, but a struggle to rediscover their true sense and hypostasis. I will never forget the shock I experienced when I visited, years ago, an old ascetic on Mount Athos whom I had never met, and who had never known me before. He greeted me with an overflow of joy at the gate of his hermitage by prostrating in front of me, a young strange man, and kissing my feet. Later on, as he was feeding his ants, he talked to me with great enthusiasm about them which kept him company, while teaching him about industriousness, solidarity, and silence! I honestly felt, for the first time in my life, that I was, indeed, a special being, a person, as pointed out to me by his veneration. If he was convinced that I, an unknown, was a person with a special place in creation, what right did I have to deny this dignity to myself and to others?

The dignity of human nature is ascertained by the testimony of the Bible that God, the first icon-maker, created man according to his own image and likeness; but it is proven by the fact that God himself became one of us, taking up to himself our own nature.[17] The ultimate glory of human nature and its gift of personhood became manifest by the incarnation of God-the-Word. It was because God-the-Word "became flesh and dwelt among us"[18] that the Resurrection became inevitable. If in Christianity the Resurrection is the miracle *par excellence*, the essential truth which Orthodoxy has preserved more faithfully than all other traditions, the Incarnation, is its unfathomable mystery. One cannot experience the Resurrection without being first dumbfounded by the

---

[17]Cf. Daniel J. Sahas, "Icône et anthropologie chretienne. La pensée de Nicée II," in F. Boespflug et N. Lossky, *Nicée II. 787-1987* (Paris), pp. 438f and in *passim*.

[18]Jn 1.14.

Incarnation, and the event of the restoration of human personhood.

Relationships

We need to rediscover the trinitarian foundation of relationships and the restoration of such relationships for humans in the sacraments. In other words, we need to rediscover the meaning of the sacramental character of relationships and thus to reevaluate and reinforce the sacramental tradition of our Church. All sacraments are acts of restoration of the personal characteristics and qualities of the individual to enable one to experience one's own personhood and live.[19] Essentially and very briefly:

a) *Baptism* restores man to his primordial beauty that enables him to encounter God personally, face to face, as well as other human beings as true persons made in the image (icon) and the likeness of God.

b) *Chrism* enriches man with the gifts of the Spirit to enable him to achieve this encounter, and share the life and richness of the Spirit with others.

c) *Communion* enables man to be united with God and with his fellow human beings in a "communion of saints."

d) *Confession* enables man to reconcile himself with God, with himself and with others and thus relate to them in the best possible and constructive way.

e) *Ordination* enables man to discover and appropriate the gift of servanthood, the power of letting himself, as the grain of wheat, fall into the earth and die,[20] for his own fulfillment

---

[19]There seems to be a direct inter-dependence between relationship and personhood. Apart from personhood, relationships become meaningless, wasteful, and void. Indeed, the loss of personhood is a preamble to the loss of relationship, that is to death. Personhood and being are interwoven. God is *what* he is — meaning he is a *personal* being; and God *is* — meaning he exists and he is life. No surprise, therefore, that for Maximos the Confessor it is the Father, the source of Being and Life who distinguishes the hypostases (or, in the Western terminology, the "persons") in an eternal movement of love. *Scholia in the Book of Divine Names,* 2. 3. Lossky, *The Mystical Theology,* p. 60. Someone else, who is an expert on human relations and psychology, might want to look into the question of the relationship between the loss of relationship with one's self and others, and suicide.

[20]Cf. Jn 12.24.

and for the sanctification of others.[21]

f) *Marriage* enables man to lend himself to somebody else fully, and accept someone else equally fully.

g) *Holy Unction* enables man to strengthen his physical and spiritual stamina, in order to continue relating to others fully and meaningfully.

In all sacraments, the restoration of personhood and the enrichment of interpersonal relationships are the underlying concerns and the benefactors. But where a restoration of the sense of personhood and of interpersonal relationships become particularly manifest are in the sacrament of confession which, ironically, has been seriously undermined and undervalued in our days.[22] By maintaining through the ages the *personal, tête-à-tête,* encounter between the penitent and the confessor, that is, the Church (in itself a *personal* being as the Bride of Christ and the mystical body of Christ), the Orthodox Church has explicitly manifested that interpersonal relationships lead to God. In doing so, the Orthodox praxis has become the forerunner and has set the standards for interpersonal relationships for modern-day psychiatry, psychotherapy and group therapy, and it is changing the mind and practice of the Roman Catholic Church on the sacrament of confession.

In its spiritual tradition also the Orthodox Church has stressed the spiritual character and the significance of interpersonal

---

[21]At this point, I would like to stress the eucharistic, ministerial nature of priestly authority: the priest does not face the congregation; he leads but also he shares as one of the participants in the paschal meal. He is constantly *offering* blessings, communion, *antidhoron,* etc. He constantly sets himself the example: he asks for forgiveness, he kneels, he receives communion first, he declares himself unworthy, he lifts up his own heart first. The entire liturgy is a constant calling of the congregation to do what he does first. There can be no better description of the priest's role in the parish and in the world but that prescribed by the Orthodox liturgical experience. One may want to study sometime the question of interpersonal relatons as highlighted by the *sylleitourgon,* and by the Orthodox liturgical tradition in general.

[22]There have been recorded some early Byzantine practices which, although rare and unusual, show the emphasis given on confession and penance as a way of bringing out a person from his or her spiritual isolation, and experiencing human solidarity. Cf. Robert J. Barriger, ''Penance and Byzantine Hagiography. Le répondant du péche'' in *Studia Patristica,* vol. 18, ed. E. A. Livingstone (Oxford, 1982), 552-57.

relationships, as the relationship between the *gheron* and novice indicates. This relationship is the presupposition and the foundation for the monastic ascesis and spirituality.

The Orthodox experience and praxis, therefore, have shown that relationship is a characteristic of personhood, and that only persons can relate to and integrate with each other and be in association with God. God cannot be but One, because he is personal; otherwise he is abstract and non-existent. The problem with dynamic monarchianism is that, in essence, it denies the existence of God by abstracting him; or it makes him a non-person, like "a piece of wood or a stone,"[23] by denying in him the Word and the Spirit with whom he is and relates. Both denials are denials of personhood and thus reductions and rejections of Godhead. Relationship is not defined by the physical substance; otherwise personhood would not be a characteristic of God who is spirit. Relationship among angels exists in their convergence in ministering and praising God.

Humans are vested with a body which is neither a prison nor an impediment to a relationship. On the contrary, the body is a means by which personhood is discovered, realized and shared. Although sexual relationships represent a limited aspect of human life and do not constitute a universal experience, one has to affirm the profound and unique character, as well as the beauty, of sexual relationships, and the discovery of personhood in marriage. However, there are other, more "mundane" encounters which are expressions of and contributors to interpersonal relationships. I am pleading once more,[24] for a comprehensive and sensitive study, for example, of the phenomenon of discovering one's own personhood and that of others in the context of a meal, the most existential of human activities and functions. Nothing mundane is irrelevant to interpersonal relations. Food is something more universally accepted and binding than sex and even religion. Not everybody enjoys or practices sex or religion. Everybody eats.

---

[23]Cf. John of Damascus in referring to Islam, *On the Heresies*, PG 94.768C.

[24]Daniel J. Sahas, "The Experience of God in the Orthodox Tradition," in Robert Barriger, ed., *Rome and Constantinople. Essays in the Dialogue of Love* (Brookline, 1984), p. 40, n. 14; "A Response to Darrol Bryant" in John W. Miller, ed., *Interfaith Dialogue: Four Approaches* (Waterloo, Ontario, 1986), pp. 25-26.

It is remarkable that one of the expressions used by Jesus himself is that he is "the *bread* of life,"[25] not the "religion of life." An encounter in the context of a meal can unfold persons to each other and unite them with their creator. It is antinomical that such a seemingly material and base function can contain such dynamics of personal, social, and spiritual awareness. The biblical tradition is flooded with examples and images of this message: it was in the context of a hospitality meal that Abraham discovered and encountered angels, which for the New Testament is a prefiguration of the mystery of the Holy Trinity. It was in the context of a meal that Cleopas and the other disciple recognized the risen Christ.[26] It was in the context of a meal that the disciples recognized the risen Christ.[27] It was in the context of a supper that the disciples were called to become eternal communicants of Christ.[28] And this is, precisely, what the Eucharist, the central act, mystery, and sacrament of the Christian Church, is all about: a paschal *meal,* an existential encounter and union with Christ, a union of a person with others. We may want to rethink the value of a meal in the context of pastoral ministry, parish life, and interpersonal relationships.

Our age is an age of communication, symbols, images, and figurative language. It is an age of profound quest in search for rediscovering the person and restoring meaning to interpersonal relationships. People today are expressive, communicative, globally conscious of each other. They use figurative language, pictures, images, and all sorts of symbols and "gimmicks"; they make gestures, do things (at times, incomprehensible and antinomical); they send flowers, cards (the art and the intensity of card-making — a modern icon-making? — must be noticed as a phenomenon of our times), all in order to communicate personally with themselves and with each other.

As Orthodox we need not shy away from the theological precepts, and especially from the tradition and praxis of our Church in order to discover principles and means of interpersonal relationships today; we need to rediscover them and reapply them. The Orthodox experience and praxis is full of messages and wholistic ways of affirming personhood and enriching interpersonal relationships.

---

[25]Jn 6.35,41,51,58.
[26]Lk 24.13-35.
[27]Lk 24.36-43.
[28]Mt 26.20-29.

Women in the Church

DEBORAH MALACKY BELONICK

A HYMN AT PENTECOST IN THE ORTHODOX CHURCH PROCLAIMS: "The Holy Spirit is light and life, a living fountain of knowledge . . . God, and making us God." In the midst of controversial discussions regarding women — social, political, and theological — the Church must ask particularly: What is woman when she is cleansed by the Spirit, when her image is restored? The Apostle Paul writes: "And we all with unveiled face, reflecting the glory of the Lord, are being changed into his likeness from one degree to another; for this comes from the Lord who is the Spirit" (2 Cor 3.18). What does woman become as she ascends from one degree of glory to another?

Not only must the Church *ask* these questions, it must begin to answer them. For the past fifteen years, the feminist movement has strengthened itself in almost every Christian denomination and wrought changes in worship, education, and polity. Notably, however, the Orthodox Church has not yet produced a consistent theological stance toward most feminist theological beliefs and trends. It has not sorted out the scattered information in patristic, scriptural, liturgical, and historical sources to come up with even basic affirmations concerning feminine ontology or polity in regard to women. As a result, the Orthodox faithful assimilate information from the media, social movements, friends, and heterodox theologians to form their own ideologies.

I cannot forget conversations I have had with Orthodox Christian women who favor female ordination, do not understand why the Church is insistent on the term "Father" for God, view the marriage service as archaic, and politically are pro-choice on the abortion issue. Although faithful to liturgical services and major doctrinal statements of the Church, these women have not had access to discussions of women's issues in a Christian context, nor easy access to historical sources which could provide them with needed information.

Moreover, Orthodox Christians are misunderstood in ecumenical circles because of ill-defined positions. I remember well a Roman Catholic theologian quoting to me from Saint Gregory Palamas:

> Christ has become our *brother* by union to our flesh and our blood . . . he has also become our *father* through the holy baptism which makes us like him, and he nurses us from his own breast, as a *mother,* filled with tenderness, does her babies. . . . [1]

Accordingly, he said, since this indicates Christ manifests all human relationships, it would be proper to carry in a Holy Friday procession a *Christa* instead of a *Christos.* In addition, he congratulated me on having such a "rich" theology which allows women to view Christ as the androgynous model for humanity!

In fact, many theologians discovering "Orthodoxy" choose, out of context, patristic statements about woman *transfiguratus* which lead them to conclusions far afield from the *kerygma* of the Church. Most puzzling to heterodox theologians is that the Orthodox Church, which historically "possesses" these writings, has not manifested these conclusions in its polity!

Indeed, because of the fragmentary material, scattered information, conflicting teachings and general lack of interest in forming a genuinely Orthodox position *vis-à-vis* women, both those inside and outside the Orthodox Church pick and choose sources which bolster their own philosophies and support their intended directions for women in Christian communities. These ideologies and directions range from fundamentalist stricture to feminist excess.

The purpose of this paper is to demonstrate the confusing, often contradictory material which exists in Orthodox sources, and to call for resolutions to troubling inconsistencies. It will particularly concentrate on the ontology of women; the reality of womanhood

---

[1] Jean Meyendorff, *Introduction a l'etude de Gregoire Palamas* (Paris, 1959), pp. 247-48; italics mine.

must be distinguished from theological error and secular philosophy. Since practices regarding women naturally grow out of how they are viewed by the Church, church polity should be congruous with the reality of womanhood.

The Ontology of Woman

The general hymn of the Church to women (and men) who have been declared among the saints states: "In thee, O Mother (Father) was carefully preserved what is according to the image, for thou didst take the cross and follow Christ. By so doing thou didst teach us to disregard the flesh for it passes away, but to care instead for the soul for it is immortal. Therefore O Blessed (Name), thy spirit rejoices with the angels."

When a woman is cleansed, her image is restored, the renewed image of the first Eve. Does this imply she is no longer differentiated from the renewed Adam? Does she become a spiritual being beyond the duality of sexual identification? Should Orthodox Christians "care for the soul and disregard the flesh" to the point of believing womanhood and manhood, femininity and masculinity, have been expunged by Christ (Gal 3.18)?

Some church Fathers imply this. Saint Clement of Alexandria stated: "Souls are in themselves not male or female but only souls, and thus it may be that women will in the end be transformed into man, and become non-female, manly and perfect" (*Stromata* 6.12). Saint Gregory the Theologian said Christ's salvific acts occurred so " . . . that we might no longer be male or female, barbarian or Scythian, bond or free (which are badges of the flesh), but might bear in ourselves only the stamp of God, by whom and for whom we were made, and have so far received our form and model from him, that we are recognized by it alone" (*Panegyric on His Brother Saint Caesarios*, Sec. 23). One of the desert dwellers, Amma Sarah herself said: "According to nature I am a woman, but not according to my thoughts." She chided her brother ascetics, "It is I who am a man, and you who are women."[2]

However, other patristic writers express the opposite — a continuity between soul and body and a continuance of sexual distinction in the heavenly realm. Saint Irenaios acknowledged that the

---

[2] *The Sayings of the Desert Fathers,* trans. Benedicta Ward, SLG, (Kalamazoo, MI., 1975), p. 193.

perfect human was a union of soul and body vivified by the Spirit of God: " . . . the perfect man consists in the commingling and the union of the soul receiving the Spirit of the Father, and admixture of that fleshly nature which was molded after the image of God" (*Against Heresies,* Vol. 6). Anatomical image is related to the soul, making the person an integrated whole. In the fourth century, Saint Gregory of Nyssa restated the dogma that the soul is the inward image of the body (*Dialogue on the Soul and the Resurrection,* PG 46.72C-76B and cf. *On the Creation of Man* 27, PG 44.225B-C). Saint Jerome succinctly stated: "If the woman shall not rise again as a woman, nor the man as a man, there will be no resurrection of the dead . . . If there shall be no resurrection of the body, there can be no resurrection of the dead" (*Letter 108 to the Virgin Eustochia* 23 (22), PG 22.900. This letter was written in A.D. 404). An early baptismal creed, preserved in *The Apostolic Tradition* of Saint Hippolytus of Rome ends with: "Dost thou believe in the Holy Spirit in the holy Church, and the resurrection of the *flesh*" (emphasis mine)? These sources imply a psychosomatic distinction between women and men which continues from conception to the resurrection.

Given these two strands of thought, one may conclude either that in Christ sexual distinction is gradually but finally obliterated as a soul unites itself to God; or that sexual distinction remains, albeit restored to proper correlation in Christ. Which is correct?

Scriptural passages regarding the creation of woman and man are essential to resolving that question. However, patristic exegetes had varied opinions even when interpreting Genesis — the book revealing God's will for creation and the division of humanity into masculine and feminine being. Patristic sources do not agree on the meaning of Genesis stories referring to the image of God in humanity, why human being is di-sexual, and the value of procreative processes.

Scripture explicitly states "male and female" are in the image of God (Gen 1.27) and God willed sexual distinction for the "good" of humanity (Gen 2.18). Still, patristic sources disagree as to God's original intention. Some make light of di-sexuality, reducing it to only bodily distinction. The idea that masculinity and femininity are also God-intended psychological differentiations is absent. These Fathers say sexual differentiation was provided for humanity providentially, because God in forevision realized that after the fall human beings would need a means of procreation. Saint Gregory of Nyssa wrote:

> He who, as the prophetical writing says, "knoweth all things before they be," following out, or rather perceiving beforehand by his power of foreknowledge what, in a state of independence and freedom, is the tendency of motion of man's will — as he saw, I say, what would be, he devised for his image the distinction of male and female, which has no reference to the divine Archetype, but, as we have said, is an approximation to the less rational nature (*On the Making of Man* 16, PG 44.185A; cf. Saint John of Damascus, *Orthodox Faith*, Book 4.24).

Saint Gregory further suggests that sexual union in paradise was unnecessary for the multiplication of the human race; in paradise humanity would have multiplied as angels do (*On the Making of Man* 17, PG 44.189D).

Upon considering these passages, it is no wonder that theologians today use them to justify cultural trends and psychological theories which make light of sexual distinctions in woman and men. If God willed gender distinction for the sole purpose of procreation, then differences in women and men are reduced to bodily function. Such thinking has justified ordination of women to the priesthood, and changing terminology for God (e.g. God embodies neither masculinity or femininity, and therefore, equally metaphorically may be called she or he). However, it must be understood that not all Orthodox scholars, patristic writers, and certainly not Scripture, are in accord with Saint Gregory's stance.

Metropolitan George Khodre wrote:

> This view is influenced by the theology of Philo and an intellectualistic concept of man which is fundamentally alien to the Bible. For other Fathers, the image of God in man is not established by his intellectual faculties only, but by his whole being. Everything in man, including sex, is redeemed and baptized . . . 'Be fruitful and multiply.' These words, it should be noted, refer to the institution of marriage in paradise. Reproduction by way of sexual intercourse is a part of God's plan. The Author of creation knows no other way of multiplying the race; even at the very beginning sexuality was not placed

outside his design.[3]

Orthodox theologian Vladimir Lossky concurs with Khodre: although dissension and the power struggle between fallen woman and man have been healed by the love of Jesus Christ and union in Christian marriage, sexual distinction remains. He says:

> One cannot, however, follow Gregory when, arguing about this 'preventive' character of sexuality, he affirms that the division into male and female is 'super-imposed' upon the image. It is in fact not this division only, but all the divisions of creation which have acquired, in consequence of sin, a character of death and separation . . . but the new creation in Christ, the second Adam, allows us to perceive the profound meaning of a division which certainly had nothing 'super-imposed': Mariology, the love of Christ and the Church, and the sacrament of marriage bring to light a fullness that originates in the creation of woman — fullness not glimpsed however, except in the unique person of the Virgin, for our fallen condition always endures, demanding for the accomplishing of our human vocation not only the integrating chastity of marriage but also, and perhaps primarily, the sublimating chastity of monachism.''[4]

Likewise, Orthodox *professor emeritus* of dogmatic theology at Saint Vladimir's Orthodox Theological Seminary, Sergius Verhovskoy wrote tenderly of the God-willed differentiation of the sexes: '' . . . the definition of marriage as a physical union was proclaimed in paradise immediately following the creation of woman. We must conclude therefore from this that the sensual desire which a husband and wife have for each other can be pure, and so then not a cause of shame.''[5] He also intensely asserted sexual differentiation in the human race on psycho-physical levels

---

[3] George Khodre, "A Great Mystery: Reflections on the Meaning of Marriage," *St. Vladimir's Seminary Quarterly* 8 (1, 1964) 33.

[4] *Orthodox Theology: An Introduction* (Crestwood, NY., 1978) 77.

[5] Sergius Verhovskoy, "Creation of Man and the Establishment of the Family in the Light of the Book of Genesis," *St. Vladimir's Seminary Quarterly* 8 (1964) 11.

as God-willed. Saint Gregory of Nyssa is incorrect in belittling the distinctions.

Genesis 1.27 states: "So God created man in his own image, in the image of God he created him; male and female he created them." In the Hebrew text the word for "man" is *adam*. Verhovskoy notes:

> *Adam* is therefore not only the name of the first man, but also of man in general. . . . Further on in Genesis it is said that God gave the name . . . *Adam* to both man and woman . . . Since the Holy Scriptures call the first man simply "man (*adam*), does this not suggest that he was created first without sex? Or, perhaps, that he contained both sexes within himself, was an androgynous being? The Book of Genesis dismisses this notion by saying that God created man as "male and female." The words *zakar* and *negebah* are used here in the Hebrew text, which mean *man* and *woman* precisely in the sexual sense. (In Hebrew these words may be used equally well in reference to male and female animals.) Nowhere in Holy Scriptures is there a trace of the idea of sexlessness or hermaphroditic nature of Adam. (This idea did appear in the later theology of Judaism.)[6]

In further comment, Verhovskoy says not only was *adam* created to be di-sexual, but that man and woman were to form a psychosomatic union as the result of their distinctiveness. Genesis 2.18 emphasizes the psychological distinctions between woman and man: "It is not good that the man should be alone; I will make a helper fit for him." A "helper fit" (in Hebrew, *eser keneodo*) implies a "suitable partner." "Only in mutual relationships do men attain the fullness of being," Verhovskoy continues, "and no communion between men is as complete as the communion between husband and wife. We have in mind here, of course, not those elements of personality which are independent of sex, but the personal correlation of husband and wife in the union of their masculine and feminine natures."[7]

All these Orthodox theologians stress the psycho-somatic

---

[6] Verhovskoy, p. 6 and notes 1-2.
[7] Ibid. p. 9.

complementarity of di-sexual humanity. Nevertheless, a unified Orthodox voice advocating and defining this complementarity is absent or unavailable to laity. They generally are forced to choose an anthropological stance from either a feminist view that we are "just persons" who are all "a little bit masculine and feminine"[8] or from a fundamentalist model which would direct women and men into defined roles.[9] An Orthodox ontology based on Scripture — asserting women and men have all the same human traits, but a different mode of using and expressing those traits to create a true face-to-face complementarity — has gained little exposure. Additionally, *what* the complementarity *is* has yet to be defined.[10]

---

[8] This view is based on the Jungian school of psychology which defines "masculinity" and "femininity" according to which human traits a person has acquired. An aggressive, intellectual individual (no matter which gender) could be described as "masculine" for example. George H. Tavard, a Catholic priest and author, takes this position, claiming: "There is no intellectual and active and no sensitive and passive, no reasoning and no intuitive section of mankind. Each person can be both, the variations depending not on sex but on the congeries of heredity and circumstances which make up the individuals of either sex. On this point, the findings of contemporary psychology, at least those in the Jungian school, and those of physiology corroborate the conclusion that we have arrived at theologically." *Woman in Christian Tradition* (Notre Dame, 1973), p. 206.

[9] Stephen B. Clark says the "complementarity" expressed in Genesis implies both an equality and a difference. "The partnership of man and woman is based upon a community of nature and an interdependence due to a complementarity of role. That partnership and sameness of nature, both of which together make possible the creation of a race or people, are the central concerns of Genesis 2," *Man and Woman in Christ* (Ann Arbor, 1980), p. 23.

[10] Here, I would favor repeating what Edith Stein and Andre Feuillet say later in this paper, and the further study in the biological sciences to discover this complement. Biologists Jo Durden-Smith and Diane DeSimone studied the structure of male and female brains, and wrote of differences that are *independent* of culture and upbringing: woman are more sensitive to context in problem solving while men are more rule-bound, the hemispheres of the brain in male and females communicate to each other differently, for example. In other terms, physiologically females and males are arranged to have a different outlook on life and to go about problem solving in distinct ways, *Sex and the Brain* (New York, 1983), especially pp. 45-88. Some of these ideas are also advocated by Orthodox theologians: Thomas Hopko, "On the Male

Some traditional Roman Catholic exegetes have attempted definitions of complementary being.

> The Hebrew text in literal translation [of *eser keneodo*] means a helpmate for man who is perfectly face to face with him, his perfect partner (word for word: "as before him"). In Genesis 2.18-25, what is accentuated is the irreplaceable spiritual aid that woman brings to man: man stands in need of a being of the same nature as himself, who can make him emerge from his spiritual isolation thanks to a mutual communication of thoughts and a mutual outpouring of affections. . . . She is another "face" of his own being . . . he will not be able to express to himself what he is and thus realize himself without entering into relation with another person. . . . Through her love, the women in some way calls man into existence both with respect to himself and to others. . . . [11]

Here author Andre Feuillet stresses there is "nothing arbitrary" about the differentiation of woman and man,

> the differentiation is inscribed in their very being. . . . As for woman, the function attributed to her is different, and in many respects nobler. She is born not from the slime of the earth as is man but from one of the ribs of the first man, therefore at the very heart of what is human; it is then toward all that is human that she is primarily oriented in order to foster its growth by turning it toward God! Did she not already cause the first man to advance in the knowledge of his vocation? It is only when he sees her that he comprehends fully what he is in himself and in regard to the Creator (Gen 2.23-24). [12]

A modern Roman Catholic "martyr," Edith Stein, concurs:

Character of the Christian Priesthood," in *Women and the Priesthood,* ed. Thomas Hopko (Crestwood, NY., 1983), pp. 97-134; Kyriaki Karidoyanes FitzGerald, "The Ministry of Women in the Orthodox Church: Some Theological Presuppositions," *Journal of Ecumenical Studies,* 20 (4, 1983) 564ff.

[11]Andre Feuillet, *Jesus and His Mother,* trans. Leonard Maluf (Still River, MA., 1974), pp. 194-95.

[12]Ibid. 196-97.

I am convinced that the human species develops as a double species of "man" and "woman," that the human essence in which no trait should be missing shows a twofold development, and that its whole structure has this specific character. There is a difference not only of bodily structure and of certain physiological functions, but the whole somatic life is different, as well as the relation of soul and body; and within the psychological sphere there is a similar difference of relationship between intellect and sensuality and between the various intellectual faculties. The female species is characterized by the unity and wholeness of the entire psycho-somatic personality and by the harmonious development of the faculties; the male species by the perfecting of individual capacities to obtain record achievements.[13]

Many contemporary female authors — in various sciences — also are advocating recognition of this dimorphic state of humanity, and are emphasizing its value. Within their fields, they seem to formulate what is expressed by the Spirit in Genesis. Psychologist Diane McGuinness has found major differences between males and females, *independent* of culture:

... men are more "rule-bound" in solving problems, less sensitive to situational variables, more narrowly focused, more persevering ... Women, by contrast, are *very* sensitive to context ... They're good at picking up peripheral information. And they process the information faster.[14]

Biopsychologist Jerre Levy, after studying the hemispheres of female and male brains suggested:

... it's entirely possible that females are much better than males at integrating verbal and nonverbal information — at reading the emotional content of tones of voice and intensities of facial expression ... at quickly fitting all sorts of peripheral

---

[13]*The Writings of Edith Stein,* trans. Hilda C. Graef (Westminster, MD., 1955), pp. 142-43.

[14]Jo Durden-Smith and Diane DeSimone, *Sex and the Brain,* p. 59.

information ... This may be at the root of what we call female intuition.[15]

Surrounded by all these comparative scientific, exegetical, patristic and psychological views, the Church must take a stance. The tradition of the Church implies an inherent complementarity in di-sexuality, but explicit dogmas are absent. When they do occur, they appear as negative injunctions in canons: "Women may not . . . " — usually misinterpretations of Pauline thought or Levitical laws.[16] It is time for the Church to express a positive dogma regarding the dignity of femininity, as willed by God. It is time to comment on and classify patristic sources. Do we believe di-sexuality was instituted for procreation only, to be obliterated as souls draw near to Christ? Do we believe di-sexuality implies a complementarity willed by God in order to form a psycho-somatic union *necessary* to the definition of human being, of *be-ing human*?

A firmer dogmatic stance would guide Orthodox Christians in their lives both within the Church and world community. It would guide women and men toward their common and distinct ministries in all spheres of life. Given her common human nature with man, yet her unique femininity, what activities would be compatible with the reality of womanhood?

From tradition, Orthodox Christians do have clues regarding the common and unique ministries of women. Saintly women have manifested both individual talents (common also to men) and specifically feminine vocations.

Women have comprised a variety of "precious stones" in the spiritual house of God. According to 1 Cor 12.8-11, they have been apportioned gifts for the "common good" — those of wisdom, knowledge, faith, healing, miraculous works, prophecy, discernment, speaking in and interpreting tongues. According to 1 Cor 12.28, they have functioned as apostles, teachers, helpers and administrators besides. A hymn to Saint Euphemia, the Much-pleased (†304) reads: "O all glorious Euphemia, you are bedecked with

---

[15]Ibid. p. 73.

[16]Veselin Kesich, "St. Paul: Anti-Feminist or Liberator?" *St. Vladimir's Theological Quarterly,* 21 (3, 1977) 123-48. Deborah Belonick, *Feminism in Christianity: An Orthodox Christian Response* (Syosset, NY, 1983), pp. 45-48.

virtues. You have manifested reason . . . by the visitation of the Holy Spirit you instructed the assembly of the Holy Fathers." Saint Thekla, Equal to the Apostles, and Great Martyr, is honored for her courage: "O most blessed Thekla, you trampled down the enemy by a valiant struggle, and you escaped his contrivance. You conversed with Paul and contended with Stephen." The virgin Justina instructed and enlightened the hieromartyrs Dionysios and Cyprion, who were disciples of the Stoic philosophers and Gnostics. Saint Katherine (fourth century) was a great orator, martyred for winning so many pagans to the Christian faith. Saint Irene (eighth century) was the empress who called together the Seventh Ecumenical Synod in Nicea to restore icons to their proper place of veneration. Saint Tamara (twelfth century), Queen of Georgia, was said to have fought with Georgian armies against Turkish invaders and passionately spread the good news of salvation in Jesus Christ. She likened herself to a myrrhbearing woman. Desert Amma Synkletika, Amma Sarah, and Amma Theodora are consulted by monks about monastic life.[17] Blessed Athanasia, a schema-nun and disciple of Saint Seraphim of Sarov, was known for her "gift of counsel and clairvoyance."[18]

In keeping with history and tradition, the Church must recognize women imbued with the Holy Spirit and authorize them to use their talents for the building up of the body of Christ. Given our surrounding culture, this may necessitate formal recognition for women to function in certain fields. For example, if a woman was called by God to begin a prison ministry or ministry in a psychiatric hospital, she may have to be recognized as an official "lay minister" of the Orthodox Church in order to obtain a job and function within that framework. In am in no way implying she should be ordained to the cultic priesthood, but I do not believe there is anything inconsistent with the New Testament or church tradition by saying there ought to be in the Church both *priests*, and *ministers* of the royal priesthood.

When Saint Paul writes about the distribution of the gifts of the Spirit to the saints, he says: "Now there are varieties of gifts, but the same Spirit; and there are varieties of service, but the same

---

[17]*The Sayings of the Desert Fathers*, p. 71.

[18]Father Alexander Priklonsky, *Blessed Athanasia, Disciple of St. Seraphim*, (Platina, CA., 1980), p. 31.

Lord; and there are varieties of working, but it is the same God who inspires them all in every one" (1 Cor 12.4-6). The Greek text says literally: "Now differences of gifts there are, but the same Lord" (Διαιρέσεις δὲ χαρισμάτων εἰσίν, τὸ δὲ αὐτὸ πνεῦμα καὶ διαιρέσεις διακρονιῶν εἰσιν, καὶ ὁ αὐτὸς κύριος). In his Letter to the Romans, he likewise says, "I commend to you our sister Phoebe, a deaconess of the church at Cenchreae, that you may receive her in the Lord as befits the saints, and help her in whatever she may require from you . . . " (Rom 16.1-2). The Greek word for "deaconess" again is "διάκονος," literally, "minister." It is within the very nature of the Church to have "lay ministers" — saints who have been apportioned spiritual gifts for the upbuilding of the Church. In the present culture, where these spiritual gifts can overlap with secular professions, it would be, in my opinion, helpful to many people to receive the extra, recognized credential from the Church — as "lay minister" — to operate within some of these special counseling fields.

Such recognition must not be conferred on nominal church members who happen to have received a secular degree. Recognition must originate within the church body. The Church should recognize that certain faithful members have been endowed with the gift to operate in certain pastoral areas — for example, healing ministries — and authorize them as "lay ministers." A true charism of the Spirit must be present.

The Church has recognized spiritual gifts in women and has authorized them to use these individual charisms for the upbuilding of the body of Christ. At the same time, it also has recognized that women as a whole contribute uniquely to church life and have occupied special positions by virtue of that fact. Bishop Kallistos Ware notes:

> Although it is the calling of every Christian, male as well as female, to pray for others and to listen to God, yet women by virtue of her gift for direct and intuitive understanding seems especially blessed to act as intercessor and prophet. It is no coincidence that the symbolic figure of the *Orans* on the walls of the Catacombs, representing the Christian soul waiting upon the Spirit, should take the form of a woman.[19]

---

[19]"Man, Woman and the Priesthood of Christ," in *Women and the Priesthood,* p. 10.

While developing their individual talents and using their individual gifts, women must not decry or demean their basic nature. The fact that woman complements man means that she has unique qualities for the upbuilding of humanity. Translated into practical terms, it means she will likely develop different methods of leadership and handling of people if she is employed outside her home. In the political arena, she may propose different solutions to problems, or in the Church, to the managing of the ecclesial household. In her home life, she must be the mother of the family (practicing the meaning of *teknogonia* in 1 Tim 2.15), turning all members to the Holy Trinity. Morally, she must stand against pornography, fornication, adultery, abortion, and forms of contraception harmful to her, since all of these degrade her nature and cause her to despise the functioning of her own body. Especially, women must guard against the insidious cultural suggestion that motherhood is a meaningless, boring activity. A woman certainly should have active interests besides her immediate family, but a job which significantly separates her from her child-raising and home life stunts the growth of her very being. Unfortunately, our economic structure and societal pressure militate against wifery, motherhood and child-rearing to the point of non-support for women who want to develop these inclinations. The dignity of being "Eve," a "mother of the living" is lost to the present culture. The dignity of being *ishshah,* a different form of humanity than *ish* (Gen 2.23), also will be lost if women disregard their psychological and physiological inclinations and needs natural to them.[20]

Woman in Relation to the Holy Spirit

In further exploration of womanhood, the tradition of the Orthodox Church, and the image of God in humanity, I am struck more and more by a growing tendency among theologians to tie women ontologically to the third Person of the Trinity, the Holy Spirit. In other words, does the male and female human community have as its archetypal pattern Jesus Christ and the Holy Spirit, as many contemporary theologians claim?[21] Is there a divine

---

[20]*Sex and the Brain,* pp. 227-43.

[21]Thomas Hopko, "On the Male Character of the Christian Priesthood," in *Women and the Priesthood,* pp. 97-134; Paul Evdomikov, *E Gynaika kai E Soteria tou Kosmou,* trans. Nicholas Matsoukas (Thessalonike, 1958), p. 23; Vladimir Lossky, *Orthodox Theology,* pp. 69-70.

pattern for the feminine mode of life? Is our di-morphic state some-how a reflection of trinitarian life?

In the patristic period, the Fathers related the procession of the Holy Spirit from the Father with the "procession" of Eve from Adam.[22] Saint Basil the Great poetically described the Holy Spirit as a mother bird when commenting on the Genesis account: "And the the Spirit was borne upon the face of the waters" (Gen 1.2) means . . . it cherished the nature of the waters as one sees a bird cover the eggs with her body and impart to them a vital force from her own warmth . . . [the Spirit] prepared the nature of water to produce living beings" (*The Hexameron*, Homily 2,6). In later centuries Saint Athanasios wrote: "Eve, who proceeded from Adam, signifies the proceeding hypostasis of the Holy Spirit. This is why God did not breathe in her the breath of life: she was already the type of the breathing and life of the Holy Spirit" (*On the Image and Likeness*, PG 89.1145BC). A third-century Syriac work, *The Teaching of the Apostles*, suggests a link between the deacons and Jesus Christ, and the deaconesses and the Holy Spirit: "The deacon stands in the place of Christ; and do you love him. And the deaconess shall be honored by you in the place of the Holy Spirit.[23]

Some scriptural passages support these patristic meditations. The author of the Wisdom of Solomon used a feminine personification to depict the Spirit of the Wisdom of God.

> I called upon God, and the spirit of Wisdom came to me . . .
> All good things came to me along with her, and in her hands
> I had uncounted wealth. I rejoiced in them all, because wisdom
> leads them; but I did not know that she was their mother . . .
> For she is a breath of the power of God, and a pure emana-
> tion of the glory of the Almighty . . . a spotless mirror of the
> working of God, and an image of his goodness . . . and while
> remaining in herself, she renews all things; in every genera-
> tion she passes into holy souls and makes them friends of God,
> and prophets (Wis 7.7, 11-12, 25-27).

---

[22] Lossky, *Orthodox Theology*, pp. 69-70.

[23] *Didascalia Apostolorum*, ed. R. H. Connolly (Oxford, 1929), p. 88; *Apostolic Constitutions* 2.26.5-6, ed. F. Funk (Frankfurt, 1978), p. 105.

Here, Wisdom is the eternal, moving counselor who "orders all things well" (Wis 8.1). She enters the souls of holy men, and guides them in righteousness. Many of these qualities are directly comparable to the Holy Spirit. For example, Wisdom is called the breath of God, as is the Spirit: "The Spirit of God made me; and the breath of the Almighty gives me life" (Job 33.4). The New Testament itself reveals the Spirit as the Counselor eternally proceeding from the Father (Jn 15.26); as guide (Jn 16.13); as a rushing wind (Acts 2.2) which teaches the dumb to speak (Acts 2.3-4; cf. Wis 10.21).

Saint Theophilos of Antioch (second century), in Book 1, chapters 1-7, to the pagan Autolykos, identifies "Wisdom" with the Holy Spirit. He states: "Thus God, who created all things by the Word and by Wisdom, can be known in his providence and in his works (διὰ τῆς προνοίας καὶ τῶν ἔργων)."[24] Vladimir Lossky, says Theophilos, is comparing Word and Wisdom to the Son and the Spirit respectively, who co-create with the eternal Father.[25] Other Syriac writings affirm the Spirit as a feminine entity.[25]

On the other hand, most Fathers identify "Wisdom" with Jesus Christ, and not the Holy Spirit.[27] This is based on passages such as 1 Cor 1.24 and Col 1.5. "In the New Testament, though Jesus once implies that he and John the Baptist are *children* of Wisdom (Lk 7.35), she is otherwise equated with the Logos, which is Christ (1 Cor 1.24), Col 1.5ff.), and loses her feminine identity" and identity with the Holy Spirit.[28] In the book of the Wisdom of Jesus Son of Sirach, "Wisdom" is more closely identifiable with Jesus Christ:

> I came forth from the mouth of the Most High, and covered the earth like a mist. I dwelt in high places, and my throne was a pillar of cloud . . . Alone I have made the circuit of the vault of heaven and have walked in the depths of the abyss . . . Then the Creator of all things gave me a commandment . . . And he said, "*Pitch your tent* in Jacob, and in Israel receive your inheritance" (Sir 24.3-5 ,8, emphasis mine).

---

[24]Cf. PG 6.1024-36.

[25]*The Vision of God*, (Bedfordshire, Eng., 1963), pp. 28-29.

[26]Louis Bouyer, *Woman in the Church* (San Francisco, 1979), p. 37.

[27]Saint Gregory of Nyssa, *Against Eunomius*, 3.2.

[28]Erminir Huntress Lantero, *Feminine Aspects of Divinity* (Sowers Printing Company: Pendle Hill Pamphlet 191, 1973), p. 15.

Because of such passages, some theologians give little weight to the feminine personification of Wisdom, attributing it to grammatical necessity, since in Hebrew, the word "Wisdom" happens to be a feminine noun.[29] However, a feminine identity is maintained in Semitic writings of the Church.[30] Even Saint John of Damascus writes that the word "Wisdom" may apply "jointly to the whole Godhead" (*Orthodox Faith*, 1.12). The Father is the "abyss of wisdom," the Son is the "wisdom of the Father," and the Spirit is the "Spirit of wisdom" (*Orthodox Faith*, 1.12 and 13).[31] So, further exploration and clarification seems possible.

In all this exploration, one must avoid the errors of the sophiologists such as Vladimir Soloviev (1853-1900), Jacob Boehme (1575-1624), and Sergei Bulgakov (1870-1944), who equated Wisdom with an eternally feminine "dyad" between the Son and the Spirit which in turn revealed the Father.[32] One must also avoid reducing the image of the Spirit to a human woman, feminine goddess or eternal feminine principle; and dismiss as heresy any notion that Holy Spirit is the heavenly "Mother" in sexual union with the "Father" to produce the "Son."[33] Notwithstanding there are many renowned, respected contemporary Orthodox theologians who do affirm a basic relation between the mode of life and action of the Holy Spirit, and the mode of life and action of women in general.[34]

---

[29]Paul K. Jewett, *The Ordination of Women: An Essay on the Office of Christian Ministry* (Grand Rapids, 1980), pp. 48-53.

[30]Tavard, *Women in Christian Tradition*, pp. 154-55.

[31]*The Fathers of the Church*, Vol. 37, trans. Frederic H. Chase, Jr. (Washington, D.C., 1958), pp. 195-200.

[32]Tavard, *Woman in Christian Tradition*, pp. 165ff.

[33]The Capitula of the Second Council of Constantinople (A.D. 553) reads: "If anyone shall not confess that the Word of God has two nativities, the one from all eternity of the Father, without time and without body; the other in these last days, coming down from heaven and being made flesh of the holy and glorious Mary, Mother of God and always a virgin, and born of her: let her be anathema." *A Select Library of Nicene and Post-Nicene Fathers*, Vol. 14, Philip Schaff and Henry Wace, eds., (Grand Rapids, 1974), p. 312.

[34]Vladimir Lossky, *Orthodox Theology*, pp. 69-70; Thomas Hopko, *The Spirit of God* (Wilton, CN., 1976), pp. 49-50; Paul Evdomikov, *Woman and the Salvation of the World* (1958). In addition, respected, conservative Roman Catholic authors affirm the same relationship: Louis Bouyer, *Woman in the Church*, pp. 20, 37-39; Edith Stein, *The Writings of Edith Stein*, p. 143; and Andre Feuillet, *Jesus and His Mother*, pp. 197-98.

To me as a woman, this is a valuable affirmation. It offers a link of my own femininity to one of the three Persons of the Trinity, a link grounded in unchanging reality. By meditating upon the life, mode of existence and action of the Holy Spirit, I can discover the touchstone of what true feminity is. I need not grope and select from fluctuating psychological theories and cultural values. In this meditation, I discover that woman is the life and beauty of humanity as the Holy Spirit is the inner life of God. Women are life-bearers, sustainers and preservers, as the Spirit of God is toward creation.

The Church has always upheld the Theotokos as an ideal and model for women, and rightly so, for she is "full of grace." Her imitation, I agree, is for all Christians, but especially "for women, because it will lead them to the feminine form of the image of Christ conformed to their nature."[35] Nevertheless, to be linked with the Holy Spirit is monumentally different for women than to be linked with the Virgin Mary, a woman in whom the Holy Spirit is perfectly manifested.

Again, there is conflicting, scattered information underlying a theological proposition connecting the mode of life of the Holy Spirit with women. I was never taught patristic writings on the matter in church school and faithfully use masculine pronouns in prayer to the Spirit. However, after discovering patristic meditations on this matter, I feel it imperative to pursue this proposition, particularly in this era of anthropological and theological deception.

Conclusion

Orthodox Christians must make a concerted, united effort to explore and define masculinity, femininity and their relationship to the Holy Trinity within the tradition of the Church. This requires a pan-Orthodox undertaking, to pull together and explore the scattered material which causes internal dissension, and makes us appear as a spiritual smorgasbord to those outside the Orthodox faith. I do not pretend to know these definitions; I had only hoped to show how many conflicting sources exist, and how they can lead to varied conclusions.

I do know that in a world fragmented by illusion, temptation, and misdirection, it is time to offer Orthodox solutions. It is true

---

[35] *The Writings of Edith Stein,* p. 154.

that during the great church debates of the early centuries, dogmas were slow in forming and doctrinal arguments lasted hundreds of years. Yet, publishing houses, media mania and mass communications did not exist. People did not consume and digest the amount of information that comes now as an onslaught daily. It is said that Saint Basil the Great (fourth century) was reticent about writing and publishing his work *On the Holy Spirit* because he feared the common people would misunderstand terms and the Church would be splintered further on the issue.[36] One book! Today it would be a feeble witness among the thousands of heterodox publications vying for our attention in libraries, schools and bookstores.

Women and men need guidelines for their spiritual, social and political lives — guidelines that will bring them into reality with God and their own being. For it is only within reality that we take that journey "from glory to glory" (2 Cor 3.18).

---

[36] *Word and Spirit: A Monastic Review — In Honor of St. Basil the Great* Still River, MA., 1979), pp. 143-44.

Orthodox Women and Pastoral Praxis: Observations and Concerns for the Church in America

KYRIAKI KARIDOYANES FITZGERALD

THE MINISTRY OF MEN AND WOMEN IS A TOPIC WHICH IS being discussed in many circles today. This particular paper is primarily intended for an audience within the Orthodox Christian tradition. Even more specifically, this study is directed to clergy and theologians who are graduates of Orthodox theological schools in North America. It is our intention to identify some of the significant issues related to women and to church praxis which need to be addressed.

In the previous paper delivered during this Conference, Matuska Belonick related that Orthodox Christians are continuously bombarded with ideas, values, concerns and other messages from the surrounding culture.[1] Our people, especially this generation of post-World War II, American-born Orthodox Christians, have been deeply influenced by the attitudes of contemporary society. These attitudes at times may or may not coincide or complement the fundamental affirmations of the Orthodox Christian faith. Much of our people's sense of self and perceived identity, like many Americans, has been significantly shaped by the "teachings" of the surrounding Western culture and society. To analyze these factors lies outside the scope of this paper. It is, however, very important that we recognize that every believer is susceptible to the

---

[1] My paper was delivered intentionally after Belonick's presentation because it was our mutual concern that our efforts be coordinated. This paper supports the thesis expressed in her study.

101

influence of the diverse values of our society. Women are equally affected. Orthodox women are all too frequently forced to choose between what is often called the "traditional" or the "contemporary" understanding of women. Orthodox women often prematurely assess their position and role in the Church from either one of these two perspectives, long before they can reflect upon the entire theological, historical, and pastoral tradition of our Church. This takes place simply because they have had precious little exposure to this tradition.[2]

Orthodox Christian Women and Administrative Life

The growing presence of women in various administrative positions within the jurisdictions of the Orthodox Church in this country is a development of great significance. Anyone even vaguely familiar with the early development of Orthodox parishes in the United States knows that women have played an important role which has been real but not always acknowledged. Since those early days of organizational development, women have served the Church with vigor. We know that women have been very active in many capacities within the life of the Church. They have contributed to the founding of churches, offered support to others through prayer and community service, assisted the less fortunate in times of financial duress and warmly welcomed strangers through the ministry of hospitality. Women have also been very active in teaching the faith to children and adults alike. These are significant ministries which clearly reflect and embody the gifts bestowed upon the laity by the Holy Spirit in order to build up the body of Christ.

More recently, certain administrative positions in parishes and dioceses of our Church in this country, which have in previous decades been held only by laymen, are now open to laywomen as well. For example, we see a great change in the composition of parish councils. It is now quite common to see in Orthodox parishes throughout this country a number of women serving as members of these councils. Moreover, in some parishes it is not unusual to find committed women serving as presidents of the parish council. This significant development has occurred within the last twenty-five to thirty years. While we presently take the participation of

---

[2] For an interesting sidelight on this topic, see Stephen B. Clark, *Man and Woman in Christ* (Ann Arbor, 1980), pp. 467-506.

women on parish councils and other committees of the parish for granted, this phenomenon would have been inconceivable thirty years ago.

At the same time, however, the influx of women serving on parish councils has not diminished the viability and presence of specific women's organizations at the parish, diocesan, and national church level. From a historical perspective, it is clear that these organizations were established at a time when it was expected that women would have their own specific groups within the local parish or diocese. And, throughout the many years of their existence, these organizations, such as the Philoptochos Society, have done a great deal for the Orthodox Church in North America and abroad. Now, however, at a time when male and female roles within the parish are not as highly stratified as they once were, there is a need for some of these organizations to reaffirm their fundamental mission as vehicles of Orthodox Christian philanthropy, mission, and witness. Throughout the various levels of church life in America, there are certainly important ministries to which our women's organizations can be devoted with much commitment and Christian spirit.

Wonen in Theology

Since the 1960s and 1970s both major American Orthodox theological seminaries, Holy Cross and St. Vladimir's, have totally opened their doors to women who desire to study theology. This action, in itself, is highly significant because it clearly demonstrates that the study of the various fields of theology is not open only to men or to those men who wish to serve the Church as priests. Moreover, this action is also significant when compared to the policy in effect at some Protestant and many Roman Catholic seminaries and theological schools. The question of whether women should be permitted to study theology at these institutions is not resolved fully by some Roman Catholics and Protestants.

The matriculation of women into the Orthodox theological seminaries in North America has occurred quite naturally and with relatively little discomfort. While there are some who continue to feel that women should not participate in programs of Orthodox theological education, this significant development cannot be undone or underestimated. With the approval of the hierarchs and under the direction of a number of thoughtful administrators at

Holy Cross and at St. Vladimir's, women have been encouraged to participate in the complete range of academic programs available to their seminary brothers. Women have also been encouraged to take part fully in seminary activities and organizations which are properly open to the laity. From the academic, psychological, and spiritual perspectives, the presence of women at our major Orthodox theological schools in this country has enriched the quality of the life of these institutions.

It is most encouraging to note that the vast majority of women graduates from Holy Cross and St. Vladimir's have gone on to serve the Church in a number of important roles such as monastics, pastoral assistants, ecumenical officers, official delegates and representatives to theological consultations and dialogues, religious education directors, youth ministry directors, choir directors, authors, preachers, retreat directors, seminary and diocesan administrators, teachers of theology, pastoral counselors, and spiritual directors. From these women seminary graduates, one is on the graduate theological faculty at Holy Cross and another is teaching on the theological faculty of St. Vladimir's. In addition, there are others who are engaged in education, public service, publishing, and the home with the benefit of their study of Orthodox theology. It should also be noted that almost a third of the women graduates of both our major seminaries have continued their graduate studies at other institutions of higher learning both in this country and abroad. It is clear that the women graduates of both St. Vladimir's and Holy Cross, regardless of their particular tasks in the Church, the society, or the family, are contributing greatly to the development of Orthodox Christianity in this land as persons of faith who are gifted with a valuable education in the various aspects of the Orthodox tradition.

Theology of the Priesthood

Questions regarding the issue of women and ordination are serious and are being raised at a number of different levels. The contemporary societal emphasis upon the rights of women has led many women to raise questions regarding the role of women within the institutional life of the Orthodox Church. Moreover, the daily encounters which Orthodox clergy and laity in this country continue to have with members of other Christian confessions have challenged us to reflect seriously upon the various questions being raised. Such thoughtful reflection does not take place in a vacuum. Rather, it occurs within the context of our pluralistic society. We would do well to remember that the manner in which we Orthodox respond or do not respond to these serious questions is open to the scrutiny of all.

Orthodox theologians are quick to point out that the major theological issues regarding the ordination of women to the priest-hood have not been raised primarily from within the Orthodox Church but rather from within Protestantism, especially Anglican-ism, and to a lesser degree from within Roman Catholicism. While this theological challenge comes primarily from outside of our Church, nevertheless, it provides us with an opportunity to respond to these theological issues and to explicate further or understand-ing of the priesthood for both ourselves as well as others.

At the heart of this discussion lies the Orthodox experience of the nature of the Church which during certain circumstances complements and at other times seriously differs from that of Western Christianity. For the Orthodox, the Church is a theanthro-pic community and not simply a human institution created by falli-ble and, perhaps, even less than noble human beings. The Church is ultimately the product of divine initiative and active human response, established by the Lord Jesus Christ. Our understanding of who we are is rooted in divine revelation. Both the divine and human elements of this relationship need to be taken seriously. This experience of the Church leads the Orthodox to oppose all views which may diminish either its divine or human dimension.[3] We believe this reality to have serious ramifications with regard to the Orthodox understanding of ministry and the life of the peo-ple of God. To conceptualize the Church as being merely a human community gathered around a certain doctrine, ritual, or ethical code is to misunderstand its very nature. Regretfully, such a mis-understanding can lead to numerous unfortunate consequences.[4]

A number of male Orthodox theologians have begun to address the issues associated with women and ordination. Among these are Metropolitan Emilianos Timiadis of Silybria, Bishop Kallistos Ware

---

[3] Stanley Harakas, "Orthodox Church," in David Schuller et al, *Ministry in America* (San Francisco, 1980), p. 333.

[4] Georges Florovsky, *Bible, Church, Tradition: An Eastern Orthodox View* (Belmont, MA., 1972), pp. 37-72.

of Diokleia, Bishop Maximos Aghiorgoussis of Pittsburgh and Father Thomas Hopko. Several female Orthodox theologians also have begun studying these issues. Among them are Elizabeth Behr-Sigel, Constance Tarasar, Vasiliki Eckley, Elaine Gounaris, Deborah Belonick, and the writer. Each of these authors clearly recognizes that the questions under consideration must be related to the more general issues associated with the position of women in the Church and in the society.[5]

Those Orthodox theologians who have examined the issue have concluded that women are not called to the ministerial priesthood of the Church. It is beyond the scope of these observations to discuss fully the Orthodox theological reasoning against the ordination of women to the priesthood.[6] However, it is appropriate to

---

[5] E.g., Deborah Belonick, *Feminism in Christianity: An Orthodox Christian Response* Crestwood, NY., 1981); Elizabeth Behr-Sigel, "The Meaning of the Participation of Women in the Life of the Church, *Orthodox Women: Their Role and Participation in the Orthodox Church,* Constance Tarasar and Irina Kirillva, eds., (Geneva, 1977), pp. 17-29; Vasiliki Eckley, "Male and Female God Created Them," *The Orthodox Observer,* January 7, 1976, p. 8 and "Male and Female God Created Them," *The Orthodox Observer,* February 4, 1976, p. 6; Metropolitan Emilianos Timiadis, "The Concern for Women in the Orthodox Tradition," *Diakonia,* 12 (1, 1977) 8-23; Kyriaki FitzGerald, "The Ministry of Women in the Orthodox Church: Some Theological Presuppositions," *Journal of Ecumenical Studies,* 20 (4, 1983) 558-75; Elaine Gounaris, *The Relationship Between Jesus Christ and Women in the Gospels,* (M.Div. thesis, Holy Cross Greek Orthodox School of Theology, Brookline, MA., 1977); Thomas Hopko, "On the Male Character of the Christian Priesthood," *Women and the Priesthood,* ed. Thomas Hopko, (Crestwood, NY., 1983), pp. 97-134; *idem,* "Women and the Priesthood: Reflections on the Debate," *Women in the Priesthood,* ed. Thomas Hopko, pp. 169-90; Bishop Kallistos Ware, "Man, Woman and the Priesthood of Christ," *Women and the Priesthood,* ed. Thomas Hopko, pp. 9-38; Bishop Maximos Aghiorgoussis, *Women Priests?* (Brookline, MA., 1976); *idem,* "The Ordained Priesthood: Historical Interpretation, Theological Dimensions and Contemporary Issues from an Orthodox Point of View," unpublished paper presented to the Orthodox-Roman Catholic Consultation in the United States during its January 23-24, 1976 session at Garrison, NY; Constance Tarasar, *Woman: Handmaid of the Lord,* (Thesis, St. Vladimir's Orthodox Theological Seminary, Crestwood, NY, 1965).

[6] I have discussed these specific topics more thoroughly in "The Ministry of Women in the Orthodox Church: Some Theological Presuppositions," *Journal of Ecumenical Studies* 20 (4, 1983) 558-75.

identify a number of propositions which are central to the Orthodox position. Firstly, male and female human persons are equal but different. Human nature is expressed in persons who are either male or female. Both men and women are fully human and fully equal but are not the same. The difference between men and women is not simply sexual. Rather, it is a difference of being which is rooted in the very essence of creation and manifested in the particular expression of personhood. Secondly, the Word of God became human as a male. This in no way diminishes the dignity of the female. It is simply a fact of history. As the incarnate Son of God, Christ was fully divine. Yet, his humanity had to be expressed either in the male or the female mode. To claim, as some have done, that Christ was not a male or that he was androgynous is clearly a denial of his full humanity. Thirdly, the ministerial priest of the Church represents in an iconic manner the presence of Christ within the eucharistic assembly. Likewise, it is in the name of Christ that the ordained priest is truly the father of the eucharistic community. Fourthly, ordination to the priesthood is not a "right." On the contrary, it is gift bestowed by the Spirit upon particular male persons for the well being of the entire community of faith. The Church is the divinely established community through which all the gifts of the Spirit are affirmed. And finally, by virtue of baptism, it is the goal of every believer to be conformed to the likeness of Christ. Every believer is called by God not to be an ordained priest but to be a saint.

It is clear that the fundemental understanding upon which Orthodox theologians base their position is essentially doctrinal and not simply sociological or cultural. It is important to take note of this fact especially because there are those who mistakenly believe that the Orthodox opposition to the ordination of women to the priesthood is based primarily upon cultural presuppositions. It should be remembered that priestesses existed among the pagan mystery religions and among certain gnostic sects of the early centuries of the Christian era. Thus, the clear opposition to the possibility of a woman being a priest in the Church which one may find in the writings of Saint Irenaios and Saint John Chrysostom is not founded upon cultural bias but upon doctrinal presuppositions.[7]

---

[7] See Deborah Belonick, "The Spirit of the Female Priesthood," *Women and the Priesthood*, ed. Thomas Hopko, pp. 135-68; Thomas

Orthodox theologians, nonetheless, must continue to investigate the issues being raised. The propositions put forward against the ordination of women to the ministerial priesthood need greater elaboration. Whether we like it or not, we are being challenged to articulate more thoroughly our understanding of the human person, the meaning of masculinity and femininity and the significance of the ordained priesthood. Indeed, it would appear at times as though our fundamental affirmations regarding the Trinity, the Person of Christ, and the Church together with its Scripture and tradition are being challenged.

The Orthodox theologians in North America have a particular responsibility to examine the various issues being discussed even though these concerns may originate outside the Orthodox Church. Indeed, it is within the context of North America that the issues associated with the rights, responsibilities and dignity of the human person are most prominently discussed. Therefore, as we explicate the content of the Orthodox faith, we must do so with a clear understanding of the nature and characteristics of this society. Our society is not as highly stratified as was that of Byzantine or Imperial Russia, nor does it appear that it will ever become so. Our present culture places much value on the fundamental equality of persons. And, this was not necessarily the case in previous societies. We are clearly challenged to profess our faith and to express our *phronema* within this unique cultural context.

Women and the Diaconate

There has been growing interest in recent years among Orthodox in the historic position of the female deacon and the possibility of reviving this ministry. Clearly, there has been a very remarkable development in this area of theological investigation. It

---

FitzGerald, "An Orthodox View on the Ordination Question," *The Living Church* (February 8, 1976) 9-14; Thomas Hopko, "On the Male Character of the Christian Priesthood," pp. 97-134; *idem*, 'Women and the Priesthood: Reflections on the Debate," pp. 169-90; Bishop Kallistos Ware, "Man, Woman and the Priesthood of Christ," pp. 9-38; John Karmiris, Ἡ Θέσις καὶ ἡ Διακονία τῶν Γυναικῶν ἐν τῇ Ὀρθοδόξῳ Ἐκκλησία (Athens, 1978), especially pp. 7-46; Bishop Maximos Aghiorgoussis, *Women Priests?*; Veselin Kesich, "St. Paul: Anti-Feminist or Liberator?" *St. Vladimir's Theological Quarterly* 21 (3, 1977), pp. 128 and 146.

is now common to find many Orthodox theologians openly discussing this issue. For the most part, they find no doctrinal reason against the rejuvenation of a genuine order of women deacons. Orthodox theologians who have carefully examined the issue find a clear distinction between the possibility of ordaining women as deacons and the impossibility of ordaining women as presbyters or bishops. Because these theologians see no doctrinal reason to keep the Church from reactivating the diaconate of women, this is a recognition which is, in itself, highly significant.[8]

The most extensive and fundamental research by an Orthodox scholar on the topic of the order of the deaconess has been done by Professor Evangelos Theodorou of the University of Athens. Through his analysis of Byzantine liturgical texts, Theodorou has clearly demonstrated that the female deacons were actually ordained at the altar and within the context of the Eucharist. While this question was once debated among Orthodox theologians, Theodorou has forcefully shown that the female deacon did not simply receive a blessing (χειροθεσία) but received the laying on of hands (χειροτονία) as was the case of the male

---

[8] Elizabeth Behr-Sigel, "The Meaning of the Participation of Women in the Life of the Church," *Orthodox Women: Their Role and Participation in the Orthodox Church*, eds. Constance Tarasar and Irina Kirillova (Geneva, 1977), pp. 26-27; Bishop Chrysostomos, "Women in the Orthodox Church: Brief Comments from a Spiritual Perspective," *The Greek Orthodox Theological Review* 26 (2, 1981) 199; Metropolitan Emilianos Timiadis, "The Concern for Women in the Orthodox Tradition," *Diakonia* 12 (1, 1977), 20; Alexander Golubov, "On Deacons and the Diaconate — A Response," *One Church* 5 (1986) 194-200; Sergei Hackel, "Mother Maria Skobtsva: Deaconess Manquee?" *Eastern Churches Review* 1 (3, 1967) 264-266; Bishop Kallistos Ware, "Man, Woman and the Priesthood of Christ," pp. 32-34; Constance Tarasar and Irina Kirillova, eds., *Orthodox Women: Their Role and Participation in the Orthodox Church*, p. 50; Evangelos Theodorou, Ἡρωΐδες τῆς Χριστιανικῆς Ἀγάπης (Athens, 1949); *idem*, Ἡ «Χειροτονία» ἤ «Χειροθεσία» τῶν Διακονισσῶ (Athens, 1954); Militsa Zernov, "Women's Ministry in the Church,' *Eastern Churches Review*, 7 (1975) 34-39. See also my study on this topic in "The Characteristics and Nature of the Order of the Deaconess," *Women and the Priesthood*, ed. Thomas Hopko, (Crestwood, NY., 1983), pp. 75-96. Appreciation for research assistance is expressed to Proto-Deacon Michael Roshak and Hiero-Deacon Peter of New Skete Monastery.

deacon.[9]

According to the Byzantine liturgical texts, the ordination of the woman deacon occurred as any other ordination to major orders. It took place during the celebration of the Eucharist and at the same point in the service that the male deacon was ordained. She was ordained at the altar by the bishop and, later in the service, received Holy Communion at the altar with the other clergy.[10] Depending upon the need, location and situation in history, the deaconess ministered primarily to the women in the community in much the same way that the male deacon ministered to men.[11]

While the expression of the deaconess' work varied in both form and content throughout the life of the Church, it is important to note that the hallmark of this ministry had always been loving service to others. This is because the female deacon, just as the male deacon, was ordained to *diakonia* or ministry.[12] And, as was the case with her male counterpart, she was ordained to unconditional service to the Lord and his Church. The woman deacon had to always be receptive to the many changing needs of the Church and the promptings of the Holy Spirit.

There is no clear evidence to explain why the order of the deaconess gradually was deemphasized sometime after the twelfth century. It should be noted, however, that there does not exist any canon or church regulation which opposes or suppresses the order. Writing in 1954 Professor Evangelos Theodorou noted that one could find at that time convents of the Church of Greece in which there were ordained deaconesses. This observation is certainly an important one.[13]

Before going any further in our discussion, it is important to emphasize here that we must not misunderstand the diaconate to

---

[9] His highly significant work, Ἡ «Χειροτονία» ἤ «Χειροθεσία» τῶν Διακονισσῶν, and an earlier study, Ἡρωΐδες τῆς Χριστιανικῆς Ἀγάπης, have become standard texts concerning the study of this issue. See also Panagiotis Trempelas, Δογματικὴ τῆς Ὀρθοδόξου Καθαλικῆς Ἐκκλησίας, 3 (Athens, 1961), pp. 291-92; and my discussion regarding this concern in "Characteristics," pp. 84-89.

[10] Theodorou, Ἡ Χειροτονία, pp. 40-65.

[11] E.g., *Didaskalia Apostolorum*, (*Syriac Didaskalia*), Robert Connolly, ed. (Oxford, 1929) 4.3.12, p. 146, and 4.3.13, p. 148.

[12] Theodorou, Ἡ Χειροτονία, pp. 55-56.

[13] Ibid. pp. 37 and 95-96.

be merely a stepping stone to the ordained priesthood. This is still a fairly common, yet mistaken, assumption expressed by many within the Church. This kind of thinking is essentially alien to the proper Orthodox Christian understanding of ordination. The diaconate is a genuine and full order in and of itself. It has its own particular justification for existence and its own unique ministry within the life of the Church. While we know that certain male deacons may be called to pass from the order of deacons to the orders of presbyter and bishops, the nature and vocation of the ministry of the ordained deacon is permanent, complete and unique. Yet, the ministry of the deacon does not entail presiding at the celebration of the Eucharist as the father of a community of believers. Thus, it was quite possible for both women and men to be ordained to the order of the diaconate.[14]

The ordained diaconate is the only ministry of higher orders which has been, and could be, open to women in the Orthodox Church. Although women have in fact been ordained deacons in the Orthodox Church, they have never been ordained to the orders of priesthood and episcopacy.

Those persons who presently believe that there is no need for the diaconate in general and, more particularly, for women deacons would find the prayers of the Orthodox Church of special interest. In the Orthodox ordination service of the deaconess, the following prayer is offered by the ordaining bishop.

O God, the Holy and Almighty, you have blessed woman through the birth in the flesh of your only-begotten Son and our God from the Virgin and you have given the grace and visitation of the Holy Spirit not to men only, but to women as well; Lord, look now upon this your servant and call her to the work of your ministry (εἰς τὸ ἔργον τῆς διακονίας σου). Send down upon her the rich gift of your Holy Spirit. Preserve her in the Orthodox faith, that she may fulfill her ministry in blameless conduct according to what is well pleasing to you. For to you are due all honor, glory and worship, Father, Son and Holy Spirit, now and forever and unto the ages of ages. Amen.

---

[14]Tarasar and Kirillova, *Orthodox Women*, p. 50. For an interesting discussion on the nature of the diaconate, see Louis Bouyer, *Women in the Church* (San Francisco, 1979), pp. 82-87.

And, as the ordination service continues, the bishop offers this prayer prior to vesting of the deaconess with the diaconal stole.

> O Lord and Master, you do not reject women who are willing to offer themselves, in so far as it is fitting, to minister in your holy houses, but rather you accept them into the rank of ministers (ἐν τάξει λειτουργῶν). Grant the grace of your Holy Spirit also to this your servant who desires to offer herself to you and fulfill the grace of your ministry, just as you gave the grace of your ministry (χάριν τῆς διακονίας σου) to Phoebe, whom you called to the work of ministry (ἔργον τῆς λειτουργίας).[15]

While a full analysis of the service of ordination of the woman deacon is beyond the scope of this paper, studies of these and other prayers clearly indicate that the witness of the liturgical life of the Church does not limit this particular visitation of the Holy Spirit to men only, nor to certain privileged women who lived during a certain time in history, never again to be repeated. There are no constraints imposed upon the Holy Spirit in these prayers! These prayers tell us that the Lord accepts women "into the rank of ministers" with no restrictions as to time and place.

Certainly, there are a number of issues related to the order of the women deacon which must be studied. Among these are the disciplinary canons which set various ages and conditions of life for the prospective deacon. Yet, these studies should not prevent us from seeing the great good which the rejuvenation of the order of the woman deacon would be for the Church today. We need only look around us and see the spiritual needs that exist within the parishes and in the larger society. Even with the assistance of the most devoted laypersons, our priests cannot be expected to meet the many demands of parish life. Therefore, it can be argued that the present situation requires that we also consider rejuvenating this special ministry for qualified women who, following a genuine discernment of their call, would be willing ot make a permanent commitment to the ordained ministry of the Church.

---

[15]See "The Ordination Rite of the Byzantine Deaconess," in Theodorou, *Ἡ Χειροτονία,* pp. 55-56. This service dates from the eighth to the tenth centuries and is taken from the Barberion Codex and the Bessarionos Codex. I have offered a translation of this service in "Characteristics," pp. 93-95.

A decision by the Church to rejuvenate the order of the women deacons would certainly not be an action contrary to Scripture and tradition. Rather, such an action would be in complete harmony with the Scripture and tradition of the Church.

Perhaps the rejuvenation of the female (as well as the male) diaconate will also provide us with a witness towards an even deeper spiritual reality. The woman deacon would take her appropriate place as a living sacramental presence in the life of the Church. This act in itself would serve as a powerful reminder that the fullness of the life of the Church is not meant to be solely expressed by what may appear to be a monolithic, male clerical presence at the Eucharist. Rather, this invitation of striving to share this fullness of the life of the Church (i.e., holiness) is at the very heart of the vocation of every baptized Christian. The rejuvenation of the female diaconate could serve as an important living testimony to this fact.

Those who have discussed the possible rejuvenation of the order of the woman deacon do not appear to have a clear perception with regard to how this might take place. Would it be possible, for example, for a particular diocesan bishop to simply begin to ordain women as deacons? This appears to be precisely what Saint Nektarios did. He ordained at least two deaconesses for the convent on the island of Aegina for which he was the spiritual father.[16] Or, some may argue, it may be necessary for a particular local church, rather than the pastoral initiative of an individual

---

[16]Theodorou, ʽΗ Χειροτονία, p. 96. Not too many years ago (1979), my husband and I had the opportunity to visit this same monastery as part of a Lenten pilgrimage. The nuns who escorted us spoke very respectfully about the sanctity of these deaconesses. The monastery's last surviving deaconess, they related, had recently died. Because of the respect they had for this office and for the persons who held them, the nuns told us that they had reverently preserved the cuffs and stole of the last surviving deaconess. When asked if they thought the order was a good and needed one for the Church in these present times, we were given the reply, "Of course." When asked if any of their nuns would be ordained in the near future, the response we received was, "No, because this is a very sacred office and none of us are worthy; even so, we are still under the loving care and protection of the great Saint [Nektarios]." While they verbally stated that they felt they were not worthy, their devotion and humility inspired us and left us with a powerful lasting impression.

bishop, to make the decision to rejuvenate the order of the deaconess.[17] Indeed, some may argue that the decision would have to be made by the entire Orthodox Church. Clearly, the issue is related to an even deeper one regarding the manner in which the Orthodox Church, either locally or internationally, is to act upon important questions which affect her life in the twentieth century.

Women and "Uncleanliness"

This issue is probably the most difficult and sensitive topic to be discussed. This is so because of two basic reasons. Firstly, the issue of the pastoral understanding of menstruation is one which

---

[17]In the case, we note the example of the Armenian Apostolic Church in America, more specifically, the Diocese of the Armenian Church of America, which recently accepted to authorize the ordination of women deacons: "Diocese of the Armenian Church of America Seeks Ordination of Women to the Diaconate," The Diocese of the Armenian Church of America, News Release, July 7, 1986. Cf. "Restoring Women to their Proper Role in the Armenian Church," Yedvard Gulbekian, *Outreach* 8 (October 6, 1985) 3. Recently, I had a noteworthy experience where I could personally observe this very issue of ecclesial "initiative" first hand. At a national Greek Orthodox Archdiocesan conference, I was approached by a well-respected and highly placed clergy friend with the following unexpected salutation, "Hello! . . . So, how soon do you think we will have our first class of deaconesses ordained?" I was stunned with such a greeting, since I had not seen him in several months and expected another kind of reception. "What do you mean?" I asked him. He replied, "Haven't you ever considered that we could probably have at least a dozen pious, eager, and qualified female seminary graduates from our Archdiocese who would, tomorrow, present themselves for ordination to the diaconate, if they could?" Never having considered this in such explicit terms before, I was surprised with his statement and deeply moved by the serious reflection this older clergy friend had put into his comment. Not quite sure about the intention behind his statement, however, and remembering our friendship, I slowly replied, "You know . . . that would be like having a whole 'extra' graduating seminary class of clergy being able immediately to respond to the needs of the Archdiocese." "Precisely," he answered. Although still feeling a little self-conscious, I desired to explore how committed he was to this idea, since he had initiated this conversation. I asked my beloved clergy friend, "It appears you have given this a good deal of thought; do you personally plan publicly to make this proposal?" He froze for a second, and then replied in a controlled, quiet and firm manner, "My friend, for now I refuse to comment on this issue; I will speak up only at the required time." So ends this personal observation on ecclesial initiative.

personally affects every Orthodox woman during part of her life. And secondly, it is an issue of pastoral theology which has not been fully explored by Orthodox theologians. Because of this, it is an issue which is little understood and often associated with a form of superstition which frequently passes for church teaching. Contemporary Orthodox women who are knowledgeable about the functions of their bodies understand the menstrual cycle to be a normal and natural part of their biological identity. These same women, however, are often taught by persons in the Church that the menstrual period is essentially evil and, therefore, unnatural. These women are prohibited by some from receiving Holy Communion during their period of menstruation. There are even those who claim that women during their menstrual period should not attend church, should not receive the blessed bread (antidoron), and should not even venerate icons.

As we have already said, this topic is one which certainly deserves greater examination. However, it is clear that even a cursory examination of the historical evidence indicates that there are divergences of opinion with regard to this issue. Central to this issue, however, appears to be the question of the proper Orthodox interpretation of the Old Testament view which regarded the menstruous woman to be ritually "unclean" because of her loss of blood.

There are two rather obscure canons which deal directly with this topic. These canons were not directly promulgated at an ecumenical synod. Rather, they belong to a collection introduced into the broader canonical corpus through canon 2 of the Council of Trullo in 692. The first is canon 2 of Archbishop Dionysios of Alexandria, a pupil of Origen, who lived during the mid-third century. Apparently answering the question asked of him, Dionysios states in his canon: "Menstruous women ought not to come to the Holy Table, or touch the Holy of Holies, nor come to churches, but pray elsewhere."[18] He gives no explanation for his observation. The second canon is also a response to a question put to Archbishop

---

[18]*Canonical Letter of Dionysios of Alexandria* in *The Nicene and Post-Nicene Fathers* (henceforth *NPNF*) (Grand Rapids, 1956), 14, p. 600. However, in Canon 4 he leaves it up to the discretion of the man whether or not to commune, after he had experienced "involuntary nocturnal pollutions."

Timothy of Alexandria who lived during the end of the fourth century. In response to the question, "Can a menstruous women communicate?", Timothy responds, "Not until she is clean."[19] Again, as in the first response, there is no reason given for the opinion. Subsequent Orthodox commentators, however, have related these responses to the practices of the ancient Israelites as expressed in the Old Testament.[20]

Let us compare these canons with other authoritative church documents. In his commentary on Titus, focusing on the apostolic words, "to the pure all things are pure" (Tit 1.15), Saint John Chrysostom condemns those who propagate a superstitious adherence to the uncleanliness taboo which would include the restrictions directed against women during their period of menstruation. He goes so far as to accuse these persons of being supporters of myths.

In this third homily on Titus, Saint John Chrysostom compares many examples of the uncleanliness taboo which the Church, under the new, or rather, the fulfillment of the law in Christ, need not follow anymore because "things . . . are not clean or unclean from their own nature, but from the disposition of him who partakes of them." Further on in this this discussion, Saint John states that for the Christian:

> all things are pure. God made nothing unclean, for nothing is unclean except for sin only. For [sin] reaches the soul and defiles it. . . . [And] when the soul is unclean, it thinks all things unclean. Therefore, scrupulous observances are no mark of purity, but it is the part of purity to be bold in all things . . . moral. What is unclean? Sin, malice, covetousness, wickedness.

While his discussion on this issue is a general one, and does not specifically call attention to a woman's period of menstruation, Saint John Chrysostom's teaching, nevertheless, seeks to address all of the practices associated with the uncleanliness taboo.

---

[19]*Canonical Answers of Timothy of Alexandria*, in *NPNF*, 14, p. 613. I have slightly adapted this and subsequent texts to a more readable style which conforms more readily with the spirit of the original Greek texts.

[20]E.g., Leviticus 12.1-5, and 15.19-30.

He affirms that all such observances from the Old Testament period are inappropriate for Christians to follow. With regard to these, Saint John relates that "many forms of uncleanness would be found, if it were necessary to recount them all. But these things are not now required of us." Even more noteworthy, Saint John Chrysostom makes no exceptions in this discussion, not even a woman's period of menstruation. He even goes so far as to discuss the uncleanliness taboo as related to the female birth cycle, which concerns both the generation of life as well as the loss of blood. Referring to the Old Testament practices, he states:

> You see how many forms of uncleanliness there are. The woman in child-bed is unclean. Yet God made childbirth and the seed of copulation. Why then is the woman unclean, unless something further is intimated? He intended to produce piety in the soul, and to deter it from fornication. . . . But these things now are not required of us. But all [concern] is transferred to the soul.[21]

This discussion is intimately tied to the Orthodox understanding of natural body functions. If a woman's period of menstruation is ultimately a good and necessary aspect of human physiology, then the canonical *Epistle of Saint Athanasios to the Monk Ammos* (Epistle 48) may offer us a more appropriate approach to this issue. It states that natural body functions are not sinful. To this, the text continues with the following discussion on bodily emissions:

> For what sin or uncleanliness can any natural excrement have in itself? Think of the absurdity of making a sin of the wax which comes from the ears or of the spittle from the mouth. Moreover, we might add many things and explain how the excretions from the belly are necessary to animal life. But if we believe that man is the work of God's hand, as we are taught in Holy Scripture, how can it be supposed necessary that we perform anything impure? And if we are the children of God,

---

[21]John Chrysostom, *Commentary on the Epistle to Titus*, Homily 2, *NPNF*, 13, pp. 529-31. Cf. *Women and Men in the Church* (New York, 1983), pp. 40-46.

as the holy Acts of the Apostles teaches, we have nothing in us unclean.[22]

This fundamental principle related to us by Saint Athanasios, that for Christians, "we have nothing in us unclean," may actually prove to be a more solid guideline for us; for if involuntary nocturnal pollutions are not considered sinful or unclean, neither should menstruation be considered unclean. It would seem that admonitions concerning all bodily emissions must be applied evenhandedly to both men and women.[23]

While this topic cannot be thoroughly addressed here, probably the strongest Orthodox response to this issue can be found in the early third-century *Didascalia Apostolorum*. This very significant document presents a highly developed discussion on this very concern. We will review only a few passages. Referring generallly to the uncleanliness taboo, it states:

> But you who have been converted from the people [of the Old Testament] to believe in God our Savior Jesus Christ, do not continue in your former conversation, brethren, that you should keep vain obligations, purifications and sprinklings and immersions and distinction of meats; for the Lord has said to you: "Remember not the former things" and "Behold, I make all things new, that you may know them."[24]

Directly referring to those who still observed the uncleanliness taboo concerning a woman's period of menstruation as well as other related practices, the *Didascalia* states the following:

> ... Let them tell us, in what days or in what hours they keep themselves from prayer and from receiving the Eucharist, or from reading the Scriptures — let them tell us whether they are void of the Holy Spirit. For through baptism they receive the Holy Spirit, who is ever with those that work righteousness, and [the Spirit] does not depart from them by reason of natural

---

[22]*Canonical Epistle of Saint Athanasios to the Monk Ammos, NPNF*, 14, pp. 602-03; cf. Leviticus 15.

[23]Constance Tarasar, *Woman: Handmaid to the Lord*, p. 262.

[24]*Didascalia Apostolorum*, 26.4.15, p. 216.

issues and the intercourse of marriage, but is ever and always with those who possess him, and keeps them . . . [25]

Further in the document, this position is even more succinctly articulated when it asserts emphatically:

For do you think, O woman, that in the seven days of your flux that you are void of the Holy Spirit, and if you die in those days, you will depart empty and without hope? But if the Holy Spirit is always in you, without impediment, why do you keep yourself from prayer and from the Scriptures and from the Eucharist? For consider and see that prayer is heard through the Holy Spirit, and the Eucharist through the Holy Spirit is accepted and sanctified, and the Scriptures are the words of the Holy Spirit and are holy. For if the Holy Spirit is in you, why do you keep yourself from approaching the works of the Holy Spirit?[26]

Elsewhere in the same document, we read that women are not to be separated from the rest of the Christian community because of their period of menstruation. The text supports this with the following:

She who had the flow of blood was not condemned when she touched the fringe of our Savior's cloak but, rather, received the forgiveness of all her sins. Therefore, beloved ones, avoid such foolish observances, and do not come near them.[27]

This reference to the woman with the flow of blood should remind us how important it is for us to look seriously at the words and actions of the Lord as found in the Gospels. Let us remember that this whole discussion concerning the "uncleanliness" of woman is nowhere to be found in the actions and teachings of Christ. On the contrary, it appears as though the Lord treated women in a manner which often ran contrary to the accepted practices and teachings of first-century Judaism. Not only did Jesus permit women

---

[25]Ibid. 26.4.21, p. 242.
[26]Ibid. 26.4.21, p. 244.
[27]Ibid. 26.4.22, p. 254.

to follow him and to learn from him but also he chose to appear first to the women following his resurrection. Indeed, the Lord commissioned these women to be the first evangelists of the resurrection.

Even a basic review of the New Testament witness and the documents which we have discussed raise a number of questions which await further exploration by our theologians. Firstly, it appears as though there is divergence within the tradition with regard to menstruation in particular and to bodily processes in general. Certainly the two canons in question must be examined thoroughly in the light of their particular cultural and historical circumstances.

Secondly, there appears to be a need to examine anew the proper Orthodox understanding of the Old Testament regulations especially those relating to women. It seems somewhat peculiar that the regulations referring to such issues as circumcision and diet are not binding upon Christians yet others which deal directly with women seem to have authority, at least according to the opinion of some. Clearly, it appears that we need to investigate this matter more systematically, especially with the actions of Christ as well as the observations of the *Didascalia* and Saint John Chrysostom in mind.

And finally, we must look anew at the singular importance of the Holy Eucharist. There is no doubt that we are living in a period which has reemphasized the centrality of the Eucharist. Indeed, because of the renewed appreciation of the biblical and patristic evidence regarding the Eucharist, we are called upon to reexamine our understanding of a number of practices which may have minimized the centrality of the Eucharist. Thus, the practice of those who claim that a woman should not receive Holy Communion simply because she is menstruating needs serious review. This must take place in the light of our physiological understanding of menstruation and in the light of our understanding of the centrality of the Holy Eucharist both for each believer and for the entire Christian community.

Women and the Sanctuary

Another issue which is often discussed, but seldom reflected upon theologically, is that of the apparent restriction of women from the sanctuary. There are those who fervently believe that women are not allowed in the sanctuary merely because they are women and "unclean." And conversely, there are those who with equal ardor believe that men, simply because they are men (sometimes even if they are not Orthodox believers), may enter the sanctuary virtually at will. Both views, of course, are incorrect.

The appropriate restriction placed upon women and men from entering the sanctuary area is actually directed to the laity in general. This is based upon two canons; the first comes to us from a local council held in the fourth century at Laodicea of which Canon 44 relates that, "The altar must not be approached by women." A second canon comes from the Sixth Ecumenical Synod and states that, "No layman except the emperor shall go up to the altar" (Canon 69).[28] While some have related this prohibition expressed toward women to reasons of biological uncleanliness,[29] the more accurate practice applies these restrictions to *all* those who had no appropriate liturgical or practical business for being in the altar area. This particularly pertains to the offering of the holy gifts during the Divine Liturgy. Because

> all lay persons are forbidden such action as *lay persons* . . .
> Women in particular are forbidden since they have no place
> among the bishops and priests *as women,* with canonical regu-
> lation indicating that there was an attempt to violate this doc-
> trine at some point in history.[30]

Those men and women who have both ecclesial approval and appropriate reason (e.g., for assisting the clergy with the services or for preparing the sanctuary for worship) are not prohibited from entering the altar area. What was originally intended as a practice to maintain good order and promote piety within the whole worshipping congregation has all too often been used by some as a way of encouraging attitudes which devalue the vocation of women and their equality before God merely because they are women.

As in every issue which we have mentioned, it is also necessary for us to consider this concern with full appreciation for the tradition of the Church as a whole and not simply with an eye upon

---

[28]*NPNF*, 14, pp. 153 and 396 respectively.

[29]E.g., Zonaras' comment regarding Canon 44 of the Council of Laodicea, *NPNF*, 14, p. 153.

[30]*Women and Men in the Church*, p. 45.

relatively recent, local practices. Thus, we will find that there is more at stake than may have been at first anticipated. As we have already discussed in this study, we have the tradition of women deacons. They were not only ordained at the altar but also received Holy Communion as a member of the clergy within the sanctuary. Also, we have the striking example of Saint Gorgonia, the sister of Saint Gregory of Constantinople. She was praised by her brother for her courage and faith in God. Saint Gregory notes also that when was "dangerously ill of a malignant disease," she clutched the holy altar and prayed for God to deliver her from her illness. In telling this story, Saint Gregory remembers her "declaring that she would not loosen her hold until she was made whole."[31] While the story of Saint Gorgonia may be somewhat unusual, the very fact that Saint Gregory records the incident is a vivid reminder that we must be willing to broaden our appreciation of the various elements of the tradition of the Church which may enable us to see contemporary issues in a better light.

There are some very significant pastoral, as well as liturgical, concerns which center upon this issue. The first has to do with the Service of the Forty Days at which the newborn child is formally brought to the church. Why, then, in the churching rite of infants, do most priests customarily take male infants into the sanctuary and circle the altar and only bring female infants as far as the royal doors? While some may claim that this is the "traditional" practice, it is necessary to raise the question of whether there is a valid doctrinal reason for the practice. Or is the practice simply conditioned by a cultural view which exalted the male child and devalued the female child?

Some may have heard clergy justify these actions by stating that there is always a chance that the male infant could one day serve at the holy altar as a priest. Others may state that the practice is in accord with the canon which prohibits women from entering the sanctuary. Upon closer investigation, however, both of these arguments have little merit. Firstly, as we have already noted, is the canon which prohibits *all* laypersons (except the emperor) from entering the sanctuary. Thus, it would appear that even the practice of bringing a male child into the sanctuary violates the letter of the canon. And secondly, with regard to the "future" of the

---

[31]Gregory the Theologian, *On His Sister Gorgonia, NPNF,* 7, p. 243.

child, who is to say that perhaps the female infant could one day serve within the holy altar as a deaconess?

Such argumentation both for the male infant and for the female infant, however, leaves much to be desired. Simply stated, the arguments generally put forward in this regard appear to reflect an attitude which is culturally determined and not doctrinally based. The practice of prohibiting female infants from being brought into the sanctuary at the time of their presentation may well be an act of discrimination. Since we view both the female and the male infants as being equally valuable and equally treasured by God, then it would appear that our liturgical practices must reflect this reality.

This leads us to the issue of young girls serving as acolytes. The issue has already been boldly faced by Metropolitan Emilianos of Silybria. He recommends that more women "be admitted to the minor orders such as lectors and acolytes."[32] Based upon what has already been said in this paper, especially with regard to the tradition of female deacons, there does not seem to be any doctrinal reason which would prevent girls from serving as acolytes and women as serving as lectors. Indeed, the present custom may be contrary to the Church's teaching on the dignity of the human person, and the fundamental equality of the male and female persons.

Certain members of the Church's leadership may consider the issue of altar girls as unimportant. It is a topic, however, that is discussed by many mothers and their young daughters. This issue is very important to them. Since it is a serious matter for them, so it also must be treated as an important topic by us as well.

Some of the other significant questions we will have to ask regarding this include: how necessary is it for young girls to feel just as much a part of the liturgical life as young boys? How much would an increase in the ways young girls could participate in ecclesial worship affect their future life in the Church? How would this affect the rest of their lives? This is indeed a very important pastoral challenge that we as the Church militant must face.

Conclusions

We have identified in this paper six specific issues which relate directly to the position and the ministry of women in the Orthodox

---

[32]Metropolitian Emilianos Timiadis, "The Concern for Women in the Orthodox Tradition," p. 19.

Church today. Each of them is an issue of great importance and pastoral concern which cannot be ignored. While this paper in no way assumes to be a complete investigation or analysis of these topics, it has been our intention to introduce some of the more important issues to the members of this audience. In the case of each issue, we have identified a number of theological and doctrinal concerns which can provide the basis for further exploration.

Pious, yet sometimes superficial, assumptions and platitudes concerning how women may or may not serve in the Orthodox Church will not withstand the scrutiny of our time. The Church historically responds to critical generational challenges related to Christian doctrine and praxis by creatively articulating the truth in a pastoral manner which is consistent with the reality of the Gospel. Our generation severely compromises or even betrays this pastoral responsibility when we discount the existence and importance of the issues which have been noted in this presentation. Ignoring these topics will not make them go away. Rather, we will only continue to compound our pastoral problems. And, without sufficient response, we may find ourselves alienating many faithful believers.

Our apparent lack of active commitment to discern and express the appropriate Orthodox Christian response to the issues related to the position and the ministry of women in the Church may ultimately compromise the Church's witness of the Gospel in the world. We must now attempt to respond to these questions in a manner which reflects the genuine and catholic tradition of the Church. While this can occur only after thoughtful study, it must be emphasized that this is not merely an academic exercise. Rather, this work must be an activity of the Church, for the life of the Church and for the benefit of her witness to the risen Lord. This endeavor needs also to be accompanied by an appropriate spirit of prayer and humility. This work must be undertaken with a sense of hope and joy since we know that the Lord is risen and still abides within his Church in the Holy Spirit. How we respond to these concerns now will directly affect the future integrity of the witness of the Church.

In this presentation, we have been careful not to enumerate or dwell upon the concrete and overt examples of sexism perpetuated against women in specific situations. The Church by her very nature and structure is not sexist. There are some in the Church, however, who practice this particular manifestation of sin and inflict great pain on others because of it. Unfortunately, there are all too many examples of women who have been intentionally overlooked and discounted in their service to the Church, for no other reason except for the fact that they are women. When qualified women enthusiastically desire to serve in the various ministries that are well founded upon the tradition of the Church, but are barred from doing so simply because they are women, then we encounter nothing less than a scandal and an injustice.

Sexism is not merely an affront against women or even men. Sexism is a direct offense against God because it is the triune God who has created all human beings in the divine "image and likeness." This sin ultimately denies that which is frequently prayed in our services, that all men and women are equally cared for by God who is "good and full of love for all humankind." Sexism is a sin in the fullest sense of the word: it intentionally obstructs the divine will concerning the vocation of both male and female persons. Those who callously deny or demean the vocation of women are imposing their own will over that of the will of God.

The Church calls women to experience and express this life in the triune God on an equal footing with men. The lives of the saints are a witness to this. Women will often manifest their personal appropriation of sanctity within the Christian community much in the same way male believers will. There will also be other times, however, when the personal gifts of women, including their particular gift of femininity, will present variety and complementarity to the respective gifts brought to the Church by men.[33]

The sin of sexism, however, has many faces. One such face occurs when the vitality of women's appropriate presence and participation in the life of the Church is actively opposed, stifled, or betrayed. This may have its foundation in either an exclusively androcentric conceptualization and configuration of roles and relationships for life in the Church or through clericalism,[34] both of which are foreign to fundamental Orthodox Christian tradition.

---

[33]This understanding has its roots in trinitarian theology. Orthodox Christians believe that there is a diversity in God the Trinity; one God who is also three equal and unique divine persons, yet, each person abides in the other person in an eternal dynamic of love. Our theology also affirms that there is full equality between male and female persons, expressed through a diversity of gifts bestowed to each of them, of which include their masculinity and femininity. See Thomas Hopko, "On the Male Character of the Christian Priesthood," pp. 97-134, and my article, "The Ministry of Women," pp. 561-66.

Another face of sexism is associated with the sin of omission. This occurs when we as individual persons and members of the Church neglect to encourage actively the various forms of ministry available to qualified female Orthodox Christians whose presence and service are seriously needed by the Church. We have so far failed to invest seriously our time, talents, and financial resources in this very important matter. While we may sometimes give nominal affirmation to the importance of and need for the ministry of women in the Church, our apparent lack of committed action speaks far more eloquently.

We would like briefly to conclude these observations by stating that the concern for *orthopraxia* is at the heart of this discussion. Is our praxis as fully Christian as it can be? Do our present actions begin to reflect the full reality of who we are as the body of Christ? Do our current liturgical practices totally correspond to the full Orthodox understanding of masculine and feminine persons? We may need to reflect upon these questions very carefully.

If women saw the Lord and ministered to him, if they were the first witnesses of the crucifixion and resurrection, if they were equally visible in the life of the apostolic Church, then our present constraints on women may reflect a theology very much bound to the assumptions of past cultures. We must be able to reach a point where we can recognize the difference between culturally bound assumptions and those convictions based upon Christian doctrine.

It is most appropriate that this paper is being delivered today, on the feast day of Saint Thekla. She has been honored with the title of "Proto-martyr and Equal to the Apostles." Thekla was a follower of Saint Paul and she is remembered for bringing many men and women to the faith. In this case, the Church does not call her a martyr because she died a violent death. Rather, she is called a martyr because she survived many harsh persecutions for the sake of the Gospel. Her example of courage to live and preach the Gospel serves as a great testimony to her faith and life. In some Byzantine icons, she is depicted wearing a traveler's cloak and carrying the Gospel in her left arm. This is another indication to us of the dynamism of her ministry. Her example continues to provide the Church today with a powerful Christian witness.

The challenge we face today is to recapture fully the spirit of *orthopraxia* which affirmed the person of Saint Thekla and enabled her to be a powerful presence and witness for our Lord and Savior, Jesus Christ.

The Captivity of Orthodox Christian Education

CHRISTIAN EDUCATION AMONG THE ORTHODOX CHURCHES
of North America is an *ad hoc* affair. No other term can do justice
to what is going on in the name of the educational experience in
our parishes. The first responsibility for what is or is not happening must rest with those centralized agencies, the archdiocese or
diocese, which determine the "normal" behavior for parochial life,
whether it be liturgical celebrations, the order of the church year,
or the discipline of the clergy. The second responsibility must fall
on those "professional" agencies, the seminaries, which train our
clerical and other ministers to do their jobs responsibly. The third
must fall on the pastors and parents themselves, who usually do
not know what they want and, therefore, do not know what to demand or look for.

It is indeed the case that no one single area of curriculum in
our seminaries is as potentially inclusive as Christian education.
No other area affects so directly the performance of the clergy in
serving their people and making the faith, by which they come
to be alive, if not real, at least known to them. Yet no other area
in the curriculum of our seminaries is so consistently ignored, put
on the back burner, and treated, in the worst sense of the words,
like "Sunday School stuff" as is Christian education as a category
for study. There certainly is no sense of it as an academic discipline.
The overall feeling about Christian education in the curriculum
of the seminaries runs radically counter to what is needed in the
Orthodox parishes which those schools are supposed to be serving. Consequently, the Orthodox Churches in North America have
failed to produce an academic/theological community of educator/

127

theologians who can work effectively in sharing and critiquing methods, materials, content, and research. We have in short produced no critical thinking on Christian education; pedagogues are confined to the realm of technique and the theologians to the realm of doctrine with no apparent interaction between the two groups.

The immediate academic need in the North American Church is for educators and youth workers and not for canonists, church historians, liturgists, and dogmaticians with whom we are already top heavy and who have already had too great an impact on our theological education to the exclusion of praxis. We now need Orthodox academicians, however, who are trained in pedagogy, sociology, psychology — their content as well as their methods — to enable us to apply the real faith to living situations among living Orthodox. We must come to apply the best of theology to pedagogy and the best of pedagogy to theology. In regard to this point, we must, for instance, come to understand "the human person" and "the community" as foci of our theology and our pedagogy and indeed as the interface where they can meet, learn to speak the same language, and influence one another. The remarkable thing about reading some of the church Fathers is their understanding of educational and psychological principles, centering on the growth of human personhood in the context of community. To this end we must do an intentional study of the Fathers focusing on the role of person as *object* of education and community as matrix, combining both in a relational and contextual understanding of education as *nurture* (not as learning), as *formation* (not as information). Hence, for instance, we have Gregory the Theologian understanding the limits of human person and recommending a stage developmental approach to the study of the Scriptures.[1] It is remarkable to note the manner in which patristic anthropology is consistent with the developmental stages of Erikson and the client-centered therapy of Carl Rogers. Admittedly, I have read the Fathers selectively, but I have done it carefully. It is this lack of trained personnel and the serious thought which feeds them, which permits a captivity of Orthodox Christian education to every wind of fancy that happens to be blowing.

The Orthodox Christian education is in need of liberation and

---

[1] *In Defense of His Flight to Pontos*, Oration 1, in the *Nicene and Post-Nicene Fathers*, vol. 7 (Grand Rapids), p. 214.

the form of that liberation will be directly dependent on the captivities to which it is subjected. It is best for me here, for the sake of discussion, to take a reactionary approach and consider what I see these captivities to be, and then go on to develop at a later date a positive approach to Christian education, planning, and development, an approach rooted in what I refer to as the foundational categories of Christian learning — personhood and community.

The first captivity is to the theological and pedagogical expertise of those outside of the Orthodox theological and ecclesiastical tradition, and particularly to secular researchers and theoreticians. This is especially the case with the devotion, including my own, to the developmental psychologists and their contributions to educational practice and philosophy. While devotion can be blind, it does not have to be so and, indeed, the "spoils" of Egypt and "truth" are the Church's regardless of who formulated or discovered them. Truth by its nature belongs to the Truth himself! We can usefully integrate the work of secular theoreticians into our work if we do so critically and with discernment. What we cannot allow is the wholesale adoption of one particular philosophy or, for that matter, one particular theological theme, as the foundation of our educational enterprise as if it were the only possible approach and as if it were to be "true" forever.

All researchers and practitioners have biases and these biases must be as public as possible; honest research and practice requires that the researcher and the practitioner be aware of and make his biases known. Hence, the need for a critical community of theologian/educators precisely to "test" theories against sound theological tradition and educational theory. The rejection, in principle, of the behaviorism of Skinner by Christian educators is a case in point,[2] but only the tip of the proverbial iceberg. Unfortunately, while we reject Skinner in principle, we use him in practice; we use him because he works.

It is a captivity to the programs, research, and presuppositions of such scholars as Lawrence Kohlberg and Sidney Simon in moral development and values clarification respectively and to Jean Piaget and Erik Erikson in cognitive and emotional development

---

[2] See John Elias, *Psychology and Religious Education* (Bethlehem, PA., 1975), pp. 16-27.

respectively, of which we must at least be aware. We must ask the
question: "Can we accept the methods and techniques of a particular system without accepting the philosophy of that system?"
The discerning mind must recognize that aberrant biases and presuppositions can give birth to the techniques that may be useful
to us. I am not saying we should not use Sidney Simon or Lawrence
Kohlberg, Jean Piaget, or Erik Erikson[3] but that we must be
aware of what we are doing when we use them. Such has been the
object of much of my own work in Christian education. Sidney
Simon's values clarifications, with its implied relativism, is in fact
what most effective teachers have been doing all along; the cognitive dissonance being so central. It is the case, for instance, that
Lawrence Kohlberg's stage developmental approach to moral decision making is paralleled in the techniques of many of the Fathers
of the desert.[4] Kohlberg relies heavily on cognition in moral
development and Sidney Simon relies on reflection; it is also the
case that the human mind and the "changing of the mind" (*metanoia*) is the basis of Orthodox moral life. Saint Paul himself writes
that we are to change and renew our minds (Rom 12.2). Now their
definitions of the mind might be different, but it is clear from both
of them that some sort of cognitive reorientation must take place
either before, or concurrently with, an affective or behavorial
change. Once this is clear, there is a mutual interaction between
the *lex credendi* and *lex orandi*, without giving precedence to one
over the other except in the realm of logic. It is the potential affective change which makes Simon and Kohlberg valuable, but
valuable only in the context of a living community, a community
that "knows itself" in its truths, rituals, and symbols, a community which can integrate a technique without assuming its presuppositions, a community that knows where it came from, why it exists,
and where it is going.

The problem with using the secular educational techniques is
not their secular basis or even their biases but the lack of a matrix into which we can creatively fit them. For sure, we cannot do
the research — we have neither the time, the money, nor the trained

[3] Ronald Dusk and Mariellen Whelan, *Moral Development: A Guide to
Piaget and Kohlberg* (New York, 1975).

[4] Yushi Nomura, *Desert Wisdom: Sayings from the Desert Fathers*
(Garden City, NY., 1984), pp. 9, 25.

personnel. We can, however, use what is congenial to our needs and our tradition, but we must first know what our needs and traditions as a community are, lest we become captive not only to the methods of secular education but to their values as well. We must, for instance, know what our theological and working (read pastoral) definition of "person" is.

We can use the secular as long as we know what we are looking for and possess a structure of Christian education in which we can fit what we need. It is this academic structure which we, however, lack because we lack an effective educational community which can interact with well-done theology. Instead we have tended to focus on limited aspects of our theological tradition, such as liturgy, to the exclusion of others, such as anthropology. It is a current, and slightly misplaced theme of John H. Westerhoff, an Episcopalian, that Christian educators have sold out to "valuing" and "discussing" instead of teaching values and morals. He makes the point,[5] a bit overstated, that we have betrayed the affective/intuitive approach fundamental to faith development for the cognitive/intellectual approach. This particular problem is, as Westerhoff points out, one that is serious; but it is particularly serious in the tradition from which he comes that tends to be less liturgical and more intellectual, in which children are brought into the Church after an act of confirmation in and confession of the faith. In principle, the Orthodox should not face a similar problem. We assume that the child is an active and living member of the Church, both eucharistically and socially, from the time of his baptism; due to Orthodox practice and the ethnic nature of many of our parishes we tend to focus on families in many activities and, consequently, on the whole person as part of the "family system" in which one fashions a "meaning structure." (I will develop "family systems" and "socialization" themes in the second part of this study.)

There is among Orthodox educators an insecurity and a corresponding sense of "treading water" when it comes to serious educational theory and praxis; hence, the almost compelling need to rely on the work of Protestant, Catholic, and secular educators who have the time, money, and sense of urgency to do the necessary

---

[5] John H. Westerhoff, III, *Will our Children Have Faith?* (New York), pp. 2-5. Also a lecture delivered to the Convention of the Religious Education Association, "Values for Today's Childhood," tape 21.

research. I certainly do not agree with Westerhoff's warning regarding the neglect of the affective, emotive, or intuitive element; it is not really *our* problem. Neither does the cognitive exclude the intuitive in a community context. Orthodox may have, in fact, overplayed what Westerhoff refers to as the affective element in Christian life. We must, however, become more aware of the affect of "outside wisdom" on our educational enterprise. We must be prepared to use those legitimate cognitive elements of learning and growth which can be integrated into our understanding of human personhood as the object of education and the ecclesial and familial communities as the matrix of education.

The second captivity of Orthodox Christian education in North America, and this we inherited from the sixteenth-century Reformation and Counter-Reformation, is the focus on childhood and on formal childhood education. Education, and specifically "schooling," was one of the revolutions of the sixteenth century during which schools became common and children, for the first time in history, became the wholesale objects of education. Also for the first time in history, and this is truly revolutionary, an attempt was made to change an entire people's way of looking at the world by the written word — Luther's Catechism and the Bible. An entire system of education was worked out around the catechism and the job of parents was to teach the catechism and the job of the pastor was to validate this by follow-up home visits.[6] The point here being that for better or for worse the child became the center of the educational enterprise whereas previously it had been the adult. Young children being educated, if at all formally, at home.[7] Since then education, almost by definition, has become something done by adults to children but not something done by adults to adults or even with children. Child-centered education has severely limited the education enterprise by distorting the nature of personhood and relationships within community. Education became rooted in heteronomous and authoritarian interaction.

---

[6] See William Haugaard, "The Continental Reformation of the Sixteenth Century," in John H. Westerhoff, III and O. C. Edwards, Jr., eds., *A Faithful Church* (Wilton, CT., 1981), pp. 109-73, especially p. 167.

[7] See Boojamra, "Theological and Pedagogical Perspectives on the Family as Educator," *The Greek Orthodox Theological Review* 29 (1, 1984) 12.

Childhood education as a discrete discipline violates both the mutuality of community and our developmental understanding of human person.

For better or for worse and for positive and negative reasons children receive a great deal of attention in America. They are either abused (an epidemic reality in North America) or they are cultivated, during the past two decades coming to represent a distinct multi-billion dollar market for goods and services. Childhood has been taken out of the matrix of family and community and seen as a separate entity with separate needs and separate demands and, more importantly, as an end in itself. In addition, and far more significantly socially, American families have tended to build their existences around the service of the child to the point of the "tail" wagging the proverbial "dog"; this, I believe, has resulted in an inevitable resentment of children and childhood. James Dobson even warns us about children as a threat.[8] It is this resentment which, I believe, apart from a possible inherent dislike for childhood among Americans, that has resulted in child abuse, neglect, and, among other things, the phenomenon of the "street children," who simply have been dehomed and, with the exception of the likes of Father Bruce Ritter and the *Covenant House,* largely ignored. Less obviously, but just as destructively, our captivity to childhood has led to the phenomenon of the "adultified child" (see below, note 16).

We have taken our Christian education programs only to the child and we have pedagogically and socially assumed, to the dysfunction of both processes, that education takes place before the age of sixteen after which is it is downhill until death.[9] This has put a severe pressure on the parish to "get them" while they are young; it also tells the children that nothing is effectively learned beyond the twenties, feeding a distaste of adulthood and further alienating the generation.

The point is that the focus on the child in the home (the child-centered home) and in the church school for education has been effectively dysfunctional to parents, teachers, and children. People, regardless of age, in fact do not learn until they are ready to learn or perceive a need to learn; this readiness and need is

---

[8] James Dobson, *Dare to Discipline* (Wheaton, IL., 1978), pp. 2, 82-83.

[9] Gabriel Moran, *Education Towards Adulthood* (New York, 1979), p. 8.

most prevalent in adults. This additional demand for motivation, so necessary for younger children, has strained the goodwill and talent of generations of volunteer teachers and has pressured us to produce materials without the staff to use it. It has also pressured educators to teach things children do not need to know *as* children to be Christians. They literally suffer Christian education "burn out" before they are intellectually or emotionally able to handle the content and meaning of the Christian faith. The child must be dethroned in the school and in the home before we can as a Church be liberated *for* education, before marriages and families can take on their proper proportions, and before our churches can make the necessary investment in those who learn best, the adults who have the most need to be competent.[10] I do not want to go into the value of adult education here; I do want to affirm that we have made the tremendous mistake and done a terrible disservice to both the Church and her teaching and the children and their natural development by copying the pattern of childhood education from Protestant, Roman Catholic, and secular models. We have both torn apart the value of the community and distorted the nature of personhood.

Developmental psychology has done the Church great service in that it has treated human life as a process of movement from lower to higher, from less complex to more complex, from concrete to conceptual. It has done us a great service by describing the child as more than a miniature adult. It has provided limits of what we can and should do and correspondingly what we cannot and should not do with, for, and to children.[11] It has allowed children to be children; it has placed them on a human continuum (emotional, cognitive, and ethical) with the rest of the "real"

---

[10]It is the fact that far more significant than the decline in learning ability after the age of 27 (approximately 1% per year) is the increase in motivation and the sheer quantity of experience that adults have accumulated which they usually bring to those learning situations. Issue-centered learning, learning for responsible role fulfillment, and competency learning must become the foci of a mature adult education program. See George Mouly, *Psychology for Effective Teaching* (New York, 1962), pp. 196-97.

[11]Ronald Goldman, *Religious Thinking from Childhood to Adolescence* (New York, 1968), passim.

people.[12] We have discovered that children do what they do and behave the way they behave within broad stage specific ranges that are universal, sequential, hierarchical, and somewhat age related. We have discovered that children cannot and should not learn what an adult can and/or should learn just because he is a Christian. To this end Gregory the Theologian notes:

> For some need to be fed with the milk of the most simple and elementary doctrines, viz., those who are in habit babies and, so to say, new-made, and unable to bear the manly food of the word: nay, if it were presented to them beyond their strength, they would probably be overwhelmed and oppressed, owing to the inability of their minds, as is the case with our material bodies, to digest and appropriate what is offered to it and so would lose even their original power.[13]

Gregory in the same location goes on to say:

> the wiser of the Hebrews tells us that there was of old among the Hebrews a most excellent and praiseworthy law, that every age was not entrusted with the whole Scripture, inasmuch as this would not be the more profitable course, since the whole of it is not at once intelligible to everyone, and its more recondite parts would, by their apparent meaning, do a very great injury to most people. Some portions of the Scripture were entrusted only to those over twenty-five.[14]

There are, by the nature of the structure of the human mind, limitations as what the developing child can understand; the process of trying to teach too much too soon to children inevitably results

---

[12]John Demos, "Infancy and Childhood in the Plymouth Colony," in Gordon, ed., *The American Family in Socio-Historical Perspective* (New York, 1973). See also Philip Greven, *The Protestant Temperament* (New York, 1980), pp. 35, 43-49, 46; also pp. 151-52, 159, 160.

[13]*In Defense of His Flight to Pontos,* Oration 1, in *Nicene and Post-Nicene Fathers* (Grand Rapids, 1974), p. 214.

[14]*Ibid.* p. 214. In addition to the obvious content of the passage, it does indicate that Gregory probably had had recourse to rabbis for scriptural discussion or clarification on the literal meaning of biblical texts. Such was not uncommon also among Western Fathers.

in the child's distorting concepts they cannot understand, hence
the famous malversions of the Lord's Prayer — "Harold be the
name," "lead us not into Penn Station," and so forth. The child
perceives reality in terms of what is most obvious *to him*; he tends,
for instance, to center on the most obvious element of a story or
event. He learns in ways that are different than adults and cannot
use what Piaget refers to as "formal operations." The young child
cannot reverse a process which he has begun in order to check
on it. Christianity, other than what he shares with the community,
largely remains external to him.[15]

Paradoxically, our educational techniques and content have
negated childhood by teaching them adult material and treating
them like "little adults" by teaching them adult material.[16]
Developmentalism is liberating for religious educators because it
sets up the parameters in which they can most effectively work.
It tells us that childhood is valuable not because it is charming,
but because it is the foundation of later healthy human and Christian development. For instance, children do not play because they
are children; children are children because they *need* to play. Play
is a social modifier. Play serves both a recreative and developmental
role. Play, for the Christian educator, is the child's initiation into
liturgy and moral development; play is the ability of the child to
call "time out" in a complicated world life.[17] Without a sense of

---

[15]See Milton Schwebel and Jane Raph, *Piaget in the Classroom* (New
York, 1973), pp. 10, 37. Also Barry Wadsworth, *Piaget's Theory of Cognitive Development* (New York, 1971), pp. 75-76, 93-94.

[16]See Maria Winn, *Children Without Childhood* (New York, 1983), pp.
98-99, who makes the legitimate claim that Freud is a source of the adultifi-
fication of childhood inasmuch as he ascribes the same motives, albeit passive, to children and adults (hence the centrality of "sex"). I have here taken another perspective having less to do with development and more to do
with behavior. See Dobson, *Dare to Discipline,* pp. 81-113, 145-66, 167-91.

[17]It is both notable and astounding that in an entire collection of fourteen studies in Dione Apostolos-Cappadona, *The Sacred Play of Children*
(New York, 1983), no connection is made between play and liturgy. This
would be a fruitful area for research by an Orthodox. National Institute
of Mental Health, *Caring About Kids: The Importance of Play* (Rockville,
MD., 1981) for a purely secular perception of play but applicable by any
thoughtful pastor to liturgy and moral development. See also David
Elkind, "The Role of Play in Religious Education," *Religious Education* 75 (May-June, 1980) 282.

play, a child does not grow into a healthy sense of liturgy or a healthy sense of morality. Our educational enterprise tends not to respect the needs of childhood and in fact are often part of the process of the adultified child which has occupied the attention of David Elkind in *The Hurried Child* and Marie Winn in *Children Without Childhood.*

Many of the findings of the developmentalists are valuable for adults; Gail Sheehey in her well-known book *Passages* has applied this to the growth of women.[18] This clearly points to the application of stage development to adult education and the moral, spiritual, intellectual, and emotional needs of adults as occasions for Christian education. What is obvious from the patristic tradition, the nature of the Christian faith, and contemporary education psychology is that Christian education in its methods and contents is stage dependent. The best potential learner is the adult; the best potential learning situation is any situation in which the adult happens to be exhibiting and for which he seeks competency or responsible behavior.

Paradoxically we have been told so frequently that the family is the ideal institution for rearing children that the family has focused itself around children to the neglect of the parents and the potentially nurturing value of the husband-wife relationship for all members of the family system.[19] It is not uncommon to find

---

[18]Gail Sheehey, *Passages* (New York, 1976), passim.

[19]Emile Brunner begins his study of marriage with the husband-wife relationship, while Karl Barth, whom Guernsey and Anderson tend to follow, begin their study with the parent-child or, specifically, the mother-child relations as primary. Christopher Lasch, in his *Haven in a Heartless World* (New York), takes up what is in keeping with an Orthodox approach of mutuality and companionship. See Elchaninov, *Diary of a Russian Priest* (London, 1967), p. 46, and Meyendorff, J., *Marriage*, p. 15. Children are in this approach necessary but not sufficient to a marriage. See Emile Brunner, *Love and Marriage* (London, 1970), p. 195. Barth, on the other hand, argues that marriage is subordinate to family (see *Church Dogmatics* III/4, p. 189). In Brunner, the marital pair is the basic relationship (*ibid.*, p. 198) and model of man/women relations as a community of love; to this basic relationship, all others are extra. Marriage is the highest form of human relationship for the development of authentic human growth; to this must be added ideally in an unfallen world. See Small, *Christian: Celebrate Your Sexuality* (Old Tappen, NY., 1974), p. 137.

that people who have centered their entire lives around their children have reacted against this and have determined "to find" themselves, to affirm their own freedom from children and, finally, from the family itself through various forms of legal, emotional, and spiritual divorce. In another direction, this reaction to the child-centered home has produced anger manifested as child abuse. Children have been allowed for so long, in the Freudian-inspired fear of "damaging them forever," to do what they want to do that many parents have reacted with abuse, escape, or Dobsonian disciplinarianism.[20] It is interesting that the contemporary feminist movement appears to couple a resentment/rejection of child rearing with a desire for the liberation.[21]

While Guernsey and Anderson give priority to the rearing of children in the family and the parent-child relationship as primary, I do not agree. There is a logical priority which must be given to the husband-wife relationship, both socially and theologically. Guernsey and Anderson have posited the parent-child relations as the primary one and the beginning of the theology of the family.[22] This sort of hole in the dike theology to shore up the family is not what we need now. There are convincing studies that indicate the central, though not exclusive, importance of the husband and wife relationship. Certainly for the early child the primary element of socialization is the inter-parental relationship itself.[23] The family is being replaced by the individual as the central focus of social life.

The third captivity of our educational methods and programs is to the schooling/instructional paradigm of public education

---

[20]James Dobson, *Dare to Discipline*. This theme was discussed by the author with Father Bruce Ritter of Covenant House in New York City on July 21, 1986.

[21]Christopher Lasch notes that the current fear of parenthood and of child rearing is actually a sublimated fear of the future and a manifestation of the demise of commitment in human relationships. See Lasch, *Haven in a Heartless World*, p. 139.

[22]Anderson and Guernsey, *Becoming Family*, pp. 9-11.

[23]See Lucie Barber, John Hiltz, and Louise Skoch, "Ministry to Parents of the Little Child," *Religious Education*, 74 (May/June, 1974), 264. William McCready makes the same point in "The Family and Socialization," in Andrew Greeley, *The Family in Crisis or in Transition* (New York, 1979), pp. 26-34, 26-27.

applied to Christian education. We have assumed that we can communicate all of the content of the Christian faith to the people between the ages of six and sixteen; we have assumed that we can do this in the context of what is referred to as the classroom, a euphemism for the formal teaching situation of the educational ministry — fixed desks, textbooks, formal curricula, etc. The author has opposed this scholarly instructional paradigm to a socialization model of which education is Christian formation by the community — family and parish.[24] Content is to be delivered to these children and it is to be done to them in the classroom, in a relatively passive and non-interactive fashion. We have added to this the additional limitation, the opposite side of the classroom coin, of the teacher as a formal distributor of knowledge and information to a relatively passive group of young people. We have effectively implied that legitimate teaching and learning takes place in a formal setting and we have thereby excluded the family and the community as educational matrices. We have set up the teacher as authority rather than leader, enabling growth into the faith. Once you decide on a curriculum in textbooks you are limited to the matrix in which the material is expressed. Learning takes place wherever people are and the classroom format with its accoutrements only limits this because it limits learning. Perhaps the key to this may be found in the *Shema* of Deuteronomy 6.5-9:

> Hear, O Israel: the Lord our God is one Lord: And thou shalt love the Lord thy God with all thine heart, and with all thy soul, and with all thy might. And these words, which I command thee this day, shall be in thine heart: And thou shalt teach them diligently unto thy children, and shalt talk of them when thou sittest in thine house, and when thou liest down, and when thou risest up . . .

This assumption of the schooling/instructional paradigm of education cuts out all options for the rest of the person's life and/or the child's life as educational or learning moments.

The fourth captivity is apparent in all our curricula — it is the captivity to content. It is the belief that the child becomes a Christian by acquiring information and not by living in a community.

---

[24]See Boojamra, "Socialization," *passim*.

It is a violation of his personhood as a developing reality and the nature of Christian community as nurturing. In addition, it is reductionist inasmuch as it must focus on a limited content which is often out of touch with the best of Orthodox theology and what that theology can produce by way of modeling the Christian faith and Christian life. Orthodox educational philosophy has to focus on the overall integration of the child into the total life of the Church, including moral life, Scripture study, personal faith, prayer life, social involvement, doctrine, and liturgy. On the contrary, we have assumed that Christian education is only a set of information or "stuff" about the faith — dates, numbers, facts, information, names, places, people, and so forth, and more specifically, about the liturgical life of the Church as if there was nothing else to being a Christian than going to liturgy every Sunday. Our educational process has been limited to the cognitive or to the liturgical or, worse yet, to the cognitive about the liturgical.

What is clear about our contemporary Orthodox curricular material is their objective of communicating information about the Church, or particular aspects of the Church, and not the nurture (read, formation) of the child or adult into mature Christian personhood. For instance, in the Orthodox Christian Education Commission we have finally become aware of the fact that our materials were written by people very heavily committed to theology and, in particular, to liturgical theology. We came to believe the WCC and NCC designation of the Orthodox Church as the "liturgical specialist." It is telling to note here, for instance, that the OCEC curriculum is almost completely devoid of any reference to ethical or moral development or even to ethical or moral values. This content captivity, especially to the liturgy, has led us to the mistaken belief that the longer the communion line the more effective our ministry; the one does not follow from the other.

There is no one key to teaching the Christian faith or to Christian education. There are a multiplicity of possible approaches, all of which must be integrated in a unified presentation, no one of which is exclusive. If this is not to be the case and we do choose to follow one particular approach, then we have to make our biases as clear as possible to our teachers and students. This reorientation is particularly painful pedagogically inasmuch as the eucharistic/liturgical theology we have touted for the last twenty-five years has sounded so grand but found very limited actual expression in the life of the child or of the parish. It is my firm conviction as an educator and a historian that a curriculum may focus on any one of a number of aspects of the life of the Church;[25] Christian education, as a discipline, is a multifaceted phenomenon which may legitimately focus on the social, ethical, scriptural, liturgical, historical, doctrinal, or spiritual elements of our Christian heritage or experience because any one of them can be the matrix for effectively teaching the others. It is clear in the history of Christian tradition that at particular times and in particular places one or another element was emphasized by members of the Church. For instance, it is conceivable that a curriculum could be built around baptism and through the teaching of baptism effectuate both the liturgical/eucharistic, social, and ethical aspects of Christian living. I do not mean to denigrate the value of the liturgy or teaching about it; I do mean to warn that pedagogically we have distorted the nature of the Church and the learner by focusing only on one aspect of the tradition of the Church.

These then are the four captivities of Orthodox Christian education in North America. This examination of them would be useless without taking it as a starting point to consider foundational principles. These first principles of education with which we educators and theologians must work are personhood, community (parish and family), and affective development. Building on these three foundations will enable us to meet the challenge of the four captivities which are stifling our education processes.

---

[25]See Philip Phenix, *Realms of Meaning* (New York, 1964), *passim,* who develops this approach to content in the learning situation.

Response to John Boojamra's "The Captivity of Orthodox Christian Education"

GEORGE NICOZISIN

AT THE OUTSET, LET ME SAY THAT JOHN BOOJAMRA HAS written a well thought-out and well documented paper which presents his views on the strengths and weaknesses of what we know as Orthodox Christian education here in America.

Dr. Boojamra's basic premise is that rather than having a pure Orthodox Christian base for our education ministries in our parishes, we are under a heavy influence of Protestant, Roman Catholic and secular precedents. It is his contention that this is a result of several reasons:

— the work of Christian education in Orthodox parishes of North America is an ad hoc affair.
— Religious education is a hit and miss enterprise.
— Seminaries have not provided adequate attention to Orthodox Christian education nor to curricula studies.

Dr. Boojamra makes a provocative point when he says that

the immediate academic need in the North American Church is for educators and youth workers and not for canonists, church historians, liturgists, and dogmaticians with whom we are already top heavy and who have already had too great an impact on our educational process. We now need Orthodox academicians, however, who are trained in pedagogy, sociology and psychology — their content as well as their methods — to enable us to apply the living faith to living situations among living Orthodox.

This is both an observation and complaint I myself have had in

143

the past thirty years of my priesthood as well as my seminary years. The parish priest must be familiar with the contents of books, materials, and audio visual aids in order to recommend them to his supervisor and staff of teachers. It is he who is directly responsible for what is being taught to the children and the parish flock. But the truth of the matter is that the average seminary student graduates not having a sufficient grasp of the curriculum program nor materials his archdiocese and diocese offer.

Once again our presenter is right on target when he writes, "It is this lack of trained personnel and the serious thought which feeds them, which permits a captivity of Orthodox Christian education to every wind of fancy that happens to be blowing."

Four Captivities

Dr. Boojamra proceeds to elaborate the four captivities from which we must be liberated:

> The first captivity is to the theological, pedegogical expertise of those outside of the Orthodox theological and ecclesiastical tradition, particularly to secular researchers and theoreticians. We should utilize but not allow wholesale adoption of one particular philosophy, theology, or theme as if it were "true" forever.

He then proceeds to discuss theories of Westerhoff, Kohlberg, and Piaget. He takes issue with their theories of moral development and values clarification and rightly so, because they leave out one very essential doctrine for us, the role and function of the Holy Spirit in the formation and development of our moral and earthly life.

Dr. Boojamra reminds us that we seem to have a compelling need to rely on the work of Protestants, Roman Catholics, and secular educators because they have time, money, and trained personnel to do necessary research. He is correct in cautioning us not to use them excessively. But as he aptly states, we can and should use them where applicable. But the burning question for us will always be, "How much?" Who will make that determination? And what will be our criteria for determining what is applicable?

According to Dr. Boojamra,

> The second captivity of Orthodox Christian education in North America — this was inherited from the Reformation and the Counter-Reformation — is the focus on childhood and on formal childhood education.

While his point is well taken, that is to say, that Orthodox Christian education is an ongoing process from the cradle to the grave, nevertheless, our efforts to focus on childhood and maximize formal childhood education must still remain one of our top priorities. We are reminded in Luke 2.40, 52 that young Jesus grew in wisdom and stature, and God's blessings were with him. Again, in 2 Timothy 1.5, Saint Paul mentions Timothy's formative years of Christian education, however formal or informal, which he learned from Saint Paul, as well as from his own grandmother, Lois, and his mother, Eunice. In wanting to emphasize the importance of ongoing Christian education I suspect our author has gone to an extreme he did not intend.

From Dr. Boojamra's perspective, "the third captivity of our educational methods and programs is the schooling/instructional paradigm of public education applied to Christian education." While we must all agree that there is a danger in thinking the public school classroom environment will solve all our educational problems, nevertheless, it is a great asset. If Dr. Boojamra is suggesting that textbooks, as we know them, should be dispensed with, then I am in full agreement. Textbooks with organized, consecutive lessons imply homework and activities that are both too ambitious and ineffective for a once-a-week class experience. The textbooks need to be replaced with teaching kits that will communicate the lesson objectives and visual aids and activities that will reinforce the learning experience. Dr. Boojamra is right to remind us that the teacher is not a dispenser of knowledge and information, but a facilitator in an ongoing growth process. Even so, the teacher must have a structured curriculum outline which will give both the objectives and the overview of what is to be taught.

Finally, "The fourth captivity is the captivity of content." The point he makes is that we presume because a child has learned certain information he will be a good Christian. He must both learn and live the Christian life. Then Dr. Boojamra goes on to say:

Orthodox Christian education philosophy has to focus on the overall integration of the child into the total life of the Church, including moral development, Scripture study, personal faith, and prayer life, social involvement, doctrine, and liturgy.

Comments

In all fairness to Dr. Boojamra, he did begin his paper by stating that for the sake of discussion he was taking a reactionary approach in this paper. In a future paper, he promises to deal with the specifics of how we can develop Orthodox Christian education on the basis of personhood, family, and community. He offers positive patterns for the development of materials and the programming of parishes, ones that would be rooted in Orthodox Christianity's perception of God's image in man and in the Orthodox vision of salvation. His presentation is a sophisticated and scholarly treatment of the subject. If this was his intention, then he has accomplished what he set out to do. His paper would certainly be in keeping with this auspicious occasion of the inauguration of the fiftieth anniversary of Holy Cross. But I would have liked to have seen Dr. Boojamra address the issues in more concrete and tangible ways that would give us direction for a more practical and fruitful Orthodox Christian education program here in America.

When he discussed the need for sharing Christian information and knowledge in a way that will help children and adults live a Christian life, I would have liked to have had him share with us the two dimensions of Orthodox Christian living, the contemplative and the experiential. The contemplative asks, "Why, how, when, where, and what?" The experiential no longer simply asks but "does." The former is learning knowledge and the latter is living the knowledge. The former is soul-searching while the latter is soul-satisfying. This is how we understand Romans 12.2 where Saint Paul challenges us: "Do not be conformed to this world, but be transformed by the renewal of your mind, that you may prove what is the will of God, what is good and acceptable and perfect." Our challenge is to integrate written and unwritten Scripture, church doctrine and liturgical experiential worship both as knowledge and a way of life from birth to death. Orthodox Christian education both trains us and transforms us to think, act, work, converse, grow, and progress according to what God has planned for us.

Two classic examples are the Greek adverb σήμερον (today) which proliferates in our hymnology and prayers, and the five imperatives of the second half of the eucharistic consecration prayer. Our liturgical theology uses the adverb σήμερον to help us transcend time and join the past with the present. Whether we re-enter the Saints' Hall of Fame or some biblical event, becoming one with the past is both contemplative and experiential in order that we might, according to 2 Peter 3.18, "grow in the grace and knowledge of our Lord and Savior Jesus Christ."

In the second half of the prayer of consecration we have the five imperatives of the Eucharist, inded, why we are at the Liturgy. They are both contemplative and experiential.

So that they [the Body and Blood of Christ] may be to those who partake of them for
— Purification of the soul,
— Forgiveness of sins,
— Communion of your Holy Spirit,
—Fulfillment of the Kingdom of Heaven, and
— Boldness to approach you not in judgement nor condemnation.

Conclusion

While I found Dr. Boojamra's paper informative and enlightening, I would have liked to have seen a little less theory and more practical application; a little less generalities and more specifics; and, a little less cynicism and a little more hopeful expectation. Finally, I think we owe a debt of gratitude to all those men and women, clergy and laity, who over the years shared in the Orthodox Christian education process to whatever extent and degree it may have been. While Dr. Boojamra has not stated this implicitly or explicitly, we should not be left with the impression that nothing has been done over the past fifty years. He has shared with us some of the strengths and weaknesses of our Orthodox Christian education programs. And we thank him for that.

Divergencies in Pastoral Practice in the Reception of Converts

JOHN H. ERICKSON

HOW ARE NON-ORTHODOX TO BE RECEIVED TO EUCHARISTIC communion in the Orthodox Church? This question cannot be answered simply by describing how they are in fact received. Practice today varies considerably from jurisdiction to jurisdiction and even within jurisdictions. Thus, depending on the group or individual priest or bishop receiving him, a Roman Catholic, for example, might be baptized, or anointed with chrism on various parts of the body according to the usual pattern of post-baptismal chrismation, or anointed with chrism on the forehead alone, or accepted simply upon profession of the Orthodox faith. Varied also are the theological arguments advanced to justify a given practice. For example, most Orthodox these days would not receive a Roman Catholic by baptism, but is this because they accept the "validity" of Roman Catholic baptism, or is it because they have applied οἰκονομία, or "economy," to make valid that which by strict standards — ἀκρίβεια — would be invalid? The first of these explanations shows the heavy impact which Western scholastic sacramental theology has had in the East, particularly in Russia, since the seventeenth century. But is the "economic" explanation, which has dominated Greek sacramental theology since the late eighteenth century, therefore, to be recognized as the authentic and normative teaching of the Orthodox Church? Or is this explanation, as the late Father Georges Florovsky maintained, in fact "a private 'theological opinion,' very late and very controversial, having arisen in a period of theological confusion and decadence in a hasty endeavor to disassociate oneself from Roman theology as sharply

149

as possible"?[1]

Of course, diversity of practice in reception of converts is hardly a new issue. It is enough simply to mention the Palmer affair in the nineteenth century or the great controversy between Cyprian of Carthage and Stephen of Rome in the third. But as the former episode indicates so dramatically, diversity of practive very often has been a source of scandal, driving away from the Church sensitive spirits like Palmer. And as the mention of Cyprian reminds us, important issues of theological principle are involved. Does his practice — reception of converts exclusively by baptism — reflect the proper Orthodox dogmatic strictness in this matter, rendering any other modes of reception suspect, questionable concessions to pressing pastoral considerations at best, betrayals of holy Orthodoxy at worst? So exponents of the "economic" explanation of the sacraments have argued. But is the sacramental theology of the Orthodox Church in fact Cyprianic? Or does the practice

---

[1] G. Florovsky, "The Limits of the Church," *Church Quarterly Review* 117 (October, 1933) 125. On "economy," see also my articles "*Oikonomia* in Byzantine Canon Law," *Law, Church, and Society: Essays in Honor of Stephan Kuttner, ed. K. Pennington and R. Somerville (Philadelphia, 1977), pp. 225-36*, and "Reception of Non-Orthodox Clergy into the Orthodox Church," *St. Vladimir's Theological Quarterly* 29 (1985) 115-32, and the literature cited therein, above all F. J. Thomson, "Economy: An Examination of the Various Theories of Economy Held within the Orthodox Church, with Special Reference to the Economical Recognition of the Validity of Non-Orthodox Sacraments," *Journal of Theological Studies* N.S. 16 (1965) 368-420; and, more recently, Bishop Pierre [L'Huillier], "The Reception of Roman Catholics into Orthodoxy: Historical Variations and Norms," *St. Vladimir's Theological Quarterly* 24 (1980) 75-82, and "L'economie dans la tradition de l'Eglise Orthodoxe," *Kanon: Jahrbuch der Gesellschaft für das Recht der Ostkirchen* 6 (1983) 19-38. The basic principles of the theory of sacramental "economy" are set forth succinctly by C. Androutsos, Τὸ κῦρος τῶν Ἀγγλικῶν χειροτονιῶν (Constantinople, 1903), quoted by J. A. Douglas, *The Relations of the Anglican Churches with the Eastern-Orthodox* (London, 1921), pp. 56-57: "According to the fundamental principles of Orthodoxy . . . both the baptism of those who have gone astray as regards the faith and still more their ordinations are not only legally irregular, but are also wholly invalid and worthless . . . The Church, nevertheless, either considering the expediency of many things, or to avoid some great evils, or through some necessity or other, has frequently by an exercise of economy simply admitted those who rejoined her by delivering a libellus . . . or by laying on of hands or by sealing with chrism."

of the Church over the centuries reflect a rather different understanding of the sacraments and their relationship to the Church? Cyprian insisted on the priority of truth over custom, but is his pastoral practice in fact the true one?

It has become a commonplace to point out that Cyprian's sacramental theology — like virtually every other aspect of his thought — springs directly from his ecclesiology, an ecclesiology dominated by the idea of unity. "It has been handed down to us that there is one God and one Christ and one hope and one faith and one Church and one baptism appointed only in one Church." Within this one Church, "the divine benefits can in nothing be mutilated or weakened" by irregularities like "clinic" baptism, for "in the salutary sacraments, when necessity compels and when God bestows his pardon, divine benefits are conferred completely upon the believers" (*Epistle* 69.12). Outside it, not even the martyr's "baptism of public confession and blood . . . avails anything to salvation because there is no salvation outside the Church" (*Epistle* 73.21).

Yet more can and must be said about Cyprian's idea of unity. Consider how frequently he uses words like "inside" and "outside" when speaking of the Church. Consider also his favorite imagery. The Church is a walled garden, a sealed fountain, the ark of Noah, whose charismatic and institutional limits coincide exactly. And as d'Halleux has tartly observed, "the Church which Cyprian imagines here is not the people which God has called to salvation but the institution through which he dispenses it to them.[2]

Was this the conviction of the early Church as a whole? This is asserted in most expositions of economy, from the rather simplistic *Pedalion* onward. Cyprian's sacramental theology, so deeply rooted in his ecclesiology, and also his sacramental practice are regarded as typical, perhaps even as normative, notwithstanding the claims to antiquity and universality asserted by Stephen in the famous phrase, "nihil nisi quod traditum est." Yet the sources give only very limited support to these claims. Certainly it is possible to find occasional patristic texts which sound "Cyprianic" — for example, Saint Ignatios' statement that "it is not permissible to

---

[2] "Orthodoxie et catholicisme: Un seul baptême?" *Revue Théologique de Louvain* 11 (1980) 416-52 at p. 435.

baptize . . . without the bishop'' (*Smyrneans* 8). It is also possible
to find quite a number of passages from early Christian writers —
ranging from Tertullian on one end of the theological spectrum
to Clement of Alexandria on the other — that indicate widespread
rejection of heretic baptism. It is important, however, to keep in
mind what these writers mean by ''heretic.'' They have in mind
the gnostics, who — one may assert without greatly exaggerating —
do not confess the same God and the same Christ as Christians
do. Such are indeed to be rebaptized. But what of those whom
we today would describe as schismatics rather than heretics? What,
for example, of Novatian, who — as Cyprian's opponents argued —
''holds the same law as the Catholic Church holds, baptizes with
the same symbol with which we baptize, knows the same God the
Father, the same Christ the Son, the same Holy Spirit . . . '' (*Epistle* 69.7)?

To be sure, ''heresy'' and ''schism'' were not always sharply
distinguished in the early Church, but this does not mean that they
were never distinguished or that they were generally regarded as
indistinguishable. In Rome in the early second century, Justin Martyr set the pattern for later heresiologists when he distinguished
the gnostic and Marcionite αἱρεσιῶται from real Christians (*Dialogue* 80.3-5). But among the real Christians he can also distinguish
those who share the ''pure and pious outlook of the Christians''
only in a general way (80.2) from those who are ''entirely correct
in outlook'' (80.5), i.e., those who share his chiliastic eschatology
as distinct from those who oppose it. For Justin at least, disagreement on certain points — on the formulation of certain aspects
of the Christian message, one might say — did not in itself make
one a heretic. Later in the second century, Irenaios drew a similar
distinction, between ''heretics of perverse minds,'' ''who bring
strange fire to the altar of God — namely strange doctrines,'' from
''schismatics puffed up and self-pleasing'' and ''hypocrites, acting thus for the sake of lucre and vain-glory,'' ''who look to their
own special advantage rather than to the unity of the Church, and
who for trifling reasons, or any kind of reason which occurs to them,
cut in pieces and divide the great and glorious body of Christ,
and insofar as in them lies, destroy it'' (*Against Heresies* 4.16.2-5).
Here again, schismatics, however wicked, are not equated *tout court*
with heretics.

In the third century, arguments like those of Cyprian's

opponents were heard more and more frequently, as first the Montanist crisis and then disputes over penitential discipline divided those who were otherwise united in their opposition to the gnostic and Marcionite heresies. While most churchmen agreed that all heretics are outside the Church and therefore to be (re)baptized, relatively few adopted the Cyprianic position that all who are outside the Church are heretics. Even Cyprian's ally Firmilian and his colleagues are perhaps less "Cyprianic" than they appear at first sight. Their policy of rebaptism seems to have been prompted above all by the Montanists, who in their judgment were not simply schismatics but heretics, having a false doctrine of God and of his relation to creation. To be sure, Cyprian uses a similar approach. He repeatedly is forced to argue that the Novatianists are indeed heretics: they falsify the faith professed at baptism, for "when they say, 'Do you believe in the remission of sins and life everlasting through the holy Church?' they lie ... " (*Epistle* 69.7). Yet even if Cyprian's argument takes an old and familiar form, its focus has shifted. With Cyprian, attention has turned from the first article of the symbol to the last, from the doctrine of one God the Creator to the doctrine of the Church. The Novatianists are heretics precisely because they are "outside" that universal episcopal confederation which for Cyprian is the one Church.

Though Cyprian was not the first or only churchman to insist that heretics must be (re)baptized, he certainly was one of the first to insist categorically on the (re)baptism of all those baptized "outside." In this insistence, he in fact appears to have gone beyond what was traditional, beyond "what had been handed down." In support of his position he appealed from custom to truth, as revealed above all in the many scriptural passages which he sees as prefiguring the unity of the Church. But if his position has demanded serious attention from his own day until ours, it is not so much because of these proof-texts as because of the cogency and logical clarity of his arguments, brilliant products of his legal training. Cyprian's immediate opponents, on the other hand, frequently seem confused if not illogical and inconsistent. Following traditional practice — or was it merely "custom without truth," as Cyprian claimed? — they rejected (re)baptism of schismatics and called instead for imposition of hands. But what was the significance of this imposition of hands? What did it imply about baptism administered "outside"? Those who initially addressed these questions did not come up with altogether satisfactory answers. They maintained traditional practice, but their arguments in defense of this practice resulted in significant shifts in the theology of baptism itself, above all in the understanding of the place of the Holy Spirit in the baptismal mystery.

Stephen, reflecting what may well have been the traditional Roman understanding of the matter, spoke of the imposition of hands as *in paenitentiam,* i.e., as a rite of reconciliation. Those baptized among the Novatianists thus were to be treated as repentant sinners. He appears not to have considered the implications of this understanding of the theology of the sacraments and their relation to the Church, however. Cyprian's African opponents and the anonymous author of the treatise *On Rebaptism,* on the other hand, developed a different line of argumentation: The imposition of hands is *ad accipiendum spiritum sanctum.* Like Cyprian, they were convinced that "outside the Church, there is no Holy Spirit" (*On Rebaptism* 10). But unlike him, they did not believe it necessary to repeat the complete rite of initiation when a schismatic sought to enter the Church. Reiteration of the initial water baptism was unnecessary, since the all important baptism of the Spirit was conferred by the bishop's imposition of hands which followed.

Cyprian's opponents thus maintained a high ecclesiology, but at the price of fragmenting the baptismal mystery. In this respect, it is they and not Cyprian who may justly be accused of innovation, for while they may have conformed to "what has been handed down" in their baptismal practice, the theological interpretation which they gave to this practice was indeed novel. Christian initiation in the West on the eve of the baptismal controversy, as seen in such sources as Tertullian's *On Baptism* and Hippolytus' *Apostolic Tradition,* involved many elements — ritualized preparation, the three-fold immersion in water, anointing with chrism, hand imposition, ... — yet *baptismum* remained a unity. When someone like Tertullian sought to associate the various aspects of Christian initiation — cleansing of sins, regeneration, reception of the Holy Spirit — with specific actions, he did so with great difficulty.[3]

---

[3] E.g., in *On Baptism* 4, Tertullian speaks of the role of the Spirit in sanctifying the baptismal waters, but then in 6 he must add: "not that the Holy Spirit is given to us in the water, but that in the water we are made clean by the action of the angel, and made ready for the Holy Spirit."

Now, however, in their efforts to link the gift of the Holy Spirit exclusively with the imposition of hands, Cyprian's opponents come close to claiming that the Holy Spirit has nothing whatever to do with the water baptism. In interpreting phrases like "of water and the Spirit," they take the "and"as indicating a disjunction. Against such arguments, Cyprian might insist that the water baptism and the hand imposition, the Christ-event and the Spirit-event, cannot be separated (cf. *Epistle* 74.5). Yet even he now begins to speak of them as two distinct "sacraments" (cf. *Epistle* 72.1). A new stage in the development of sacramental theology has been reached, leaving theologians henceforth with the task of explaining the relationship of "confirmation" to "baptism."

Following the baptismal controversy, the views of Cyprian's African opponents and of the work *On Rebaptism* appear to have been widely held in the West. The Council of Arles (314), at which the African Church abandoned its earlier insistence that repentant schismatics be received by reiteration of the entire rite of initiation, decreed that, in the case of a heretic baptized in the name of the Trinity, "it shall be sufficient to lay the hand upon him that he may receive the Holy Spirit" (c. 8 [9]). Similar statements can be found in the letters of Popes Siricius and Leo the Great.[4] Such texts indicate how widespread was the notion that converts from schism or heresy were to be received by reiteration of what we today would call confirmation or chrismation. Yet there is often some ambiguity about the significance of the imposition of hands in the rite of initiation. For example, Pope Innocent I speaks of receiving Arians "under the symbol of penitence and sanctification of the Holy Spirit, through the imposition of the hand (*sub imagine paenitentiae ac sancti Spiritus sanctificatione per manus impositione*)."[5] Is this penance or confirmation? The question — obviously an anachronistic one — is impossible to answer.

This underlying ambiguity, along with certain shifts of emphasis in Africa within the rite of initiation itself, helps to explain why Augustine could arrive so easily at his own portentous reassessment of the meaning of baptism administered outside the true Church. Baptism — which for Augustine means Christian initiation in its entirety — is Christ's; its existence does not depend upon

---

[4] Siricius: PL 13.1133; Leo: *Epistle* 159.7, cf. 166.2 and 167.18.
[5] PL 20.550.

the earthly minister. The sacrament is given *quadem consecratione,* and its recipient, even if a schismatic or heretic, acquires the *character dominicus,* the indelible mark. But if baptism administered outside the Church is valid, it is not efficacious. The schismatic is baptized but not *utiliter*; he has received the *sacramentum* but not its *effectus* or *usus.* For the manifold benefits of baptism cannot be appropriated outside the unity of the Church (*On Baptism* 3.16.21). Unlike the author of *On Rebaptism* and so many other earlier churchmen, Augustine would not maintain that only the three-fold immersion in water could be validly administered outside the Church and that the imposition of hands upon the convert represented the perfecting or "confirming" of water baptism by the gift of the Holy Spirit, as though the Holy Spirit had nothing to do with the earlier stages of initiation. The Holy Spirit was indeed given to the convert by the imposition of hands, but in order to pour God's love into his heart (cf. Rom 5.5), that love which is "the special gift of catholic peace and unity," without which other gifts are inoperative. Hands are imposed as an effective sign of reconciliation to the Church, whereby the repentent schismatic or heretic receives the full benefit of the baptism which hitherto he has possessed inefficaciously: remission of sins, regeneration, gift of the Holy Spirit . . . They are not imposed in order to complete his baptism with a "valid confirmation." This Augustine makes quite clear: "The case of the imposition of hands is different from that of baptism, which cannot be repeated. What in sum is the imposition of hands except a prayer said over a man?" (*On Baptism* 3.16.21).

In the East, just as in the West, churchmen from at least the third century onward faced the problem of how to receive convert schismatics and heretics. They sometimes differed from their Western counterparts in their approach to the liturgical, disciplinary, and theological aspects of this problem. But despite differences, there are also important similarities. Broadly speaking, in antiquity and continuing well into the Middle Ages, developments East and West proceeded analogously; similar problems produced similar solutions and explanations. These similarities give the lie to those who would sharply contrast Eastern ecclesiology and sacramental theology (Cyprianic tempered by liberal doses of "economy") and Western (Augustinian and scholastic).

In the West, Pope Stephen (if Cyprian is quoting him correctly) advocated acceptance of the baptism of all heretics whatsoever, while Cyprian urged the rejection of all baptisms performed outside the Church, whether by heretics or schismatics. In the East in the third century, both positions may have found some support: Textbooks note Firmilian of Caesarea's support for Cyprian and Dionysios of Alexandria's for Stephen. It would be incorrect, however, to regard Eastern churchmen of the period as neatly divided into two camps. Many — e.g., Dionysios — seem simply perplexed, not holding singlemindedly to any position; and, as was noted earlier, someone like Firmilian could reach the same practical conclusions as Cyprian without necessarily sharing all his ecclesiological presuppositions.

From the fourth century onward, confusion and improvisation by no means disappear in the East, but it does become possible to detect certain underlying principles governing the acceptance or rejection of baptisms administered "outside" the Church — principles not precisely those of either Stephen or Cyprian but rather in line with the older views of Justin and Irenaios. Above all, there was a clear inclination to draw distinctions. Thus, the Council of Nicea prescribed rebaptism for followers of Paul of Samosata (canon 9) but evidently accepted the baptism of the Novatianists and Meletians (canon 8 and the synodal letter to the Church of Alexandria). So also, canon 8 of the "Council of Laodicea" prescribed baptism for convert Montanists while canon 7 prescribed only anointing with chrism for convert Novatianists and Quartodecimans.[6] Acceptance or rejection of baptism seems to have depended above all on whether the group in question had maintained intact right trinitarian doctrine. The cause of nullity was heresy, not schism, as it had been with Cyprian. But heresy nullified even if Father, Son and Holy Spirit were correctly named in the administration of baptism — this in contrast to the convenient but crude criteria of Stephen. Athanasios testifies that the followers of Paul

---

[6] The "canons of the Council of Laodicea," which were included as part of the *corpus canonum Antiochenum* assembled under Meletios in the 370s, comprise two series of texts which conceivably present in epitome the fourth-century canonical collection of the Church of Laodicea. On the subject, see most conveniently Bishop Pierre L'Huillier, "Origenes et developpement de l'ancienne collection canonique grecque," *Messager de l'Exarchat du Patriarche Russe en Europe Occidentale* 93-96 (January-December, 1976), 59-60.

of Samosata (like the Montanists and the Manichaeans) used the right baptismal formula but gave it a false meaning — it was this that rendered their baptism invalid — and for a time at least, he urged rejection of Arian baptism on the same grounds (*Against the Arians* 2.43).

Canon 1 of Basil the Great's "canonical epistles" reveals the same concern for careful distinctions and right trinitarian doctrine. Many, however, have claimed to discover in it a fundamentally different approach, the foundations of "the Orthodox doctrine of baptismal economy" — a claim rendered all the more persuasive by the fact that here, if nowhere else in the ancient sources referring to reception of converts, the term οἰκονομία appears. A closer examination of the text therefore is in order.

1. Basil's interlocutor, Amphilochios, had inquired concerning reception of the Novatianists, but before discussing them Basil goes into a long digression concerning Montanist baptism. He explains that "the men of old decided to accept that baptism which in no wise deviates from the faith." Hence they made a three-fold distinction between heresies (e.g., Manichaeism, Valentinian gnosticism, Marcionism), schisms, and illegal congregations, rejecting completely the baptism of heretics, blasphemers against the Holy Spirit; even their baptismal formula is incorrect, reflecting their blasphemy. Hence their baptism must be rejected.

2. Returning to the Novatianists, Basil points out that they belong to the number of the schismatics (i.e., by the criteria of the "men of old" their baptism can be accepted). He observes that Cyprian and Firmilian rejected their baptism and gives a brief account of the theological reasoning behind this position. (Here we must keep in mind that Basil is simply reporting; he is not necessaril y advocating the theology in question.) "But since on the whole it has seemed best to some of those in Asia that οἰκονομίας ἕνεκα τῶν πολλῶν, their baptism be accepted, let it be accepted." What is meant by the phrase in question? Probably just "for the sake of the discipline (or: practice) of the majority."[7] Such translations

---

[7] Thus R. J. Deferrari in his translation of Basil's *Letters* (Loeb Classical Library, Cambridge, MA., and London, 1962), vol. 3, p. 17. Unless otherwise noted, English translations from Saint Basil in this presentation are Deferrari's.

as "pour le bien d'un grand nombre"[8] or "par motif de condescence pour beaucoup"[9] are sheer eisegesis.

3. Basil then turns to the Encratites. No clear rule has been
established concerning them; but their baptism should be rejected,
he argues, since they have deliberately altered its form "in order
to render themselves unacceptable to the Church." "If, however,
this shall prove to be injurious τῇ καθόλου οἰκονομίᾳ, we must
follow the Fathers who have dispensed legislation that pertains
to us." The phrase in question is best rendered as "to the general
discipline" or even "to the universal practice." It does not mean
"au bien général"[10] or "a une condescence générale."[11]

4. Basil returns to the Encratites in canon 47, again arguing
that they should be (re)baptized. "But if among yourselves rebaptism is prohibited, just as it is among the Romans, οἰκονομίας τινος
ἕνεκα, nevertheless let our reason have force." And he goes on
to explain that the Encratites are an offshoot of the Marcionites
and hence suppose God to be the maker of evil. Here again, οἰκονομία refers simply to some "arrangement."

From the foregoing, it is clear that, though Basil recognizes
a variety in practice and is not particularly alarmed by this, he
in no wise teaches that an otherwise invalid baptism can be made
valid "by applying economy." He relies, first of all, upon the
schema laid down by "the men of old," with its three-fold classifica-
tion of those outside the Church's communion; and with these "men
of old," he is adamant about rejecting the baptism of heretics —
here meaning above all those who hold a false doctrine of God
and of God's relation to creation. In line with this conviction, he
is determined that acceptance or rejection of a particular baptism
should be based on solid theological evaluation of the group in
question, even if this at times means going beyond the customary
classifications. Unlike some of his counterparts in the West, he
would hardly accept an exaggerated *ex opere operato* approach,

---

[8] P. P. Joannou, *Discipline général antique* (= Pont. Com. per la Reda-
zione del Cod. Dir. Canon. Orientale, *Fonti*, fasc. 9, Grottaferrata, 1963),
vol. 2, p. 97.

[9] P. Dumont, "Économie ecclésiastique et réitération des sacrements,"
Irénikon 14 (1937) 228-47, 339-62, at 236.

[10] Joannou, p. 98.

[11] Dumont, p. 97.

one content with simply determining whether the correct form had been employed. The right content must also be intended. But Basil does find correct form important. As a general rule he can declare: " . . . those who have been baptized in names not handed down to us have not been baptized at all" (cf. 1). For the baptismal formula is directly linked to the faith. According to Basil, one might say, the Church accepts that baptism which it can recognize as its own, in both form and content. It is this conviction that leads Basil to reject the baptism of the Encratites as well as that of the Montanists in canon 1: They have deliberately established *their own* baptism, as distinct from the Church's baptism. It is also this conviction that leads him to reject their baptism again in canon 47: They have invested the baptismal formula with a false content, a content reflected less in dogmatic treatises than in an entire way of life.

This insistence on right content as well as right form can be found in other fourth-century Eastern texts as well, such as *Apostolic Constitutions* 6.15 (along with the dependent Apostolic Canons 46 and 47), the Procatechesis of Cyril of Jerusalem, several orations of Gregory the Theologian, as well as the passages from Athanasios cited earlier. These texts clearly reject heretic baptism, sometimes in very forceful terms and hence are often regarded as indicative of "Cyprianic" tendenciess in the East. In fact, the position taken in these texts is quite compatible with that of Basil and his "men of old." In the fourth-century East, rejection of heretic baptism did not necessarily mean rejection of all baptism performed "outside," as Cyprian had maintained. This is certainly so of Cyril: "Only the heretics are rebaptized, since the first was no baptism" (*Procatechesis* 7). Presumably others were not rebaptized. And who were these heretics? Elsewhere the great catechist warns his hearers against the Montanists and against "the Marcionites, the Manichaeans and the rest of the heretics" (*Catechesis* 16.7, 16.8, 18.26). He appears not to have regarded, e.g., mainstream Arians as belonging to this category. The position of Gregory the Theologian also should be noted. His strictures on Arian baptism make it sound little better than that of the old-time heresies so long condemned in the East: Baptism into a faith that is doctrinally wanting results in drowning, not cleansing (*Orations* 40.44). But this does not mean that with Cyprian he would identify the charismatic and the institutional limits of the Church. As one recent writer has pointed out, for Gregory, "baptism is more of a dogmatic confession than an ecclesial act."[12] The point of departure for his doctrine of baptism is the relation between baptism and faith, not that between baptism and the Church.

This fourth-century Eastern concern for the faith-content of baptism coupled with insistence on the need to draw proper distinctions — to determine whether or not the Church's baptism and faith is present in a given case — is echoed in later Byzantine writers. Though some texts categorically rejecting heretic and/or schismatic baptism were incorporated into Byzantine canonical collections (Apostolic Canons 46-47, Cyprian's baptismal council), they were not regarded as normative. For example, in the early ninth century in the course of the moechian controversy, the monk Naucratios questioned his master Theodore the Studite on this very issue, presumably because it seemed odd not to insist on rebaptism of those baptized by the moechians if, as Theodore insisted, they were truly heretics. Though his contemporaries might accuse him of "Cyprianizing,"[13] Theodore here shows no inclination to put Cyprian's ideas on baptism into practice. Naucratios had said that the Apostolic Canon "by no means makes distinctions, but rather definitively declares that those who are ordained or baptized by heretics are neither clerics nor Christians." But take note, says Theodore, that the Apostolic Canon calls "heretics" those who are not baptized and do not baptize in the name of the Trinity. Saint Basil, he continues, teaches the same thing. He calls "heretics" those wholly cut off and estranged with respect to the faith itself. These he distinguishes from "schismatics," whose separation can be remedied — who are still "of the Church," to use Basil's own words; and from "illegal congregations." As an example of "heretic," Saint Basil gives the Montanists who baptize into names that have not been handed down to us" and therefore are not baptized at all. These and others of their kind the Apostolic Canon, Saint Basil, and the Fathers call "heretics." They are heretics properly so-called; others are called "heretics" by

---

[12]D. Winslow, "Orthodox Baptism — A Problem for Gregory of Nazianzus," *Studia Patristica* 14.3 (Berlin, 1976) 371-74 at p. 372, against J. Korbacher, *Ausserhalb der Kirche kein Heil* (Munich, 1963), p. 212.

[13]*Epistle* 2.63, PG 99.1281C: Ἐγὼ δὲ Κυπριανίζειν . . . ᾠήθην.

extension.[14]

Similar explanations can be found in the standard commentators of the twelfth century. Balsamon pointed out the necessity of distinguishing how the terms "heretic" and "schismatic" are used in different contexts;[15] and both he and Zonaras call attention to the role of correct form as a criterion for true baptism.[16] At the same time, abuses arising from an exaggerated reliance on form were avoided. Manifestly falsified content invalidated baptism even if the proper form was employed. Thus certain Saracens who had themselves and their children baptized in the belief that this conferred invulnerability were to be regarded as unbaptized.[17]

But what of Cyprian and his position? While the text of his baptismal council circulated in Eastern canonical collections from antiquity onward, in the Byzantine period it was frequently abridged and abbreviated, the full text returning to prominence only with the *Pedalion,* and commentators tended to regard its provisions as obsolete. "This synod is the most ancient of all," write Balsamon and Zonaras; it has considerable historical interest, but it was exclusively an African affair, not universally accepted, and more recent canons have taught us to distinguish in our ways of receiving those who turn from heresy.[18]

The Eastern tendency to distinguish and categorize groups on the basis of their proximity to orthodoxy can be seen above all in the continuing practice of the Church of Constantinople, as witnessed in a series of canonical and liturgical texts from the fourth century onward: the "Letter to Martyrios," widely circulated in slightly modified form as I Constantinople canon 7;[19] the

---

[14]*Epistle* 1.40, PG 99.1052D-1053B, referring to Basil the Great canon 1.

[15]Commentary on I Constantinople canon 6, PG 137.337A.

[16]Commentaries on Apostolic Canons 47 and 49, PG 137.132B-133C, 137AB.

[17]G. Ficker, "Erlasse des Patriarchen von Konstantinopopel Alexios Studites," *Festschrift der Universität Kiel zur Feier des Geburtsfestes Seiner Majestäts des Kaisers und Königs Wilhelm II* (Kiel, 1911), p. 14.

[18]PG 137.1096-97, 1104.

[19]On the text, see especially the analysis of L. Ligier, *La Confirmation* (Théologie Historique 23, Paris, 1973), pp. 135-61, 282-91, who provides a convenient account of earlier research into the historical origins and development of this text.

presbyter Timothy's treatise, "On the Reception of Heretics" (ca. 600);[20] canon 95 of the Synod of Trullo (691); and the *Euchologion's* service for the reception of converts.[21]

The first and earliest of these texts places converts in two categories, with the mode of reception corresponding to that prescribed in canons 7 and 8 of the "Council of Laodicea."

> Those who from heresy turn to orthodoxy, and to the portion of those who are being saved, we receive according to the following method and custom: Arians, and Macedonians, and Sabbatians, and Novatians, who call themselves Cathari or Aristeri, and Quartodecimans or Tetradites, and Apolinarians, we receive, upon their giving a written renunciation [of their errors] and anathematize every heresy which is not in accordance with the holy, catholic, and apostolic Church of God. Thereupon, they are first sealed or anointed with the holy oil upon the forehead, eyes, nostrils, mouth, and ears; and when we seal them we say: "The seal of the gift of the Holy Spirit." But Eunomians, who are baptized with only one immersion, and Montanists, who are here called Phrygians, and Sabellians, who teach the identity of Father and Son, and do sundry other mischievous things, and [the partisans of] all other heresies — for there are many such here, particularly among those who come from the country of the Galatians: all these, when they desire to turn to orthodoxy, we receive as heathen. On the first day we make them Christians; on the second day, catechumens; on the third day, we exorcise them by breathing thrice in their face and ears; and thus we instruct them and oblige them to spend some time in the Church, and to hear the Scriptures; and then we baptize them.[22]

At first glance we appear to have here a practice exactly parallel

---

[20]PG 86.9-74; better edition: V. Beneshevich, *Drevne-slavianskaia Kormchaia XIV Titulov bez tolkovanii* 1 (St. Petersburg, 1906), pp. 707-38.

[21]J. Goar, *Euchologion siue Rituale Graecorum* (Paris, 1647), pp. 694-95; new edition M. Arranz, "Les Sacrements de l'ancien Euchologe constantinopolitain," *Orientalia Christiana Periodica* 49 (1983) 53-59.

[22]Translation of canonical texts here and throughout this paper, unless otherwise noted, are taken from *The Seven Ecumenical Councils*, Nicene and Post-Nicene Fathers, second series, vol. 14.

to that prevailing in the West in the same period: Converts who have a Christian baptism are received by reiteration of that part of initiation which is specifically associated with the gift of the Holy Spirit — imposition of the bishop's hand in the West and sealing with chrism in the East. It is because of this essential identity of practice that Gregory the Great later is able to remark, "Arians through the imposition of the hand in the West and through the unction of the holy chrism in the East are admitted to the holy catholic Church."[23] Initially, however, the situation was not so simple.

We have seen how the basic shape of Christian initiation in the West — water-bath/anointing and hand-imposition — permitted separation of a "sacrament of confirmation" from the "sacrament of baptism" and, for a time at least, suggested a disjunction between mere water baptism and "baptism of the Spirit." In the East, however, in the regions of Antioch (West Syrian) and Edessa (East Syrian) but also including Palestine, Cappadocia, Pontos, and Constantinople, the basic shape of initiation was different, at least until well into the fourth century: Anointing and hand-imposition either preceded or were simultaneous with the water-bath, and emphasis lay on the closeness of the relationship of Son and Spirit, on their reciprocal work in creation and redemption — and baptism — so that the anointing itself was not simply a misplaced confirmation/chrismation, the sacrament of the Spirit as distinct from that of the Son. Rather, throughout the one sacrament of Christian initiation the Spirit was seen as present and active, pointing to the Son, making him presenting, refashioning men and women into him.[24] The first evidence for the post-baptismal chrismation of neophytes in the East occurs only in canon 48 of the "Council of Laodicea," the very council which first prescribed chrismation of converts (canon 7).[25]

---

[23]Book 40, *Epistle* 67, PL 77.265-66.

[24]See especially G. Kretschmar, *Die Geschichte des Taufgottesdienstes in der alten Kirche* (Leiturgia: Handbuch des evangelischen Gottesdienstes, vol. 5, Kassel, 1970) pp. 1-348 at pp. 115-36. A convenient appreciation of the early Eastern tradition from an Orthodox perspective is provided by B. Bobrinskoy, "Le mystère pascal du baptême," in *Baptême: Sacrement d'unité* (Maison Mame, 1971), pp. 85-144.

[25]The third of the mystagogical catecheses attributed to Saint Cyril of Jerusalem, which refers to post-baptismal anointing, is now generally recognized as the work of Cyril's successor, John, and hence subsequent to "Laodicea."

Very quickly, however, both practices became generalized, above all because the canons of "Laodicea" came to be included in the very influential Antiochian *corpus canonum* (ca. 370).

It is difficult to determine precisely what significance was given to these new practices. At least initially, the chrismation of converts appears to have been linked specifically to catechesis and right profession of faith: Chrismation signified the presence of the Spirit who arouses faith in Christ, who enables us to say, "Jesus is Lord."[26] Chrismation would have marked full incorporation into the community of faith which is the Church. In the anonymous *Quaestiones et responsiones ad orthodoxos,* chrismation thus becomes precisely a *sui generis* rite of correction and reconciliation: "The fault of the heretic coming to orthodoxy is set straight in the following way: the fault of cacodoxy by change of opinion, the fault of baptism by application of holy myron . . . " (cap. 14). At the same time, the practice of also chrismating neophytes resulted in the transference of much of the rest of the Spirit-imagery formerly associated with the *pre*-baptismal anointings to the new post-baptismal rite. In addition, allusions and images particularly appropriate to *post*-baptismal anointing, long prominent in the West but hitherto unknown in the East, also were developed (e.g., the theme of diverse gifts of the Spirit ordered to the life of the church community). Above all, the very formula employed, "seal of the gift of the Holy Spirit," would serve to make chrismation a "sacrament of the Spirit" distinct from baptism. As a result, the same tendency toward disjunction of Christ and Spirit, baptism and confirmation which we noted earlier in the West appears in the East as well, at least for a time. The "chrismation" of converts in the East in this period thus is as ambiguous as their "confirmation" by imposition of hands in the West. While initially and essentially it seems to have been a rite of reconciliation, as the *Quaestiones et responsiones ad orthodoxos* suggests, it could also be taken as the second "sacrament" of initiation. This at least was the position of Didymos the Blind in Alexandria: Those with a baptism invalid because of defects of form and content are to

---

[26]Cf. the text of "Laodicea" canon 7 and also the very pertinent comments of J. Daniélou, "Chrismation prébaptismale et divinité de l'Esprit chez Grégoire de Nysse," *Recherches de Science Réligieuse* 56 (1968) 177-98.

be (re)baptized; those with a valid baptism are anointed with chrism, not so much because they need reconciliation or convalidation of an otherwise invalid baptism as because the group that originally baptized them lacked a valid "sacrament of chrismation," apparently because it also lacked "valid orders."[27]

We have seen how Augustine quietly revolutionized the Western understanding of the significance of baptism administered outside the Church and hence also the significance of episcopal imposition of hands on converts. A similar revolution became possible in the East when a "third category" for converts was recognized. In canon 95 of the Synod of Trullo (691) we find the following addition to the text of "I Constantinople canon 7" ("Letter to Martyrios"):

> But Nestorians, and Eutychians, and Severians, and those from similar heresies must present certificates and anathematize their heresy, and also Nestorios, Eutyches, Dioskoros, Severos, and other chiefs of such heresies, and those of like mind, and all the aforementioned heresies; and so they become partakers of the holy communion.

In the fourth century Basil the Great (canon 1) had already employed a three-fold distinction between heresies, schisms, and illegal congregations, a distinction already drawn by the "men of old"; and the text on which the presbyter Timothy based his own work made the Meletians — identified specifically as schismatics — a third category, to be received simply by anathematizing their schism. But only in the wake of the christological controversies of the fifth century did this third category become important. Regardless of their understanding of christological orthodoxy, moderate churchmen preferred to regard their opponents as pathetically deluded rather than willfully hostile to the triune God and his Church, particularly when their quick reintegration into the true Church appeared not just desirable but also possible. Reception simply by profession of the right faith and admission to communion was the obvious remedy for their situation. But what was their ecclesial status, if not only their water baptism but also their chrismation/confirmation was to be accepted?

---

[27]*On the Trinity* 2.15, PG 39.720-22.

The most noteworthy attempt to deal with this question came from among the opponents to Chalcedon, with Severos of Antioch's polemic against "the self-created religion of the re-anointers,"[28] who apparently were insisting that chrismation unto the reception of the Holy Spirit was necessary in order to perfect and complete the baptism of repentent Chalcedonians. According to Severos, "there must be no thought either of second baptism or of chrism" when dealing with converts from among the Chalcedonians.[29] To be sure,

> no one is so devoid of the sacred teachings of orthodoxy as not to call baptism given by any heresy imperfect and spurious: but those who know this look at the regulations of the holy Fathers, and reflect that according to the character of the heresy treatment also must be applied, and the stain must be purged and expiated either by another baptism, or by chrism, or by an anathema of the heresy, and the judgment of the orthodox priests and reception by them. The utterance of those who officiate with orthodox mind, whatever it may be, is accompanied also by the curative treatment and grace of the Spirit: since the word of the baptizer perfects baptism also and causes the Spirit to come down upon the water, on account of him who graciously allowed us who creep upon the earth to share in his power. . . . So also the word of the anointer is mingled with the chrism, and applies curative treatment and brings the grace of the Spirit into play. After the same fashion also an anathema of the heresy, when enjoined upon those who utter the condemnation upon order of orthodox high priests, and proferred by the mouth of those, as well as entrance into the holy of holies performed in accordance with the judgment of those who receive them brings healing to the sore, and causes the pure and sincere grace of the Spirit to flash invisibly upon those who have been accepted.[30]

Converts, therefore,

---

[28]*Select Letters* 1.60, ed. and trans. E. W. Brooks, *The Sixth Book of the Select Letters of Severos, Patriarch of Antioch* 2 (Oxford, 1904), p. 185.

[29]5.15, p. 352.

[30]5.15, p. 353.

if they repudiate by anathema the Nestorian and Jewish heresy of the Diphysites, and by sincerely repenting place themselves within the bounds of the orthodox Church, and are included among the sheep of the great God and chief shepherd Christ, will immediately cast from them everyone soever who is an alien, and will be invisibly adorned with the manifestations of the Holy Spirit. If a man on entering by night a house full of torches is completely pervaded by the flashing light, who doubts that the Church of the orthodox, which is full of the gifts of the Holy Spirit, causes the man who opens the eyes of a repentant heart to be pervaded by the light that is supra-sensual and divine?[31]

Severos' response to the re-anointers is similar to Augustine's to the Donatists in several respects. For Severos, entrance into the true Church indeed brings adornment with "the manifestations of the Spirit," just as for Augustine reconciliaton to the Church brings that love which is "the special gift of catholic peace and unity." But for Severos, just as for Augustine, this is no longer linked with exclusively with "the sacrament of confirmation/chrismation." In turn, the "sacrament of baptism" is no longer set apart as somehow an exception, considered in isolation from the rest of the Church's sacramental life as though absent of the Spirit. Rather, the Holy Spirit is seen to be at work in all the sacraments, within the Church at least. So also outside the Church, baptism is like all the other sacraments: "imperfect and spurious,"[32] "without foundation and insubstantial," indeed "invalid."[33] But here we should not be misled by a terminology differing from that of a later age.[34] Outside, the sacraments are ineffectual, but they are not necessarily non-existent, *nichtig*, invalid in an absolute sense. They can be healed by the right spiritual medicine.

Unlike Augustine, Severos left no systematic treatise on baptism. His sacramental theology, set forth only in his letters, was

---

[31]1.60, p. 184.

[32]5.15, p. 353.

[33]1.60, p. 183.

[34]Cf. J. A. Gurrieri, "Sacramental Validity: The Origins and Use of a Vocabulary," *The Jurist* 41 (1981) 21-58.

never fully elaborated, and in any case his direct influence was confined to non-Chalcedonian circles on the fringes of the empire. Within the imperial Church there were some who developed much the same position — e.g., Eulogios of Alexandria — but on the whole we find very little energy expended on formulation of a comprehensive sacramental theology. Converts from a variety of groups continued to be received into the Church's communion by a variety of means, yet neither theologians nor canonists dealt systematically with the implications of their reception. Works of a mystagogical nature were abundant enough, but they considered only "normal" initiation within the Church, not the status of the convert. While the three-fold categorization of converts in Trullo canon 95 might have prompted the canonical commentators like Balsamon and Zonaras to explore its ecclesiological implications, an accident in transmission of the canon produced a garbled text which obscured the very existence of the third category.[35] As a result, "Constantinople canon 7," with its simpler two-fold categorization, perforce formed the point of departure for their presentations of the reception of converts.

In the absence of systematic treatises on sacramental theology and ecclesiology, one must rely on inferences drawn from the actual practice of reception of converts in Byzantium. Yet this must be done with great caution. Inconsistencies or shifts in practice may be explained on the basis of theories of sacramental economy, but in fact they may simply be the result of the Byzantine propensity for identifying new heretical groups with long-dead ancient heresies, most often on the basis of altogether fanciful etymologies.[36]

In fact there is a certain fluidity in the reception of converts

---

[35]Due to an early scribal error, a substantial omission occurs in manuscripts of the family most widely circulated and commented upon during the Middle Ages, so that the text becomes confusing, to say the least: "And the Manichaeans, and Valentinians and Marcionites and all of similar heresies [. . .] must present certificates and anathematize their heresy, and also Nestorios, Eutyches, Dioscoros," etc. As a result, commentators like Balsamon and Zonaras took "I Constantinople canon 7," with its two-fold categorization, as their point of departure for discussion of converts and fitted Trullo canon 95 to it as well as they were able.

[36]See especially J. Gouillard, "L'hérésie dans l'Empire Byzantin des origines au XIIe siècle," *Travaux et Memoires* 1 (Centre de Recherches d'Histoire et Civilization Byzantines, Paris, 1965), pp. 299-324.

in Byzantium. Those baptized in the name of the Trinity were by no means to be rebaptized unless — as in the case of the Saracens cited above — there was manifest lack of the proper "intention." But were they to be anointed or simply received by profession of faith? Certain groups — those for whom anointing with chrism had been prescribed in the ancient canons or who could plausibly be assimilated to such groups — appear always to have been received in that way. In a sermon for Holy Saturday Photios reports on the reception of a group of Quartodecimans: chrismated and robed in white, they were led into the Haghia Sophia with the neophytes in the solemn baptismal procession.[37] In the thirteenth century, Niketas Choniates describes an almost identical scene involving a group of converts from the Lizikian heresy, a messalian group which because of their failure to observe Easter with the Orthodox were also identified as Quartodecimans and treated as such.[38] But converts from other groups — especially the non-Chalcedonian Armenians and Jacobites — were also frequently received by anointing with chrism even though the canons had assigned them to the "third category," to be received by libellus and profession of faith.[39] Is this to be interpreted as a denial of the "validity" of the "sacrament of confirmation/chrismation" among them (and by implication also as a denial of their orders and of their ecclesial character generally), as though they were thought to be in the same position as the Quartodecimans, i.e., a position roughly analogous to that of a person baptized in an emergency by a layman?[40]

There is little evidence to support such an interpretation. Chrism was used generously in Byzantium, for more than just the post-baptismal anointing which modern textbooks label the "sacrament of chrismation." In the ninth century, anointing with chrism accompanied by the formula, "Seal of the gift of the Holy Spirit,"

---

[37]*Homily* 17.1, ed. and trans. C. Mango (Cambridge, MA., 1958), pp. 288-89.

[38]PG 140.284.

[39]Cf. the invective against the Armenians ascribed to one "Isaak, Catholikos of the Armenians," but in all likelihood the work of the monk Euthymios of the Peribleptos monastery, PG 132.1155-1217. Other examples are given in J. Kotsonis, Ἡ κανονικὴ ἄποψις περὶ τῆς ἐπικοινωνίας μετὰ τῶν ἑτεροδόξων (Athens, 1957), pp. 130-32.

[40]On the status of baptisms performed by laymen, see especially Photios, canonical responses to Leo of Calabria c.1, PG 102.773-75.

comes to be prescribed for the reconciliation of apostates.[41] In the same century, it apparently was also demanded by Patriarch Methodios as the appropriate means for reconciling the Studite schismatics,[42] and in the tenth century it was used for the reconciliation of persons baptized among the Orthodox who subsequently joined the bogomils. Certainly these apostates and schismatics were not anointed with chrism because the "validity" of their original post-baptismal chrismation was somehow in question. Rather, they were anointed above all to give a tangible expression to their reconciliation with and reincorporation into the fellowship of the Church. The rule of thumb which determined when anointing with chrism was to accompany abjuration of errors and profession of faith seems to have been roughly this: Chrism is to be employed when a period of *catechesis* is required.[43]

Variations in the reception of Latins in the Middle Ages — ranging from rebaptism to simple admission to eucharistic communion — are particularly noteworthy and have loomed large in discussion concerning sacramental "economy." Certainly it is difficult to single out any one practice as normative or even customary through the entire Eastern Church at any point. This is due in large part to the nature of the estrangement of the churches in the Middle Ages. No single issue or event divided East and West the way that, e.g., Chalcedon divided Christians in antiquity. Differences of doctrine and practice were inextricably linked to a host of shifting socio-political differences, making it hard for anyone to pinpoint the significance of any of these differences for relations between the churches and hence for reception. Quite simply, the Latins did not fall neatly into any of the categories provided in the service books and canonical collections. They had been

---

[41]Text in Goar, 876-79; cf. M. Jugie, "La Réconfirmation des apostats dans l'Eglise gréco-russe," *Echos d'Orient* 9 (1906) 65-76.

[42]Cf. Patriarch Methodios' *Testament* as quoted by Niketas of Heraklia, *On the Heresiarchs,* ed. J. Darrouzes, *Documents inédits d'ecclésiologie byzantine* (Archives de l'Orient Chrétien 10, Paris, 1966), pp. 294-95.

[43]Cf. Patriarch Methodios, *Testament,* and Mark of Ephesos' *Encyclical* c.4, ed. J. Karmires, Τὰ δογματικὰ καὶ συμβολικὰ μνημεῖα τῆσ ὀρθοδόξου καθολικῆσ ἐκκλησίας 1 (Athens, 1960), p. 426. *Catechesis* here would mean "indoctrination" or "reeducation," a process as much disciplinary as pedagogical.

regarded as disagreeably "different" long before any final break in normal ecclesiastical relations occurred, and while antipathy mounted with the passing centuries, particularly when Latin military aggression threatened the very foundations of the Byzantine world, this did not automaticaqlly entail their "unchurching." To be sure, some controversialists did seek to identify a precise time and cause for the rupture, a point after which they were presumably "outside" the Church. Yet in fact for centuries no official pronouncements defined their status, whether in the wake of the tragic events of 1054 or in the thirteenth century following the fall of Constantinople to the knights of the Fourth Crusade, notwithstanding claims to the contrary by rigorists from at least the eighteenth century onward.

Several medieval Latin sources accuse the Greeks of practicing rebaptism — Cardinal Humbert already in the eleventh century, Hugo Etherianus in the twelfth century, IV Lateran Council in 1214 . . . — and since then advocates of rebaptism and proponents of theories of economy in the East have taken these accusations at face value: this indicates the "real" attitude of the Orthodox toward the Latin heretics, the ἀκρίβεια which has ruled when circumstances have not necessitated dissimulation and οἰκονομία. In fact in the Middle Ages there is much more evidence of Latins rebaptizing Greeks than vice versa.[44] Rebaptism of Latins by Greeks may have taken place, but if so, it was not encouraged by official policies or sanctioned by canon law or theological reasoning any more than rebaptism of Greeks by Latins was. It was a visceral reaction, a way of venting long-standing grievances —regrettable but perfectly understandable.

The attitude of official ecclesiastical circles is revealed in a series of responses to Patriarch Mark of Alexandria which were delivered in the name of the Permanent Synod of Constantinople

---

[44]It might be noted here that, while there are numerous references in the Greek and Slavic sources to reception of Latins by anointing with chrism in this period, there are few if any to rebaptism, despite Latin accusations on this point at Lateran IV and elsewhere. Better documented are instances of Latin rebaptism of Easterners: cf. J. Meyendorff, "Projets de concile oecuménique en 1367: un dialogue inédit entre Jean Cantécuzéne et le legat Paul," *Dumbarton Oaks Papers* 14 (1960) 49-177; and E. Przekop, "Die 'Rebaptizatio Ruthenorum' auf dem Gebiet Polens vor der Union von Brest (1956)," *Ostkirchliche Studien* 29 (1980) 273-82.

by Balsamon in 1195. When asked whether Latin captives in the East could be given the eucharist should they so desire, he replied: "Since the Western Church has been separated from spiritual communion with the other patriarchs for so long, no Latin should be admitted to communion unless he first presents a declaration rejecting their doctrines and customs and is instructed according to the canons."[45] What would this delcaration have included? Some lists of Latins errors — e.g., that of Constantine Stylibes — go on for pages, but it is unlikely that anything so comprehensive was demanded. In the capital in the fourteenth century the requisite abjuration and profession of faith was relatively brief: the convert declared his adherence to the dogmas and canons laid down by the ecumenical synods, denounced any deviation therefrom, and confessed the Creed without the interpolation of the *filioque*.[46]

Were Latins also customarily anointed with chrism? Neither the patriarchal archives nor Balsamon mention this, yet it was not likely. Another of Balsamon's responses to Mark of Alexandria, this one concerning reception of non-Chalcedonians, strongly suggest that these at least were anointed upon presentation of their profession of faith[47] — like most of his contemporaries Balsamon seems to have ignored Trullo's "third category" (reception simply by profession of faith) altogether. It seems unlikely therefore that he would not also have encouraged the anointing of Latin converts. Other sources also suggest that anointing with chrism was widely advocated, though not necessarily practiced. On the northern fringe of the Byzantine world, Archbishop Niphon of Novgorod (1130-1156) describes in detail the procedure to be followed in his eparchy: the anointing with chrism is accompanied by many rites associated with normal baptismal initiation — a rite of naming, clothing in the white robe of the neophyte . . . — and the convert is to be treated "like one newly baptized."[48] In the fourteenth century both Makarios of Ankyra and Nilos of Rhodes prescribe anointing, though they give no indication of what

---

[45]*Response* 15, PG 138.968.

[46]V. Grumel, *Les Regestes des Actes du Patriarchat de Constantinople* 1.5 (Paris, 1977) no. 1650, cf. no. 2659.

[47]*Response* 29, PG 138.981-83.

[48]Ed. L. K. Goetz, *Kirchenrechtliche und kulturgeschichtliche Denkmaler Altrusslands* (Stuttgart, 1905, repr. Amsterdam, 1963), pp. 223-24.

subsidiary rites, if any, were to be employed; and in the following century Mark of Ephesos regards reception of Latins by anointing as a normal practice of long standing.[49]

At the same time, reasons *why* Latins are to be received by anointing rather than simply by profession of faith are seldom spelled out. For many (e.g., Balsamon), it may have been simply because profession of faith without use of chrism was not regarded as an option. For others, it was because the Latins had fallen into one or another ancient error. In his *Alphabetical Syntagma* the fourteenth-century canonist Matthew Blastares likens the Latins (with their practice of fasting on Saturdays) to the ancient Sabbatians (whose name in fact derives not from *sabbaton* but from the personal name Sabbatios); and for this reason he would place them with the Sabbatians in the second category, among the schismatics and heretics of the second magnitude who are to be received by chrismation.[50]

While anointing with chrism seems to have been common, it should also be noted that Balsamon's generally negative attitude toward the Latins was not shared in some ecclesiastical circles. Two of the leading canonists of the early thirteenth century, Demetrios Chomatenos and John of Kitros, both remark that not all experts on canon law in Constantinople agreed with the position taken by Balsamon in his responses to Mark of Alexandria. No synodal judgment against the Latins has ever been made, argues Comatenos; and besides, the very fact that those Latin captives in Alexandria were asking to receive the eucharist from the Orthodox suggests a certain detachment on their part from the unleavened bread of the Latin usage. As Theophylact of Bulgaria pointed out more than a century before, the real difference between us concerns the procession of the Holy Spirit. While full intercommunion is ruled out until that issue is resolved, we do hold virtually everything else in common, and therefore we recognize

---

[49]Makarios: in Dositheos, Τόμος Καταλλαγῆς (Iasi, 1692), cited by I. Karmires, Τὰ δογματικὰ καὶ συμβολικὰ μνημεῖα τῆς ὀρθοδόξου καθολικῆς Ἐκκλησίας 2 (Athens, 1960) 981; Nilos: ed. A. Almazov, *Inedite canonica responsa Constantinopolitanae Patriarchae Luca Chrysovergis et metropolitae Rhodi Nili* (Odessa, 1903), p. 61; Mark: in Karmires, Τὰ δογματικὰ καὶ συμβολικὰ μνημεῖα . . . 1 (Athens, 1960), p. 425.

[50]PG 144.1036.

eucharist, ordinations, and other ministrations.[51]

Such openness seems to have been on the decline by the fifteenth century, but it was only with the Council of Ferrara-Florence (1438-39) that the full extent of the estrangement of the Eastern and Western churches was revealed. Cautious optimism about the prospects for reunion had led even notable conservatives like Mark of Ephesos to attend the council. Now such hopes were dashed for good: the Latins really did hold false doctrines, like that behind the *filioque,* and they intended to go on holding them. In 1484, following the Turkish conquest, a synod was held in Constantinople at which a special rite for reception of Latin converts by means of anointing with chrism was established.[52] For the first time an official policy was adopted. Yet as the above survey of the use of chrism in Byzantium suggests, this development should not be given undue weight, as though it completely redefined the ecclesial status of Roman Catholics. While the rite prescribed anointing with chrism and use of the formula, "seal of the gift of the Holy Spirit," the accompanying prayer was not that of the post-baptismal rite of chrismation but rather one of reconciliation. Altogether absent from the rite are the baptismal elements prescribed by Niphon of Novgorod. Also noteworthy is the fact that Latin clergy converting to Orthodoxy continued to be received in their orders, without reordination.

Only in the seventeenth century, with the work of Peter Moghila, was there a significant development in the way in which the ecclesial status of Roman Catholics and other non-Orthodox was evaluated: Because their church has "valid" orders and therefore a "valid" sacrament of confirmation/chrismation, Roman Catholics and Eastern Rite Catholics are to be received simply by profession of faith, chrismation according to the usual post-baptismal rite being reserved for those coming from Protestant groups which have only a "valid" baptism. Of course, Moghila's theology these days is often regarded as hopelessly Latinized. Nevertheless he did see the need — and there was a need! — to develop a sacramental theology which would account for the relation of the sacraments

---

[51]Ed. J. Darrouzes, "Les résponses canoniques de Jean de Kitros," *Revue des Etudes Byzantines* 31 (1973) 319-34 at p. 325.

[52]Text in Karmires, *Τὰ δογματικὰ καὶ συμβολικὰ μνημεῖα . . .* 2 (Athens, 1960) 987-89.

to the Church and thus explain the significance of sacraments administered outside the Church's canonical limits. Latin categories of validity and liceity did this very efficiently. In fact they offered — and perhaps still offer — a very convincing way of interpreting the relevant canonical and liturgical data. Moghila may have erred in adopting Latin scholastic theology uncritically, with little sensitivity to the Eastern liturgical, canonical, and spiritual tradition. For example, his preoccupation with the formula requisite for "valid" baptism causes him to ignore the Eastern patristic emphasis on the faith-content of baptism. But he did at least recognize the need for theology.

While Moghila's scholastic approach came to dominate Russian theology, in the Greek-speaking world quite a different approach developed. The mid-eighteenth century controversy over Latin baptism led not simply to another change in practice. It led to a comprehensive new sacramental theology. Arguments for rebaptizing Latins were found easily enough, just as they had been when rebaptism was occasionally practiced in earlier centuries: They teach a heretical doctrine of the Trinity, and in any case, by not immersing, they are not really baptizing at all. But how was the fact that hitherto Latins generally had *not* been rebaptized to be explained? The answer, of course, lay in the theory of sacramental "economy." External pressures of various sorts had led to the application of οἰκονομία, but now a return to ἀκρίβεια, as represented by Cyprian, is in order.

This sacramental theology, like Peter Moghila's, responded to a definite need. Like the Orthodox in Russia, Orthodox in the Greek-speaking world had to explain the ecclesial status, if any, of Christians outside their communion. But unlike Moghila's self-consciously Latinized theology, the "economic" explanation put forward in the *Pedalion* and elsewhere has claimed to represent the perennial teaching of the Orthodox Church. *This claim is in no way supported by the canonical, liturgical, and historical evidence which has been presented above.* If Peter Moghila may be accused of mutilating the Church's practice, the proponents of "economy" are certainly guilty of mutilating its history. In Byzantium, at least, Cyprian's views on heretic baptism were by no means regarded as normative. While no comprehensive sacramental theology was elaborated, the merely defective or incomplete was in practice distinguished from the non-existent. Those whose baptism the

Church could recognize as her own — and who therefore were still "of the Church" even if not precisely *in* the Church — were not placed in the same category as those who were unbaptized or whose "baptism" was of their own devising. While the word οἰκονομία does sometimes occur in connection with reception of converts, it does not refer to a limitless power to make what is invalid to be valid, should that prove expedient. Rather, οἰκονομία was seen as prudent pastoral administration on the basis of the canons and the example of the Fathers, a task above all demanding discernment, the ability to distinguish what is real from what is spurious. Recovery of this true sense of "economy" is desperately needed today if confusion and equivocation are to be avoided in our practice of receiving converts.

Response to John Erickson's "Divergencies in Pastoral Practice in the Reception of Converts"

LEWIS J. PATSAVOS

PROFESSOR ERICKSON IN HIS CHARACTERISTICALLY ERUDITE way has effectively dealt with a subject which should cause us no little concern. In his comprehensive treatment of the material, he sheds clarity on what the Church's practice has been in the past. He also gets to the heart of the matter with bold strokes and a facility for illustration. Because he is gifted with a remarkable knowledge of history, his paper is marked by pertinent quotations which illumine the subject matter and enhance its exposition. These are the attributes inherent in two similar studies of Professor Erickson on the topic of this presentation.[1]

It is not often that I disagree with Professor Erickson on fundamental issues of canon law. Again, rather than having to disagree with the thrust of his paper, I should like to affirm most of what he has said, highlighting some of it perhaps in as dramatic a way as possible. I call it an appeal because I believe it should raise our consciousness to the scandal often created by our divergencies in our pastoral practices, all presumably the practical expression of a theological truth. The question that needs to be asked is: Are all these theologies equally valid and true? If they are, then the divergencies in our pastoral practices are legitimate and there is no problem. If they are not, the question must be asked: Which theology is lacking and how do we correct it?

---

[1] "Reception of Non-Orthodox into the Orthodox Church," *Diakonia* 19 (1-3, 1984/85) 68-86 and "Reception of Non-Orthodox Clergy into the Orthodox Church," *St. Vladimir's Theological Quarterly* 29 (1985) 115-32.

Professor Erickson's well researched paper is heavily dependent upon historical analysis and therefore theoretical, as indeed
it should have been in order to illustrate its point. Yet even
my distinguished colleague, I am certain, would agree that theory
which does not issue forth in practice may remain a dead letter.
Afanasiev said something similar about the holy canons, i.e., that
they are the practical expressions in time of eternal truths. If they
do not express those truths, they are in fact defunct.[2] So it is
with the historical evidence presented to us in Professor Erickson's
paper. And here I return to my earlier appeal. If we are to profit
from the scholarly research on our topic, we must be ready to learn
from it and, having learned, we must be ready and willing to
change, if that is what is necessary to harmonize practice and
theory.

The point was made that variety of practice was a fact in the
ancient Church. One might therefore be tempted to justify and
even legitimize the phenomenon experienced today. Nevertheless,
it ought not to be forgotten that the world of the ancient Church
was a vastly different world than that of the contemporary Church.
Given the limited means of communication which existed in the
ancient world, it is understandable that the ambiguity surrounding the teaching of certain heresies should have led to a variety
of practice from place to place for the reception of converts. Can
this be said, however, of the situation existing in our midst in which
variety is practiced among Orthodox in the very same place? Or
does this reality say something about *us specifically* as a church
in America, something which reaches to the very core of our particular existence here? These are difficult questions which, painful though they may be, must be raised.

Divergencies in pastoral practice, as has already been intimated,
is not limited to the reception of converts to eucharistic communion alone. In his equally provocative article, "Reception of Non-
Orthodox Clergy into the Orthodox Church," Professor Erickson,
writing on how non-Orthodox clergy are to be received into the
Orthodox Church, says: "Practice in America and elsewhere varies
from jurisdiction to jurisdiction and occasionally even within
jurisdictions. Thus, depending on the group or bishop receiving

---

[2]N. Afanasiev, "The Canons of the Church: Changeable or Unchange-
able?" *St. Vladimir's Theological Quarterly* 11 (1967) 61-62.

him, a Roman Catholic priest, for example, might be rebaptized and reordained; or chrismated and reordained; or chrismated whether wholly or partially and then accepted in his orders; or be received in his orders simply upon profession of the Orthodox faith. . . . Varied also are the theological arguments advanced to justify a given practice; two groups might follow the same practice but justify this practice in altogether different ways."[3] In the event a Roman Catholic priest were accepted in his orders, for example, some might attribute this to the "validity" of Roman Catholic orders. The very category "validity" as a criterion in assessing the status of non-Orthodox sacraments indicates the degree to which some Orthodox have been influenced by Western scholastic sacramental theology. On the other hand, there are others who might explain acceptance of Roman Catholic orders by the application of "economy." In other words, that which by "exactness" would be considered null and void is recognized as now being a channel of grace. The question to be posed here is how expressive of authentic Orthodox theology is either of the above two explanations?

The whole issue of the status of heterodox sacraments takes an especially serious side when referring to the sacrament of marriage. Owing to the number of persons thereby affected, it would seem that some kind of accomodation needs to be agreed upon among all Orthodox, especially here in America. The situation with regard to the status of heterodox marriage — under consideration here are only those sacramental acts performed in churches of the classic catholic tradition of the undivided Church, such as the Roman Catholic Church — is not unlike that already encountered in the Church's varying practice towards the reception of converts and the recognition of heterodox orders. Here, as there, there are Orthodox jurisdictions following the lead of mother churches abroad which require (re)marriage of converts. Other jurisdictions clearly do not. A consequence of the former practice is that heterodox marriages are not counted when calculating the number of allowable marriages. Thus, it is conceivable that one might be married more than the legitimate number of three times, albeit not in the Orthodox Church.

Part of the reason for this state of affairs is due to the ambiguity

---

[3]Erickson, "Reception of Non-Orthodox Clergy," 115.

which exists regarding the status of sacramental marriage outside the Orthodox Church. There is a deep reluctance to ascribe "ecclesial reality" to other churches in a formal, documentable way. Against such a background — if no ecclesial reality is recognized in another church, neither can its sacraments be recognized — one understands the viewpoint which does not recognize the sacramentality of heterodox marriages. This reluctance derives less from differences in theological understanding about the sacrament of marriage and more from the complete separation of our churches as communities of faith. Unofficially, some Orthodox hierarchs and theologians may recognize ecclesial reality outside the limits of the Orthodox Church. The practice of not (re)marrying converts affirms this conviction. On the other hand, it is at the least confusing both to the Orthodox faithful and to our partners in dialogue to speak of "sister churches" (referring to the Orthodox and Roman Catholic Churches), and then to require (re)marriage of former Roman Catholics in the Orthodox Church.

There is, we must admit, a certain ambiguity in all this, an ambiguity which is most evident in what we do with regard to the reception of converts. As has already been pointed out, a Roman Catholic upon entering the Orthodox Church might be baptized, or anointed with chrism on various parts of the body as in the act of chrismation following baptism, or anointed with chrism on the forehead alone, or accepted simply upon profession of the Orthodox faith.[4] The mode of acceptance depends upon the group or individual bishop accepting the convert. The practice of Ecumenical Patriarchate calls for anointing with chrism on various parts of the body. I assume this is the prevalent practice of most jurisdictions here in America, although I suspect anointing with chrism on the forehead alone is not unknown. As has also been pointed out, debate over the proper way to receive converts can be traced at least as far back as the mid-third century (Cyprian and Pope Stephen). It is heartening, indeed, that some semblance of uniformity and agreement — at least in the Church in America — does exist. What does not appear to be sufficiently clear now as in the ancient Church is the meaning of the act of anointing. Is this the sacrament of chrismation as is properly held? Professor Erickson provides us with incontestable historical proof of the generous use

---

[4]See Erickson, "Reception of Non-Orthodox Clergy," 68.

of chrism in Byzantium. The anointing with chrism required for the restoration to communion of apostates and schismatics did not place in doubt the authenticity of their post-baptismal chrismation. Rather, it gave tangible expression to their reconciliation with and reentry into the Church. Generally speaking, one could say that anointing with chrism has traditionally taken place whenever reincorporation into the fellowship of the Church has followed a period of catechetical instruction. This same principle is operative today in the reception of converts by anointing with chrism.

Finally, a word about "economy" as it has come to be understood, especially in certain Greek theological circles. They would explain the Church's reluctance to rebaptize trinitarian Christians due to the application of "economy." In other words, through the application of "economy," that which by "exactness" would be considered null and void is now recognized as valid. The theory of "economy," as we have seen, is the basis upon which much of our sacramental theology — at least in the Greek Church — is practiced. Such is its prevalence, in fact, that it has been an object of study in our dialogue with Roman Catholics regarding the mutual recognition of sacraments. Is it, however, the normative teaching of the Orthodox Church? Or, as the late Father Georges Florovsky has written, is it "a private theological opinion, very late and very controversial, having arisen in a period of theological confusion and decadence in a hasty endeavor to disassociate oneself from Roman theology as sharply as possible?"[5] In response, I can only affirm my colleague Professor Erickson's opinion that according to the authentic canonical tradition of the Orthodox Church, " 'economy' was seen as prudent pastoral administration on the basis of the canons and the example of the Fathers, a task above all demanding discernment, the ability to distinguish what is real from what is spurious."[6] Furthermore, I could not agree with him more that "a recovery of this true sense of 'economy' is desperately needed today if confusion and equivocation are to be avoided in the reception of non-Orthodox to eucharistic communion in the Orthodox

---

[5]Georges Florovsky, "The Limits of the Church," *Church Quarterly Review* 11 (1933) 125.

[6]Erickson, "Divergencies in Pastoral Practices in the Reception of Converts."

Church.''[7] I might add that an encouraging sign is to be seen in the response of several Greek theologians to the study on "economy" submitted several years ago by the Church of Romania to the First Preconciliar Panorthodox Conference convened in Chambesy, Switzerland.[8] In strong reaction to the thesis that the ancient undivided Church made "lavish use of economy" in the sense understood only since the late eighteenth century, and other such erroneous claims, a faculty committee of the Athens University School of Theology prepared a lengthy, well-documented response. It disowned the erroneous claims just cited and reflected fully the essence of the authentic canonical tradition of the Orthodox Church regarding the application of "economy" articulated above.[9]

One of the main purposes of my response has been to highlight the facts reported and documented for us by Professor Erickson in his informative paper. What ought particularly to have caught our attention is that variety of practice in the reception of converts is a common phenomenon in contemporary Orthodoxy, as it was in the distant past. To draw comparisons with the past can be dangerous because of the temptation it provides to justify a pastorally scandalous situation, not to speak of the scandal of disunity it betrays. Besides, can one honestly identify parallels in this regard between the present and the distant past?

We have heard the practical suggestions regarding the reception of certain converts put forth. Although I agree in principle with these recommendations given the reasons presented, I would only caution against too broad an inclusion of heterodox to be received solely by profession of faith. It must be quite clear that the sacramental theology of the communion from which they come corresponds to our own.

My appeal, in conclusion, is that we begin — at least in this continent — to think and act like one Church, the Orthodox Catholic Church we are in faith, as a prerequisite for our unity one day in structure.

---

[7]*Ibid.*

[8]*Towards the Great Council: Introductory Reports of the Inter-Orthodox Commission in Preparation for the Next Great and Holy Council of the Orthodox Church* (London, 1972), pp. 43-52.

[9]See Ἐκκλησιαστικὴ Οἰκονομία. Ὑπόμνημα εἰς τὴν Ἱερὰν Σύνοδον τῆς Ἐκκλησίας τῆς Ἑλλάδος (Athens, 1972).

The Monastic Vocation in America

MOTHER ALEXANDRIA

MONASTICISM HAS ALWAYS BEEN AN INTEGRAL PART OF THE Orthodox Church, an extremely vital part of its spiritual life. Without spirituality the Church may tend to become a dead letter and parochial. Worse, being still partly an immigrant church, parishes can slip into becoming a national club instead of being the house of God.

For close to 2000 years, monasteries all over the world have been centers of spirituality and culture, the abodes of peace — peace as Jesus gave it, not as the world gives it. Through all vicissitudes of history this has held true, through storm and fair weather, in persecutions and prosperous times.

Only here in America has this vital source of spirituality been lacking in our Church. Why is easily explained. Our people were mostly immigrants and the parish church an all-important unifying center of their lives. Many came from the Austrian-Hungarian Empire where Orthodox monasticism was discouraged, so that few had ever heard of the many monasteries of Greece, Romania, Serbia, Bulgaria, and Russia, or had ever seen an Orthodox monastic.

Only during the last two or three decades have Orthodox monasteries, both for men and women, begun to appear on the American continent. The Russian Church Outside Russia has been here the longest and came with monasteries already constituted but has kept very much to itself and the propagation of the monastic life for *all* Orthodox faithful in general seems not to have been one of their objectives. Therefore it became generally taken for granted that only Roman Catholic monastics existed.

The question now arises, "Is there any place for monasticism

185

in the American way of life?'' Our contention is that yes, indeed, monastics not only have a place, but are urgently needed.

As monastics we have no long history in this hemisphere although we have a long and glorious past in our countries of origin. Therefore it is the present and the future that we must consider and find out what our role is in the New World.

We can bring stability, something permanent, a glimmer of the unchanging Truth, for God's Truth is the same yesterday and forever. We stand for the presence of Christ in our midst. We are men and women who have dedicated our lives irrevocably to God, people who have put God and their neighbor first, who pray when no one else prays, whose home (that is to say, their monasteries) belong to God, where hospitality to all who knock is a way of life.

The prayer life of the monasteries is continuous. Monastics follow David's words, ''Seven times a day do I praise Thee.'' These seven praises are gathered into three groups so as to give time for work, in which time inward prayer is practiced.

The monastic seeks to make his or her life a continual prayer, an unending praise of God, imitating on earth what the angels do in heaven. Hence their habit is called the angelic habit, not because we are angelic but because we try to imitate the angels in formal and private prayer and also in prayer during physical work. Monastics pray for all those who cannot or do not pray themselves. They pray for the sick and dying, captives and free, for travellers and those who sit at home, and also for themselves. If we would serve God we have to try and be as worthy an instrument of his grace as we are able.

Yes, we are needed in the modern world in which people are so confused by all the clamor and events churning around them. They thirst for quiet and peace, after something positive and certain. They long to have their problems and fears calmed if not solved. The monasteries are islands of peace in a troubled world where people may drink of the living water of which Christ spoke to the Samaritan woman.

Who can say that he or she does not at times want to find some rest, loving and uncritical understanding, the need to unburden himself or herself? The monasteries provide answers to many troubling questions and teach the faith. They give answers to many of the ever growing needs.

For such centers to exist, devoted faithful souls trained in the spiritual life must inhabit the monasteries. We need monks and nuns steeped in prayer and guided by the Holy Spirit. If they are not so guided they cannot help others or themselves. They have to be people who, having put their hands to the plough, do not look back but have truly renounced everything for God.

Orthodox monasticism never changes, though it adapts to places and circumstances. Although the monastics of today cling as ever to the inward and outward peace and keep their monasteries the center of their spiritual life, they will go out into the world as missionaries. They wear their habits at all times; it is as if in this way they carried their monastery walls with them. Also the habit sets them apart; anyone seeing them recognizes them as people who have given their lives to God. They awake in the mind of the beholder at the very least a question as to the why and wherefore of such a person, and are reminded inevitably of God. Thus they are almost a sermon without having uttered a word.

There is nothing very remarkable about us. We are simply people who have taken up our cross to follow Chirst in love and obedience for he is "the Way, the Truth, and the Life" (Jn 14.6).

Reflections on Orthodox Monasticism in America Today

ARCHIMANDRITE LAURENCE

ANY CONSIDERATION OF MONASTICISM IN CONTEMPORARY Orthodox life in North America must reflect on why there is so little. Orthodoxy without a thriving monasticism is almost a contradiction in terms, it would seem! Yet, this is a fact of our church life, and the reasons for this deficiency are complex and multifaceted. However, after thirty years in monastic community, I believe that there are two basic reasons for this deficit, reasons which we do not, as a church, appear to be noticing.

The first and most serious reason is the general crisis of faith which confronts our society today — and that includes our Orthodox faithful as well — especially in the more developed and sophisticated populations of the world. Obviously, this crisis of faith has variant appearances from individual to individual, from group to group. But, it is really a universal phenomenon caused and aggravated not only by the world as it has developed but by the general failure of the Church to perceive and come to grips with this as it was coming about.

Any discussion of this crisis of faith cannot be done in a presentation so brief as this. Nevertheless, by this phrase we mean simply that more and more people the world over no longer simply believe. People no longer simply believe as they were taught. They frequently believe, if at all, independently of the household of faith, i.e., the Church. They are seldom so sure that the Church really knows what life is all about. And more and more they tend to believe less and less, both in substance and in degree. The circumstances that have given rise to this phenomenon are beyond our allotted time to discuss here, but the fact remains that it is more and more difficult to find people (even rather well educated people) who have a mature faith supported by conviction. Most often, one finds that where faith does seem to exist, it is either an inferior substitute or on the point of suffocation from the extreme sentimentality and uncontrolled emotions that accompany it. Yet, there are those who refuse to associate themselves with the community of faith, the Church, but who, in their own way, are still thirsting after Christ and his message, however incompletely or incorrectly they understand it. So, it is not simply that people do not care about faith, but, it would seem that we, the Church, are failing in our mission to our own and to outsiders, but in a manner we don't even suspect!

Most people do not really understand what faith is. In fact, if the truth be known, many clergy fail to have a correct idea of what it is. This lack of true understanding carries with it an ignorance of what true faith expects of the believer. One of the corollaries of this is that many people are so confused they no longer know whether they are able to believe, let alone willing to believe. Yet, today, more than ever before, our technologically geared and ever-shrinking world impels more and more people to seek more and more understanding on all levels and in all areas of life. This should, it would seem, imply a desire for more understanding of religion and its truths and imperatives also. But those who have this desire, this drive for understanding, meet only a dead end in the Church.

Further, the traditional discussions and explanations of faith and how it works in the human condition — all this is fruitless. For, in fact, little of these erudite and scholarly words on the subject lead people to true faith, but to some kind of empty intellectualism, at best. And when it seems to lead them to faith, it turns out that the result is questionably true, mature, and free of superstition. Thus, what faith many people may have had in their youth shrivels and dies as they pass through adolescence into adulthood. Many, therefore, don't believe because they *think* they *cannot* believe. Or, they *will not* believe because they see our explanations and encouragements to believe as an invitation to intellectual prostitution.

So, the only people who believe at all and actually practice their faith are either those who have had to overcome some personal crisis in this area, or those who simplistically believe because of some deep-seated impulse such as need or fear of God and what (sic!) he may do to them and those they hold dear. And finally, for those who find faith a difficult hurdle at its easiest, the behavior and conduct of believers all around them drives them further and further into some kind of agnosticism, if not atheism.

These have been my observations throughout the years of my priestly and monastic life. My reception into the Orthodox Church has revealed to me that this situation, far from being better, is in many ways more clearly evident among our clergy and people than among other Christian denominations. It should not be so! Sincerity is a prerequisite of true spiritual life, but it is not alone sufficient; some understanding and growth in understanding is absolutely essential.

So, without doubting the sincerity of our clergy and people, it is nevertheless a truth that faith among us is very immature. Most of our Orthodox faithful never seem to have had to struggle for their faith, and when they have had to engage in this battle, there comes about in them a curious loss of reason, an essential human power to reason which is not at all opposed to the act of faith, but which actually supports it. Many of our clergy, for example, seem to fear any kind of natural human doubt or difficulty when it comes to faith, for they seem to think that such doubts and difficulties are inherently sinful. Sin, rather than being understood as the *willful* turning away from God, becomes confused with the infinite difficulties of life, all very natural and normal. This is shabby theology, to say the least, and psychologically very harmful and detrimental to any attempt at living a spiritual life and growing in the love of God and neighbor.

With this in mind, one can readily imagine the painful lot of people who experience real or imaginary problems in their life of faith life. Approaching their priest, they are so often told that their doubts and difficulties are either sinful themselves or the result of personal sin. And we must recall that this advice is administered because so often the priest himself does not understand the mechanics and dynamics of faith and how the healthiest of faith is necessarily intertwined with all the rest that is human within us. Often the persons who are having problems with believing are confronted with gibberish, namely that their lack of faith is a result of lack of faith! The poor souls may be told that faith is a free gift of God (whose ways, we must recall, are totally inscrutable — here, one must understand "arbitrary"!), the logical conclusion being that they don't qualify for this gift! What a theological masterpiece that is!

As clergy and knowledgeable laypeople, we fail to notice that today we have an infinitely greater bank of experience and factual knowledge about many aspects of human life than the Fathers had at their disposal. We fail to see that if we are indeed to emulate the Fathers, as we are constantly told, we must *do* what *they did.* We must bring this vast storehouse of advanced knowledge and accumulated experience to bear on our religious and spiritual lives. The longer we fail to do this, the greater the danger of more and more attrition in the Church and the less will there be any possibility of authentic monastic life. Accordingly, it would be well for us to learn and value the *good* effects of events among Western Christians, of the last twenty years. They have developed and matured both in their faith and in their understanding of faith in many ways, and this openness to further understanding has enabled them to *renew* their faith commitment, to *refocus* their sights on *interior* living of their faith in Christ rather than *merely* on the *external* observances to which we, on the contrary, are still so attached. There may indeed be many things to criticize in the lives of Western Christians, but if we are to be honest, we must see that there is also a great deal for us to learn for our benefit. As Orthodox — yes, as human beings! — we are in danger of leaving reality behind in our ponderous overconcern for and misunderstanding of the ritualistic and symbolic, as necessary and essential as they are to human life.

The second major reason for so little monasticism in our times lies in what I will call the failure of our Church to notice and deal with the reality of the American psyche. By psyche, we mean the dynamic of a people's way of being, a dynamic which obviously includes their thinking, their feelings, the way they perceive themselves and the world around them, the way they respond to needs and desires and aspirations. We mean peculiarities of a people and its distinct view of itself and all else. We do not here mean anything cultural or ethnic. In fact, I would like, as I have in the past, to note once again that as Orthodox, we have overkilled the horse of ethnicity. It is impossible to be human and not ethnic. Even the "wasp" is ethnic. We are all children of some other nation here in this land unless perhaps we be related to Sitting Bull or Geronimo! And every ethnic group has its culture, however like or unlike all others. But over and beyond that is what we are here calling the psyche of a people. To exemplify this, one need only to know the students of this esteemed institution to realize that as Greek as they may be, they are in varying degrees thoroughly more and more American in psyche. Our clergy and church personnel, whether simply trying to be sincere laborers in the vineyard or what we might call zealots, fail to understand that what is strangling our Church is not really the ethnic problem but the persistent attempts to impose a *foreign* and *dated* psyche on a people whose psyche is worlds and centuries away from those of the Orthodox motherlands.

In this area, it is clear that the clergy are the greatest offenders, however sincere their zeal and devotion. It was, and is, inevitable that our people, however ethnic, will gradually become more and more American in psyche, but our clergy are somehow or other locked into some sort of psychic and chronological time warp that insulates them against the natural way life has of changing our psyche through time and space. We must use some *critical thinking* to see that this is so and that it is suffocating our greatest efforts to spread the message of the Gospel. We must push on to study the whys and the wherefores of our being this way and how we may begin to change; otherwise our people will leave us in the dust of our time warp and perhaps even leave the Church because of the natural problems that will accompany the growing alienation between them and the clergy.

As necessarily brief as this consideration is, there does seem to be enough material here of such staggering implications as to make it very clear why monasticism is not thriving on these shores.

Without faith, monastic life is both a dream and a nightmare. Monastic life flows from the heartbeat of a living, mature faith of the Church both at large and in her single members. Monasticism is the *flower* of that faith and, because it is a veritable martyrdom, it is also the *seed* of faith. Thus, because of the immaturity of faith in our Church here and now, the flowering cannot be found, and that, in turn, will itself result in further attrition in faith. Overly-simplistic and self-righteous protestations that the Church is guided by the Holy Spirit *and*, therefore, possesses the full perfection of truth and the vision of God, *and*, therefore, all will be well — all this is the proverbial cop-out. It manifests not only our lack of true wisdom and understanding, but the dishonesty and arrogance that characterize our religious lives as well.

Let us therefore ask ourselves: how *authentic* and *complete* is our perception of and dedication to that vision the Church holds out before us? And do we not, without realizing it, frequently demean or belittle the monastic calling either by holding it up in such a way that it appears an impossible and inhuman ideal, or be deriding it as flight from reality?

Finally, monasticism is not a museum; it is in no way the simple transplantation of usages and practices of another time and place to our time and place. It is a *living way of life!* Therefore, it is not some kind of "let's pretend," some kind of attempt at "playing," much as children "play house." And it is therefore not the habit that makes the monk, nor the other aspects of life that can become the object of our "devotion and adoration" in countless ways. But since it is life at its deepest, it necessarily touches the psyche of the person and must therefore naturally be in harmony with that psyche. This is the rub! And this is where our attempts at monasticism in this land are tripping up. If an American monasticism is in fact to flourish for the good of our people on these shores, it cannot be *in spite* of the American psyche, but as a harmonious and integrated manifestation and synthesis of the best of tradition with the psyche of this land.

To insist stubbornly that monasticism can and must be lived here today as it was and is in Europe or the Near East now or ever is as foolish as saying that monasticism can be lived without faith. To the critical mind, this is self-evident. But that same critical mind can readily come to understand more and more of the vision of human life as it is expounded for us in the Gospels. When we begin to experience this, it will be the Church that will glow brighter and brighter before the world, exclaiming the irresistible message that has been hers from the beginning.

The Role of Orthodox Monasticism in America

CONSTANTINE CAVARNOS

THE TITLE OF OUR PANEL DISCUSSION IS "THE ROLE OF Orthodox Monasticism in America." I would modify the title to read: "The Roles of Orthodox Monasticism in America." For Orthodox monasticism traditionally has played *not one* role in the regions where it has existed, but a *good number* of important roles. In speaking of Orthodox monasticism in America, we are speaking largely of a *possible* monasticism, since Orthodox monasticism in this country is only at the beginning of its development. The actualization of its possibilities here will depend on the presence and guidance of monastics who are well known for their Orthodox Christian faith and high spiritual attainments.

When we speak of monasticism, we have in mind monastic establishments founded by monastics, and also the presence of monks or nuns living in such establishments and practicing authentic Orthodox monasticism under the direction of a spiritual father, called in Greek a *Geron* and in Russian a *Starets*.

The foremost role of Orthodox monasticism is to provide a suitable place and way of life for those who have a strong aspiration to achieve purity of soul and body, to cultivate the virtues to the highest degree possible, to achieve union with God, salvation, and who have an equally strong feeling that they are called by God to follow the path that most safely leads to these attainments. The late Abbot of the Monastery of Dionysios on the Holy Mountain of Athos, Archimandrite Gabriel, put these points very tersely, saying that the espousing of the monastic life springs from *"klisis with iota"* (that is, from inclination) and *"klesis with eta"* (that is, from a divine call).[1] Elaborating on this, he says the following: "The monastic life is a divine call, an aspiration for devotion to God, and an endeavor of man to attain as far as possible perfection in Christ, according to the statement of the Lord in the Gospel: 'If thou wantest to become perfect, renounce everything and come and follow me!' "[2] The person who has this aspiration and this call feels daily frustrated when not in a monastic setting, but finds inner rest and fulfillment when he places himself in it. He then finds himself, finds God, finds his own place in the divine plan, and is at peace, happy.

Those Orthodox in this country who do not find satisfaction in the incipient Orthodox monasticism that has appeared in this country, go to the Old World, to the ancient centers of monasticism: to Mount Athos, to Jerusalem, to Mount Sinai, but in most cases to Athos. I know of a good number of instances that confirm this statement.

Another role that monasticism can play in this country is to provide a place of temporary withdrawal from the "world," for persons who live in the "world" but love the quietness and spirituality of a monastic center, persons who thirst for holiness and want to attain to a greater measure of it than is possible in sinful society, in life among irreligious people or people who are religiously lukewarm or indifferent. Such individuals may spend several days, or a week or longer, as guests of some monastery, or successively of several monasteries, once or twice a year. In Greece, where there are many monasteries throughout the country — some for monks and others for nuns — this is a regular practice among very pious individuals. During their sojourn at monasteries they live as the monks or nuns do, and thus become for a period of time monastics by participation. They participate in the moving daily church services, and sometimes even go to the chanter's stand and take part in the chanting. They confess their sins and receive Holy Communion, if found prepared for it by the confessor. At cenobitic monasteries, they eat together with the monastics and listen to the reading from sacred texts during the meals. At other

---

[1]In his book, *He Monachike Zoe kata tous Hagious Pateras* (Athens, 1962).

[2]Pp. 4-5. See my book, *The Holy Mountain* (Belmont, MA., 1977), pp. 117-19.

times, they have the opportunity to converse with the monastics and thereby receive spiritual profit. Such a thing would be possible also in America, if we had Orthodox monasteries in many states, modeled after those in Greece and elsewhere in the Old World, those which have an outstanding spiritual tradition.

Pilgrimages and sojourns of this sort would result in a better understanding and appreciation of the Orthodox faith by those who live in the "world." It would result in greater spirituality among them, in higher spiritual attainments. The observations of those who have studied closely the effects of monasticism verify this. The consensus is that, as Photios Kontoglou — great iconographer and writer — puts it, "Where there exists true monastic life, and monasteries with a pious tradition, there Orthodoxy flourishes, and where such monasteries were absent there piety dried up."[3]

A third role monasticism could play in America would be to prepare confessors, who would confess not only monastics, but also those who live in the "world." They would confess the latter during their pilgrimages to their monasteries, or during their own pastoral journeys in cities, towns, and villages. Confession is one of the most important practices in the Orthodox Church, which unfortunately is very much neglected in this country. One main reason for this is, I believe, that we lack duly equipped confessors. And this, in turn, is due to the lack of monasteries.

Of course, one might say that *any* priest may serve as a confessor. In point of fact, however, the truly effective confessor is a rare person. In the Old World, in Greece for instance, a confessor, a spiritual father (*pneumatikos pater*), is usually an older monk. He is a man of widely recognized piety and general virtue, of experience and wisdom, of gifts such as the power of reading the deeper thoughts of a person who goes to him for confession, and of inducing him to confess sins which he is shy of confessing. Spiritually discerning, such a confessor prescribes the proper penance for the confessant's spiritual therapy.

---

[3]See my book, *Aphieroma sto Monasteri tes Evangelistrias tou Ploumariou tes Lesbou* (Athens, 1970), p. 50. Cf. Theodosios Sperantsas, Great Logothete of the Church of Greece: "If this world of ours should ever be renewed, it will be — this I believe with all my soul — the humble monks who will open the new path," *ibid.* pp. 49-50.

One of the great religious figures of modern Greece, Athanasios Parios (1722-1813), remarks: "A person should not confess indifferently to any confessor, but just as we seek out the best physicians when we are suffering from bodily illness, to resort to those skillful in the healing of the soul."[4]

An effective confessor is one who, being a person of great purity and unceasing prayer, can remain uninfected by the accounts of the sins which he listens to, and thus can keep on confessing daily, week after week, month after month, year after year, with undiminished purity and effectiveness. Being helped by divine grace, he can practice successfully spiritual diagnosis, spiritual midwifery, spiritual surgery, and spiritual therapy. Among such confessors, in recent Greek history, were Saint Arsenios of Paros (d. 1877), Abbot of the Monastery of Saint George on Paros; Saint Savvas the New (d. 1948), spiritual director of the Convent of All Saints on Kalymnos; Father Philotheos Zervakos (d. 1980), Abbot of the Monastery of Longovarda on Paros; and Father Gabriel Dionysiatis (d. 1983), Abbot of the Monastery of Dionysiou on the Holy Mountain. They were prepared for the practice of hearing confession by entering a monastery at any early age and leading an exemplary life during the rest of their years. They all confessed people both at the monastery where they dwelt and also at times in the world.

Closely connected with confession is spiritual guidance. The work of the confessor is not completed when he has listened to confession and given absolution. A good confessor will also give instruction to his confessant in such arts as that of fasting and of praying properly, and that of opposing temptations and negative emotions. This calls for spiritual love and knowledge, for wisdom, for intuitively entering into the mind of the confessant. The combination of these qualities is rare. It is found in confessors such as those just mentioned. Here, then, is another role monasticism in America could play, if and when it comes to maturity.

Related to the two roles just discussed, that of confession and that of spiritual guidance, is the role of spiritual healing. Of course, confession and absolution are forms of healing. But there is another mode of healing too, that of healing diseases of the body and the mind through the gift of miracles. Here, again, monasticism has

---

[4]*Epitome, eite Sylloge ton Theion tes Pisteos Dogmaton* (Leipzig, 1806), p. 383.

historically displayed its power. In his *Ladder of Divine Ascent,* Saint John Klimakos says: "Who among those that live in the world has ever yet performed miracles? Who has raised persons dead? Who has banished demons? Nobody. For all these things are prizes of monks, which the world cannot receive. For if it could, asceticism, withdrawal from the world, would be superflous."[5]

This assertion finds confirmation in our time in the many miracles that have been ascribed to Saint Arsenios of Paros, to Saint Nektarios of Aegina, to Saint Savvas the New, and to Saint Methodia of Kimolos (1865-1908),[6] all of them monastics.

Of course, the power of miraculous healing is a gift, a rare gift. Is is not a necessary accompaniment of the monastic life, even when this mode of life culminates in sainthood. However, monasteries of long standing always have relics of one or more saints; and pious Orthodox Christians regard them as channels of healing divine grace. Sacred relics are usually presented in Greece to pilgrims by a specially appointed monk, at the end of a church service. Many pious persons who go to these monasteries do so specially to venerate these relics, believing that they will be made well in body or soul, even when physicians in the world have given them up as incurable, "terminal" cases. Often they leave with positive results. Many "incurably" sick become well. Here, then, is a fifth role that monasticism in America might in time begin to play.

Another possibility Orthodox monasticism has in this country is to develop teachers and defenders of the true faith. Here, we need only recall that the great luminaries, teachers of the Oikoumene, and pillars of the Church, Saint John Chrysostom, Saint Basil the Great, Saint Gregory Palamas, and Saint Mark of Ephesos came out of monasteries; and that other great teachers of the Church, such as Saint John Damascene, Saint Symeon the New Theologian, and Saint Nikodemos the Hagiorite spent a lifetime in monasteries.

I will close my paper by citing one more possible role of Orthodox monasticism in America, closely related to the one just mentioned, that of preparing missionaries. In my book, *The Holy*

---

[5]Ioannes of Sinai, *Klimax* (Athens, 1979), p. 22, par. 15.

[6]See my series, *Modern Orthodox Saints,* Vol. 6 (*St. Arsenios of Paros*), Vol. 7 (*St. Nectarios of Aegina*), Vol. 8 (*St. Savvas the New*), and Vol. 9 (*St. Methodia of Kimolos*).

Mountain, I speak of more than a dozen significant missionaries that came out of the Holy Mountain of Athos, this pan-Orthodox monastic republic.[7] I will cite here three especially noteworthy examples: Saint Antony Pechersky of Russia, Saint Sava of Serbia, and Saint Cosmas Aitolos of Greece. After having lived as a monk on Athos for many years, Saint Antony was directed by his Elder, Theoktistos, Abbot of the Monastery of Asphigmenou, to return to Russia in order to transmit Athonite monasticism to the people of that country. Obeying, he returned there and established monasteries as "schools of virtue" leading to salvation.[8] This took place in the eleventh century. In the thirteenth century, Saint Sava, after having dwelt on the Holy Mountain for twenty years, returned to Serbia and there undertook the great mission of transforming the Serbs into a holy nation. To this end, he trained monks for missionary work and others for parish priesthood.[9] And in the eighteenth century, Saint Cosmas Aitolos, after having led a monastic life for seventeen years at the Monastery of Philotheou, returned to the world with the blessing of his Elders in order to do missionary work among the Orthodox in the Greek lands, in Albania, and in South Serbia. He addressed large audiences, explaining to them the basic doctrines of Eastern Orthodoxy, dissuading the people from wickedness, exhorting them to lead a godly life, stressing the need for instruction in the true Faith, and establishing for this purpose schools in many towns and villages. This he did very effectively for twenty years. Thus he became the greatest missionary of modern Greece.[10]

The lives of these three saints, as well as many others that could be cited, show the possibility that monasticism has also in a country such as this of providing spiritual leaders who can do much needed missionary work among the Orthodox, work of instruction in the Faith, of moral exhortation, and of spiritual uplifting.

---

[7] See pp. 43-59.

[8] *Ibid.* pp. 43-44.

[9] *Ibid.* pp. 45-48.

[10] See my book, *St. Cosmas Aitolos,* the "Introduction" and "The Life of Saint Cosmas."

Contributors

Mother Alexandra is retired Abbess of the Orthodox Monastery of the Transfiguration, Ellwood City, Pennsylvania.

V. Rev. Dr. Joseph J. Allen is Vicar General of the Antiochean Archdiocese and Adjunct Professor of Pastoral Theology, St. Vladimir's Theological Seminary, Crestwood, New York.

Deborah Malacky Belonick, a graduate of St. Vladimir's Orthodox Theological Seminary, is an Orthodox theologian, author, and ecumenist.

Dr. John Boojamra is Director of the Department of Christian Education of the Antiochean Archdiocese, Executive Secretary of the Orthodox Christian Education Commission, and Lecturer in Church History and Christian Education, St. Vladimir's Orthodox Theological Seminary.

V. Rev. Dr. Alkiviadis Calivas is Associate Professor of Liturgics, Holy Cross Greek Orthodox School of Theology, and Dean of Holy Cross and Hellenic College.

Dr. Constantine Cavarnos, former professor at Clark University and Holy Cross, is an Orthodox theologian, philosopher, and author.

John H. Erickson is Associate Professor of Canon Law and Church History, St. Vladimir's Orthodox Theological Seminary.

V. Rev. Stanley S. Harakas is Archbishop Iakovos Professor of Orthodox Theology, Holy Cross Greek Orthodox School of Theology.

Dr. Deno J. Geanakoplos is Professor of Byzantine History and Orthodox Church History, Bradford Durfee Chair of History, Yale University.

Dr. Kyriaki Karidoyanes FitzGerald is Adjunct Assistant Professor of Religious Education, Holy Cross Greek Orthodox School of Theology and Director, Orthodox Pastoral Counseling, Worcester Pastoral Counseling Center, Worcester, Massachusetts.

Archimandrite Laurence is Abbot of the New Skete Communities, Cambridge, New York.

Dr. Veselin Kesich is Professor of New Testament, St. Vladimir's Orthodox Theological Seminary.

V. Rev. George Nicozisin is Pastor of St. Nicholas Greek Orthodox Church, St. Louis, Missouri, and former Director of the Religious Education Department of the Greek Orthodox Archdiocese.

Dr. Lewis J. Patsavos is Professor of Canon Law and Director of Field Education, Holy Cross Greek Orthodox School of Theology.

Dr. Daniel J. Sahas is Associate Professor of Religious Studies, University of Waterloo, Ontario, Canada.

V. Rev. Dr. Theodore Stylianopoulos is Professor of New Testament, Holy Cross Greek Orthodox School of Theology.